Reference Sources
in History

Reference Sources in History

An Introductory Guide

Ronald H. Fritze
Brian E. Coutts
Louis A. Vyhnanek

ABC-CLIO

Library of Congress Cataloging-in-Publication Data

Fritze, Ronald H., 1951–
    Reference sources in history : an introductory guide / Ronald H. Fritze, Brian E. Coutts, Louis A. Vyhnanek.
        p. cm.
    Includes bibliographical references and index.
    1. History—Bibliography. I. Coutts, Brian E. II. Vyhnanek, Louis Andrew. III. Title.
    Z6201.F72 1990   [D20] 016.9—dc20   90-45169

ISBN 0-87436-164-8 (hc)

ISBN 0-87436-679-8 (pb)

97 96 95 94 93 92 91   10 9 8 7 6 5 4 3 2   (hc)
97 96 95 94 93 92 91   10 9 8 7 6 5 4 3 2 1 (pb)

ABC-CLIO, Inc.
130 Cremona Drive, P.O. Box 1911
Santa Barbara, California 93116-1911

This book is printed on acid-free paper ∞.
Manufactured in the United States of America

With Love to Our Parents

Harold[†] and Eleanor Fritze
George and Verna[†] Coutts
Louis[†] and Margaret[†] Vyhnanek

Nisi fuissetis, nihil esset
UNLESS YOU HAD BEEN, THERE WOULD BE NOTHING

Contents

Preface

Never read History without having maps, and a
chronological book, or tables lying by you, and
constantly recurred to; without which, history
is only a confused heap of facts.

That is what Philip Dormer Stanhope, Earl of Chesterfield, advised his son on 5 February 1750. It is a piece of advice that still retains its relevance in spite of the passage of time. The historian's job is to make sense of that "confused heap of facts," to recover and preserve knowledge of the past known as History, to organize it in an intelligible manner, and to explain or interpret it so that society can understand it. In the performance of that task the historian and the student of history are assisted by many different types of reference works: bibliographies, dictionaries, indexes, guides, and so forth. There are so many of these works, in fact, that it might almost be said that for every question there is a reference book to answer it. Under these circumstances, it is impossible for practicing historians and librarians to maintain in their heads a working knowledge of the existing general reference literature for history. For the beginning student of history at the undergraduate or graduate level the situation is even more bewildering. Hence the need for a reference guide that organizes, describes, and evaluates the basic reference works of interest to historians.

For many years the task of introducing the major reference works for history has been performed by Helen J. Poulton's excellent *The Historian's Handbook: A Descriptive Guide to Reference Works*. It was first published in 1972 and has gone through six printings. Since 1972, however, the enterprise of creating and publishing reference works has undergone several significant changes. The quantity of excellent new reference titles, particularly specialized historical dictionaries and encyclopedias, has increased and shows no signs of diminishing. New types of printed reference materials, especially indexes, have appeared, such as *Biography and Genealogy Master Index* and *Arts and Humanities Citation Index*. Even more revolutionary has been the vast increase in the number of microform titles available to researchers. This change has been accompanied by vastly improved photographic reproduction. Still, the greatest changes have taken place in the field of electronic publishing. Most indexes are now available in computerized data bases that can be searched by means of a telephone connection, i.e., on-line, from libraries throughout the country. Some of these on-line indexes are also available in the CD-ROM format (Compact Disc-Read Only Memory), which is even more convenient for researchers. All of this means that the time has arrived for a new reference guide for history.

The present volume is designed to provide an introduction to the major reference works for all periods of history and for all geographical areas. At the same time, since the intended audience for this book is primarily English speaking, reference materials published in the English language have been emphasized. Publications in languages other than English have been limited to works in European languages that use the Roman alphabet and are outstanding or unique in their utility for historical research. Because the intended audience of this volume will largely be Anglo-American, the geographical coverage emphasizes British, Canadian, European, and United States history. Major works for African, Asian, Latin American, and Middle Eastern history, however, have been included.

The authors of this volume have attempted to include all of the most important and generally useful reference works for historians. They have also included various specialized publications that are particularly outstanding in their quality. In fact, the great majority of the items listed in this guide are publications of the highest distinction. The only time a less than satisfactory reference work appears here is when it is the only work available on an important topic. All of the criteria used for the selection of the works listed are somewhat subjective. The authors have no doubt that many readers of this book will find that one or more of their favorite and most trusted reference works have been left out. For that omission, the authors apologize. Practical considerations of size and cost for this book caused the authors to forego listing many worthy reference works both old and new.

There are 685 reference works and related titles listed and annotated in this reference guide. The entries have been organized into 14 chapters on the basis of types of publications, e.g., bibliographies, atlases, microforms, journals. Works relating to various topics within the discipline of history, such as economic history, British history, and psychohistory, can be found by using the index, which also lists all authors, editors, and titles mentioned throughout the text. Individual entries are numbered and followed by complete bibliographic information and annotations that describe the contents of the works and provide some evaluation of their usefulness for the study of history. Whenever an annotation for one work mentions the title of another with an entry in the guide, a bracketed "see" reference including the item number of that work has been provided. Frequently annotations will also mention other similar or related titles that have not been given separate entries in the guide. Whenever this occurs, the authors have supplied the author's or editor's name, title, place of publication, publisher, and date of publication. In this way the reference guide is able to list more titles than could have possibly been listed separately.

Regarding the continuing appearance of new books, the authors established no arbitrary cutoff date for the inclusion of recent publications. Instead, they continued to sift through catalogs, reviews, book exhibits, publishers' advertisements, and new acquisitions well into early 1990. Thanks to the wonders of word processing, the chosen fruits of this labor could be added to the guide with minimal trouble. Also, without a doubt, something will have been overlooked anyway. The Preacher spoke most truly in Eccles. 12:12 when he said, "Of making many books there is no end."

Acknowledgments

Many people have helped us in the writing of this book. First, we would like to thank Heather Cameron, vice-president for acquisitions at ABC-CLIO. No one could ask for a better person to help develop a project. She is patient, attentive, and full of sound advice and suggestions. John Grenville, professor of history at the University of Birmingham, England, read and evaluated our original proposal. He stayed on to provide advice and consultation. His suggestions were always sensible, and his criticisms were invariably polite and constructive. Donald Davis of the Graduate School of Library and Information Science at the University of Texas steered us to Heather at a crucial moment. Charles Patterson and Lee Shiflett of the Graduate School of Library and Information Science at Louisiana State University introduced all of us to the librarian's point of view on reference materials. John Loos of the Department of History at Louisiana State University introduced us to reference and research materials from the historian's side. He was aided in this task by Paul Hoffman, Burl Noggle, and Fred Youngs, all from the Department of History at Louisiana State University. Rudolph Heinze and Sir Geoffrey Elton contributed to Ron's education as a historian, as did Christon Archer, Herman Konrad, and Graham Knox to Brian's, and George Mayer to Lou's. Various colleagues from the libraries of Lamar University, Washington State University, and Western Kentucky University assisted with the location and acquisition of needed materials, in particular Mary Frances Sherwood. Many thanks to Lisa Andreason of Kelly High School, Beaumont, Texas, for providing the Latin epigram on the dedication page. Brian's wife, Karen D. Greene,and Lou's wife, Kay Vyhnanek, were constant sources of support. The Faculty Senate and the Research Council of Lamar University provided grants, and Western Kentucky University and Washington State University provided research leaves and technical support, all of which aided in the completion of this book.

Acknowledgment

Reference Sources
in History

1.
Guides, Handbooks, and Manuals for History

This chapter brings together some basic reference books concerned with different aspects of the study of history that are important to anyone beginning research. A selection has been made of those basic guides, handbooks, dictionaries, encyclopedias, and bibliographies likely to prove most useful. English-language texts have been preferred if available.

Historiography

Historiography is a term that can be used in several ways. Here it means the study of the development of historical scholarship or the critical analysis of conflicting interpretations of a given period or problem in history. Historical scholarship has changed in both its methods and its concerns over the years and continues to change. For a full understanding of the study of history, it is important to know how it has developed and what the different current trends are.

001. *Dictionary of Concepts in History.* By Harry Ritter. Westport, CT: Greenwood Press, 1986. 490p. Index. ISBN 0-313-22700-4.

Although this work is called a dictionary, its entries are really historiographical, critical essays dealing with various ideas and words commonly used by historians, e.g., "frontier," "modernization," and "revolution." Each entry consists of a definition or definitions of the term followed by a critical essay with a list of references; entries end with suggestions for further reading. This book is a very good tool for stimulating thinking about the meaning and implications of commonly used words.

002. *Historical Studies Today*. Edited by Felix Gilbert and Stephen R. Graubard. New York: W. W. Norton, 1972. 468p. Index. ISBN 0-393-05453-5.

According to Graubard, it is important for historians as much as for those in any other profession to take stock of the strengths and weaknesses in their field periodically. The 20 historiographical essays by an eminent and international group of historians do just that by covering the important topics and components of historical scholarship. They originally appeared in the Winter and Spring 1971 issues of *Daedalus*, vol. 100, nos. 1 and 2. Particularly strong is their coverage of social history and the new methodologies that were becoming increasingly popular in the early 1970s, e.g., psychohistory, prosopography, and popular culture. A similar work is the collection of 11 historiographical essays edited by Charles Delzell in *The Future of History: Essays in the Vanderbilt University Centennial Symposium* (Nashville, TN: Vanderbilt University Press, 1977). The essays in both of these works are complemented by the later essays in the *International Handbook of Historical Studies* and *The Past Before Us* [*see* 006 and 007].

003. *Historiography: A Bibliography*. Edited by Lester D. Stephens. Metuchen, NJ: Scarecrow Press, 1975. 271p. Index. ISBN 0-8108-0856-0.

The purpose of this bibliography is to provide a comprehensive, although not complete, reference source for the beginning student of historiography. It contains almost 2,300 entries of books and journals, some of which are lightly annotated. These are divided into four sections: theories of history, historiography, historical methods, and reference works. Stephens' work has a strong emphasis on American history. A similar and more recent bibliography, with a British emphasis, is R. C. Richardson's *The Study of History: A Bibliographical Guide* (Manchester, England: Manchester University Press, 1988). These volumes are a good companion to *Historiography: An Annotated Bibliography* [*see* 004].

004. *Historiography: An Annotated Bibliography of Journal Articles, Books, and Dissertations*. Edited by Susan K. Kinnell. Santa Barbara, CA: ABC-CLIO, 1987. 2 vols. 858p. Indexes. ISBN 0-87436-168-0.

Containing some 8,500 entries, this work is drawn from the data bases for *America: History and Life* and *Historical Abstracts*. The first volume deals with individual historians, schools of history, and the various types of history: economic, social, political, and so forth. The second volume covers the geographical and national divisions of history, e.g., France, the U.S.S.R., and the United States. Within the broad divisions listed above, the individual entries are listed alphabetically by author and are numbered. A complete citation to the written work is provided. Most entries are annotated and signed by the abstractor. Titles of the many foreign-language entries are followed by English translations. This is an excellent source for beginning historiographical research, but it does not include the older literature.

005. *Historiography: Ancient, Medieval, & Modern.* By Ernst Breisach. Chicago: University of Chicago Press, 1983. 487p. Index. ISBN 0-226-07275-4.

This pioneering narrative work provides in one volume a survey of the development of Western historical scholarship from the ancient Greeks to the 1970s. The author sees the writing of history as an activity that is a fundamental part of Western culture: history helps to provide a balance between continuity and change in human society. The detailed index allows specific topics and historians to be located easily, while the endnotes and the selective bibliography provide guidance for further reading. An older, two-volume work that traces in great detail the development of both Western and non-Western historical scholarship from ancient times to 1900 is James Westfall Thompson's *A History of Historical Writing* (New York: Macmillan, 1942). Also related is that excellent new work *The Blackwell Dictionary of Historians* [523]. Many periods and historical topics have their own specialized histories of historical writing.

006. *International Handbook of Historical Studies: Contemporary Research and Theory.* Edited by Georg G. Iggers and Harold T. Parker. Westport, CT: Greenwood Press, 1979. 452p. Index. ISBN 0-313-21367-4.

Intended both as a follow-up and as an expansion of the collection of essays in *Historical Studies Today* [see 002], this new volume contains 23 essays. Eight of them discuss new developments in the various topical fields of history, e.g., economic, social, and political. The other 15 essays cover the historiography of individual countries such as Italy or regions such as sub-Saharan Africa. (The Middle East has been omitted because a contributor could not be found.) Although collections can date quickly, this one is still worth looking at, given the present relative stability of trends in historical research.

007. *The Past Before Us: Contemporary Historical Writing in the United States.* Edited by Michael Kammen. Ithaca, NY: Cornell University Press, 1980. 524p. Index. ISBN 0-8014-1224-2.

This volume provides a report on the state of historical research in the United States circa 1980. As such it serves as a handy guide and reference work for current historiography. Its 20 essays were written by eminent practitioners and cover all geographical areas along with many historical periods and subtopics. Inexplicably, there are no essays on ancient or classical history. This volume can be regarded as the true follow-up to *Historical Studies Today* [*see* 002]. But even this more recent volume is now somewhat dated in its analysis of the state of historical scholarship.

Methodology

008. *The Modern Researcher.* 4th ed. By Jacques Barzun and Henry F. Graff. New York: Harcourt Brace Jovanovich, 1985. 450p. Index.

The classic manual for research and writing for more than 30 years, *The Modern Researcher* has been updated regularly in every edition and so remains fresh and relevant. The book's scope is wide; written by two historians, it provides a useful guide for all researchers and writers in the humanities and the social sciences. The reader is shown the way to develop a research topic, to use the library, to take notes, to organize research materials, and to write up the findings. Barzun and Graff wrote it with style and much thought, making it the best such work available. Its size, however, could prove intimidating to many students.

Other, similar titles are available that are smaller and less expensive:

009. *Going to the Sources: A Guide to Historical Research and Writing.* By Anthony Brundage. Arlington Heights, IL: Harlan Davidson, 1989. 79p. ISBN 0-88295-865-8.

Students are introduced to the types of history, the nature and types of sources used in historical writing, the use of the library, and the writing of a historiographical essay and a research paper.

010. *A Guide to Historical Method.* 3d ed. Edited by Robert Jones Shafer. Chicago: Dorsey Press, 1980. 272p. Index. ISBN 0-534-10825-3.

A good deal of space is devoted to discussing the nature and relative reliability of various types of historical evidence; the techniques for writing a historical research paper are explained. The fact that this work has been through three editions and is still in print indicates its widespread use.

011. *A Student's Guide to History.* 4th ed. By Jules R. Benjamin. New York: St. Martin's Press, 1987. 167p. ISBN 0-312-77004-9.

All undergraduate history students, whether majors, minors, or nonmajors, would do well to read this book and to learn its lessons. Those lessons are applicable to more than history courses. Benjamin shows his readers how to do their reading assignments for class, take notes in class, study for an exam, write a book review, and write a research paper. A useful classified bibliography of reference books found in most college libraries is included.

012. *Writer's Guide: History.* By Henry J. Steffens and Mary Jane Dickerson. Lexington, MA: D. C. Heath, 1987. 211p. Index.

The contention of this recent work is that writing is the best way to learn history. It begins with various types of historical writing that students might do, i.e., keeping a journal, essays in and out of class, book reviews, and the short research paper. These chapters are followed by others dealing with library research, documentation, usage, and punctuation.

Chronologies, Calendars, and Lists of Rulers

013. *The Book of Calendars.* Edited by Frank Parise. New York: Facts on File, 1982. 387p. Index. ISBN 0-98196-467-8.

Historical researchers working with the dating systems and calendars of other cultures past and present will welcome this excellent and fascinating handbook. It provides background information on the development and evolution of 40 types of calendars from all periods of history and all parts of the world. Even more useful, it supplies tables for converting the dates of 60 calendars into their Gregorian and Julian equivalents. Among the calendars included are the Hebrew, the Islamic, the Chinese, and the Mayan. Also helpful are the lists of Easter dates, the calendar of saints, and the descriptions of attempts by revolutionary France and the Soviet Union to create new calendars.

014. *Cronologia e Calendario Perpetuo: Tavole Chronograficho e Quadri Sinottici per Verificare le Date Storiche dal Principio dell'Ara Cristiana ai*

giorni nostri. 4th ed. Expanded and Amplified. By Adriano Cappelli. Milan: Ulrico Hoepli, 1978. 606p. Index.

Although written in Italian, much of the information found in this guide is still accesssible to English-speaking readers. Basically, it is a handbook that gathers information useful for dating documents. The perpetual calendar for both the Julian and Gregorian systems supplies the date, day of the week, and religious holidays as they occurred in individual years. Further lists of saints' days and religious feasts are also supplied. Other tables allow conversions from the Islamic calendar based on the Hegira and from the French revolutionary calendar. Another large section of the book provides chronological lists of various European dynasties, including quite minor states, as well as the major dynasties of Egypt, China, Islam, and Japan. Most of this information can be found in various English-language publications, particularly the *Handbook of Dates for Students* [*see* 018], but Cappelli brings it all together in one convenient place. An English translation of this work would be useful.

015. *Chronology of the Ancient World.* By E. J. Bickerman. Ithaca, NY: Cornell University Press, 1968. 253p. Index. ISBN 0-8014-1282-X.

016. *Handbook of Biblical Chronology: Principles of Time Reckoning in the Ancient World and Problems of Chronology in the Bible.* By Jack Finegan. Princeton, NJ: Princeton University Press, 1964. 338p. Index.

Bickerman's *Chronology* is a much revised English translation of his original German work. Its historical focus is the classical Greek and Roman era from about 800 B.C. to A.D. 476. Three chapters discuss the various ancient calendars, chronography (the techniques used to determine the amount of time between an ancient event and the present), and applied chronology (the supplying of a modern date, B.C. or A.D., to an ancient event). These chapters are followed by various tables that can be used for converting ancient dates to modern equivalents, e.g., astronomical new moons from 605 B.C. to A.D. 308; a synchronistic listing of Olympic years; years from the founding of Rome; Egyptian mobile years with the B.C. or A.D. equivalent; and lists of various rulers, Athenian archons, and Roman consuls. Finegan is not so detailed as Bickerman for Greek and Roman systems of dating. But as the title indicates, this work spends more time on biblically related topics such as ancient Egyptian, Mesopotamian, and Hebrew chronology and datings used by the early Christians. It includes many tables and, unlike Bickerman, supplies a useful bibliography. *A Companion to Greek Studies,* 4th ed., edited by Leonard Whibley (1931. Reprint. New York: Hafner, 1963), and *A Companion to Latin Studies,* 3d ed., edited by Sir John Edwin

Sandys (1935. Reprint. New York: Hafner, 1963), also contain useful sections on dating and chronology along with much other information.

017. *Handbook of British Chronology.* 3d ed. Edited by E. B. Fryde, D. E. Greenway, S. Porter, and I. Roy. London: Royal Historical Society, 1986. 603p. ISBN 0-86193-106-8.

Serious students of British history will want to have their personal copy of this book. It is a series of lists of the major officeholders for the British Isles from about A.D. 400 to the present. The work begins with the monarchs and rulers of England, Scotland, Wales, and the Isle of Man but not the complicated subject of Irish kings. Next come lists of the major officers of state for England, Ireland, and Scotland. The largest section of this work lists the archbishops and bishops of England, Wales, Scotland, and Ireland. The various dukes, marquesses, and earls of England, Scotland, and Ireland are listed. Finally, there are lists of the meetings of parliament and the provincial and national councils of the English church before 1536. This work is an excellent aid for assigning approximate dates from internal evidence to undated documents.

018. *Handbook of Dates for Students of English History.* Edited by C. R. Cheney. London: Royal Historical Society, 1945. Reprint 1970. 182p. Index. ISBN 0-8476-1343-7.

This handy little book functions for students of English history as Adriano Cappelli's *Cronologia* [*see* 014] does for students of European history. It explains the Julian (Old Style) and the Gregorian (New Style) calendars along with the concept of the year of grace for beginning a new year. There are lists of English rulers, plus tables of regnal years beginning with Henry II in 1154, and lists of popes. Various saints' days and Christian festivals are also given. The dating and chronology used in the English legal system are explained, as is the Roman calendar. A series of 36 tables provides all possible dates for Easter in both Old and New Style. Finally, there is a chronological listing of Easter dates from A.D. 500 to 2000.

019. *Handbook of Oriental History.* Edited by C. H. Philips. London: Royal Historical Society, 1963. 265p. Index. ISBN 0-8476-1346-1.

Most Western students are unfamiliar with much of the basic historical terminology and the cultural practices of the Near, the Middle, and the Far East. This volume seeks to alleviate that problem for the entire Orient excluding the pre-Islamic Near and Middle East. It is divided into five geographical sections, each written by an expert on the region: Near and Middle East, India and Pakistan, South-East Asia and the Archipelago, China, and Japan. Each section supplies useful information on the romanization of that area's words and on local naming practices and titles, a glossary of frequently used terms, systems of dating and calendars (e.g., the Islamic calendar dating from the Hegira [A.D. 622]), and lists of dynasties and rulers. This clear and handy guide is a must for any student of Oriental history.

020. *Monarchs, Rulers, Dynasties, and Kingdoms of the World.*Compiled by R. F. Tapsell. New York: Facts on File, 1983. 511p. ISBN 0-87196-121-0.

Who ruled when and where are the questions answered by this fascinating book. Its scope is international and covers all periods of history back to the beginning of written records. U.S. presidents are the one group of non-monarchical rulers included in this work. Popes also are listed but not Orthodox patriarchs. The volume is divided into two sections. Section I is an "Alphabetical Guide to Dynasties and States" consisting of 1,200 dictionary-length entries, a number of them with genealogical charts. About 1,000 dynastic lists make up Section II. The lists are arranged in geographical and chronological order and provide the name, dates for the reign, and brief family information for approximately 13,000 rulers. This book's great utility is that it provides easy access to information on many minor European rulers and major and minor non-European states.

Historical Metrology: Weights, Measures, and Exchange Rates for Money

021. *British Weights and Measures: A History from Antiquity to the Seventeenth Century.* By Ronald Edward Zupko. Madison, WI: University of Wisconsin Press, 1977. 248p. Index. ISBN 0-299-07340-8.

In addition to the three chapters providing a narrative history of the evolution of standardized weights and measures in England from Roman times to 1603, the remaining half of the volume consists of four valuable appendixes for students of European economic history. Appendix A lists alphabetically goods imported and exported by the English from 1150 to 1800 and how they were bulk-rated (measured in groups). British Pre-Imperial Units are given in tabular form in Appendix B and include all units set up by statute in England, Scotland, and Ireland prior to the Imperial Weights and Measures Act of 1824. Appendix C provides tables for the units established in the British Isles by the Imperial Weights and Measures Act of 1824. Appendix D, "Pre-Metric Weights and Measures in Western and Eastern Europe," alphabetically lists the unit and tells where it was used and what its English and metric equivalents were. The classified and occasionally annotated bibliography updates the one found in Zupko's *Dictionary of English Weights and Measures* [*see* 022] and includes a large number of relevant dictionaries and glossaries.

022. *A Dictionary of English Weights and Measures: From Anglo-Saxon Times to the Nineteenth Century.* By Ronald Edward Zupko. Madison, WI: University of Wisconsin Press, 1968. 224p. LC 68-14038.

The purpose of this very helpful book is to clear up ambiguities and confusions concerning the English weights and measures used in the past. Each main entry consists of the name of the unit of measure, alternative spellings with the approximate century they were in use, an etymology of the word, and a general definition and history of the unit, including its metric equivalent whenever it can be determined. There are also numerous *see* references from alternative spellings to the main entry. The information in each entry is documented by references to items in the extensive and sometimes annotated bibliography.

023. *French Weights and Measures before the Revolution: A Dictionary of Provincial and Local Units.* By Ronald Edward Zupko. Bloomington, IN: Indiana University Press, 1978. 208p. ISBN 0-253-32480-7.

If historical English weights and measures are confusing, the French situation is even more complex, as France is a larger country with even more regional variations. Individual entries are listed alphabetically by name of the unit. Alternative spellings are cross-referenced to the main entry. The body of the entry supplies the century in which the unit was first used, variants in later centuries, an etymology of the word, and the definition of the unit with its dimensions, along with citations to the appropriate sources listed in the partially annotated bibliography.

024. *Glossary of Mediaeval Terms of Business: Italian Series 1200–1600.* By Florence Edler. Cambridge, MA: Mediaeval Academy of America, 1934. 430p. Index. 0-527-01690-X.

Italians dominated much of the international trade of the Middle Ages and early modern era. Therefore, an understanding of their business terminology and methods is essential for students of the economy and society in those time periods. The extensive glossary provides both definitions and citations to primary sources. Nineteen classified lists of terms for money, various measures, types of tolls, and other related subjects supplement the glossary. A further nine appendixes supply information on business and industrial terms and practices. This book provides clear guidance through a highly complex subject.

025. *Handbook of Medieval Exchange.* By Peter Spufford. London: Royal Historical Society, 1986. 468p. ISBN 0-86193-105-X.

Determining the relative value of money throughout history is often an impossible task. After years of research in both archives and printed documents, Peter Spufford has managed to produce a volume that provides European exchange rates for the period 1250–1500. Since the Florentine florin was the medieval equivalent of the U.S. dollar, its exchange rates form the basis for most of the tables in this book. Individual chapters are organized on a geographical basis. Commercially advanced Italy, not suprisingly, is covered in three chapters, while far more primitive Muscovy has no listings. Besides the rest of Europe, Byzantium, Levant, and the Barbary states are given detailed listings. As a tool for comparing the financial situation of the many kingdoms, regions, and cities of medieval Europe, this volume is a unique and superb work of reference. A companion volume of exchange rates for post-1500 Europe is under preparation by Professor F. C. Spooner.

026. *Historical Metrology: A New Analysis of the Archaeological and Historical Evidence Relating to Weights and Measures.* By A. E. Berriman. London: J. M. Dent, 1953. 224p. Index.

As an introduction to the study of weights and measures throughout history, this encyclopedic survey is excellent. Each chapter gives a history of various historical weights and measures and explains how they convert into modern English units. Besides the expected chapters on classical and Western European nations, there are discussions of Russian, Chinese, and Indian systems of weights and measures. Particularly useful are the chapters on ancient Egyptian and Babylonian measuring systems, which are often neglected in other works on historical metrology.

027. *Scales and Weights: A Historical Outline.* By Bruno Kisch. New Haven, CT: Yale University Press, 1965. 297p. Index. LC 65-12545. ISBN 0-8357-8315-4.

While this is not strictly a reference work, it provides an encyclopedic survey of its subject. Clearly delineated chapters and subsections supply readily comprehensible explanations and histories of the metric system, various types of scales, and specialized systems of weights, e.g., carat, pharmaceutical, and Byzantine. Particularly useful are the three appendixes: "Ancient Weight Units," "Weight Standards of the World before the Metric-Decimal System," and "Weight Standards of the World with Gram or Kilogram Equivalents." These appendixes are worldwide in their scope. The bibliography is superseded by those found in Zupko's works [*see* 021, 022, and 023].

028. *The Weights and Measures of England.* By R. D. Connor. London: Her Majesty's Stationery Office, 1987. 422p. Index. ISBN 0-11-290435-1.

This encyclopedic survey of English weights and measures ranges from earliest times to the present metric system. Its detailed subject index and numerous subheadings within chapters make it easy to locate information on specific topics. Besides discussions of the history of the mile, the foot, the acre, the gallon, and many other weights and measures, the British system of coinage is described. Various appendixes detail how weights and measures were regulated, tell the history of the metric system, and provide a table of pre-metric British measures. A useful glossary of unit-terms follows, along with a helpful bibliography.

029. *Weights, Measures, and Money, of all Nations.* Compiled by F. W. Clarke. New York: Appleton, 1894. 117p.

The purpose of this work is to supply the metric equivalent for measures of length, liquid and dry measures, and weights, as well as the gold or U.S.-dollar equivalent for coinages of various nations around the world. The first part of the book is arranged alphabetically by country. In the second part, tables are provided for measures of length, road, square measures, dry measures, weights, and money. These are arranged alphabetically by the name of the measure followed by its locality and its English, U.S., and metric equivalents. Although it is dated, this work can still supply difficult-to-find information for the historian.

Auxiliary Sciences of History

Archaeology

030. *Archaeology, A Bibliographical Guide to the Basic Literature.* By Robert F. Heizer, Thomas R. Hester, and Carol Graves. New York: Garland, 1980. 434p. Index. ISBN 0-8240-9826-9.

Although this guide has a definite bias toward New World archaeology, it is still a very useful resource for beginning research in the general subject of archaeology. Listing 4,818 books, articles, and other materials, it is divided into five broad sections: the nature and purpose of archaeology, its history, the methods and subfields of archaeology, the teaching and profession of archaeology, and reference materials. Entries are listed alphabetically by authors within the many subsections. There are no annotations. There is an author index but no subject index.

031. *The Cambridge Encyclopedia of Archaeology.* Edited by Andrew Sherratt. New York: Crown Publishers and Cambridge University Press, 1980. 495p. Index. ISBN 0-517-53497-5.

As a reasonably up-to-date and authoritative introduction to the many aspects of the discipline of archaeology, this volume is a good place to begin. Written for the educated nonspecialist and attractively illustrated, it is organized into ten chapters, which are further subdivided into 64 sections, each written by an expert in that particular topic. The first chapter and its seven subsections describe the history and current state of modern archaeology. It is followed by seven chronological/geographical chapters surveying the broad fields of prehistory; the various origins and diffusions of agricultural systems; the ancient Near East and Mediterranean; ancient East Asia; Byzantine and Islamic archaeology; the archaeology of Oceania, Africa, and the Arctic; and the New World. A separate brief chapter supplies a synthetic, interpretive overview. The final chapter discusses the systems of dating and chronology used by archaeologists. A brief bibliography supplies guidance for further reading on the various chapters in the volume. There is a detailed index of subjects, persons, and places. Maurice Robbins' *The Amateur Archaeologist's Handbook,* 3d ed. (New York: Harper & Row, 1981), is a good, practical introduction to the field and to the research techniques used by archaeologists.

032. *The Facts on File Dictionary of Archaeology*. Rev. ed. Edited by Ruth D. Whitehouse. New York: Facts on File, 1983. 597p. Index. ISBN 0-87196-048-6.

For a comprehensive dictionary of archaeology in a single volume, this work is quite scholarly. Its scope is worldwide, and the types of entries include technical terms, biographical sketches, descriptions of well-known sites, surveys of geographical areas, and the various subfields of archaeology.

Genealogy

033. *American & British Genealogy & Heraldry: A Selected List of Books*. 3d ed. Compiled by P. William Filby. Boston: New England Historic Genealogical Society, 1983. 736p. Index. ISBN 0-88082-004-7.

Although there are many genealogical bibliographies, this one is an excellent place to start research. Almost 10,000 titles concerning genealogy, heraldry, and local history are listed in this fine bibliography. While the emphasis is on American and British genealogy, this latest edition has begun listing works in English on other countries. The cutoff date for inclusion of a book is the fall of 1981. Individual entries are arranged into geographical sections: United States, the individual states, Latin America, Canada, England, Ireland, Scotland, Wales, other former British territories, and the world. There are also sections for heraldry and chivalry. The detailed index lists authors, titles, and subjects.

034. *The Dictionary of Genealogy*. By Terrick V. H. FitzHugh. Totowa, NJ: Barnes & Noble, 1985. 320p. ISBN 0-389-20565-6.

The focus of the more than 1,000 terms listed in this dictionary is British genealogy. All sorts of technical terms, like "gavelkind" and "virgate," that a person might come across in the course of genealogical research are lucidly defined. Furthermore, sources of potential information, like patent rolls, and useful repositories of genealogical materials, such as Dr. Williams' Library in London, are described. This a useful dictionary for students of both genealogy and history. A much shorter and less detailed dictionary that is intended for an American audience and lists only terms commonly found in the historical documents used by genealogists is Frances Dunfee Larson's *The Genealogist's Dictionary* (Bellevue, WA: By the author, 1986 and 1987).

035. *Genealogical Research and Resources: A Guide for Library Use.* By Lois C. Gilmer. Chicago: American Library Association, 1988. 70p. Index. ISBN 0-8389-0482-3.

Guides on how to do genealogical research comprise one of the minor growth industries of book publishing. Many are available and many are good. Gilmer's guide, published as an inexpensive paperback by the American Library Association, has the virtues of being recent, sensible, concise, and intended for the beginning genealogist. It is also designed to help librarians faced by frequent genealogical questions. Techniques of genealogical research are outlined. Next come discussions of the primary and secondary sources used by genealogists. An appendix supplies the names and addresses of various archives, societies, libraries, and publishers of interest to genealogists. There is a brief subject index. Also of interest is *Your Family History: A Handbook for Research and Writing,* by David E. Kyvig and Myron A. Marty (Arlington Heights, IL: Harlan Davidson, 1978).

Heraldry

036. *Bibliotheca Heraldica Magnae Britanniae: An Analytical Catalogue of Books on Genealogy, Heraldry, Nobility, Knighthood, & Ceremonies with a List of Provincial Visitations, Pedigrees, Collections of Arms, and other Manuscripts; and a Supplement, Concerning the Principal Foreign Genealogical Works.* By Thomas Moule. 1822. Reprint. London: Heraldry Today, 1966. 668p. Index.

Originally published in 1822, this bibliography has remained a standard for students of heraldry. More than 800 annotated entries are arranged in chronological order by date of publication and describe books on English heraldry. Another 221 entries merely list various books on Continental heraldry. The index is a simple subject one and does not list titles, although it does list authors. This work should be used in conjunction with the bibliographies found in modern books on heraldry. A plan to extend this bibliography past 1822 up to the present has not yet been realized.

037. *The Dictionary of Heraldry.* Edited by Stephen Friar. New York: Crown, 1987. 320p. ISBN 0-517-56665-6.

Intended to satisfy the needs of beginning and advanced students of heraldry, this attractive volume is an important basic resource for its subject. Its entries deal with heraldry in general and also with armory, which is the system of symbolism and presentation used in heraldry. While English topics dominate the entries, Continental heraldry is also discussed. Since heraldry was an important part of the feudal system that formed the basis of the European social structure in the Middle Ages and early modern period, this dictionary contains much to interest historians.

038. *The Oxford Guide to Heraldry.* By Thomas Woodcock and John Martin Robinson. Oxford: Oxford University Press, 1988. 288p. ISBN 0-19-211658-4.

Most people know of heraldry because coats of arms and other heraldic paraphernalia are frequently used in trademarks and decorations. Few, however, realize the actual complexity and diversity of true heraldry. Furthermore, the English practice of heraldry was considerably different from that of Continental Europe. Fortunately, beginning researchers can now turn to the *Oxford Guide to Heraldry* for the answers to most of their basic questions. Besides providing a clear and readable overview of the subject, enhanced by many attractive illustrations, this book supplies a useful glossary of terms and a brief introductory bibliography of modern books that can be used to supplement *Bibliotheca Heraldica* [*see* 036].

Numismatics

039. *The Macmillan Encyclopedic Dictionary of Numismatics.* By Richard G. Doty. New York: Macmillan, 1982. 355p. ISBN 0-02532270-2.

Numismatics is a vast and complicated subject with a specialized vocabulary and much obscure lore. The scope of this work is the terminology of coinage from ancient times to the present, including tokens, medals, and paper money along with various technical subjects regarding the making of coins. There are 500 entries with ample cross-referencing that tend to be from 200 to 1,000 words in length. There is a brief bibliography for the volume. Any student of history seeking a more detailed knowledge of numismatics will want to consult this book.

040. *Numismatic Bibliography.* By E. E. Clain-Stefanelli. Munich: Battenberg, 1985. 1,848p. Indexes. ISBN 3-598-07507-3.

Numismatics is a busy field in which new writings are appearing all the time. As a result, the publication of an exhaustive general bibliography is impossible. Instead, the present work with its more than 18,000 entries is designed to be an introduction for both historians and coin collectors. Although its scope is worldwide and encompasses all eras of history, the emphasis is on Europe and the United States. The entries are arranged quite logically, beginning with general reference works and broad monetary topics that are followed by three large sections on the ancient, medieval, and modern periods, which are arranged geographically. These are followed by specialized chapters on tokens, medals, decorations, the production of coins, important numismatic collections, the history of numismatics, and numismatic methodology. Six detailed indexes to authors, collectors, personal names, geographical terms, numismatic terms, and public collections greatly assist users of this bibliography. It updates and replaces Philip Grierson's *Select Numismatic Bibliography* (Washington, D.C., 1965). A less expensive and more accessible bibliography containing 1,100 numismatic items, which, however, is more oriented toward coin collecting, is Richard H. Rosichan's *Stamps and Coins* (Littleton, CO: Libraries Unlimited, 1974). The most recent writings on the subject can be found through the semiannual *Numismatic Literature* (1947–), a current index and bibliography.

041. *Numismatics*. By Philip Grierson. Oxford: Oxford University Press, 1975. 211p. Index. ISBN 0-19-888098-7.

Coins and medals are an important form of historical evidence, especially for the ancient and medieval periods. Numismatics is the study of coins and medals, and Grierson's book is an excellent introduction and overview of the subject. It discusses both Western and Eastern systems of coinage, the making of coins, numismatic methodology, and the importance of numismatics to the historian. There is a short glossary of numismatic terms and a brief bibliography to guide further reading. This work is available in paperback.

Paleography, Diplomatic, Epigraphy, and Sigillography

The topics comprising this section are concerned with the written word and its authentication. Paleography is the study of the handwritings of former eras. Before the advent of typewriters, handwriting was a more precise and regulated skill. It also evolved over time, so there is a need to learn how to read the scripts of the medieval and early modern eras even when they are written in English. Diplomatic is the study of the form of standardized official documents. Many government documents of the past concerning frequently occurring situations were stereotyped in their form and phrasing. A knowledge of those forms and phrases will allow the historian to read and to understand many such documents better. Epigraphy is the study of engraved inscriptions. Sigillography is the study of the seals used to authenticate documents in the past. Further bibliography on these subjects can be found in R. C. Van Caenegem's excellent *Guide to the Sources of Medieval History* [*see* 117].

042. *Bibliografia Paleografica.* By Josefina Mateu Ibars and Dolores Mateu Ibars. Barcelona: University of Barcelona, 1974. 932p. Index. ISBN 84-600-1760-5.

This massive work contains 10,000 entries and is the most comprehensive bibliography of its kind available. Although it is in Spanish, with patience and a Spanish-English dictionary the non-Spanish speaker can still find it quite useful. There are entries from all the major European languages. While its scope is all of Europe, western Europe—particularly the Iberian Peninsula—dominates. Furthermore, this bibliography goes beyond works simply on the study of paleography and includes guides to manuscript collections for various nations and subjects. There are indexes for authors, repositories, places, and journals.

043. *English Court Hand* A.D. 1066 to 1500: Illustrated Chiefly from the Public Records, *Part I: Text* and *Part II: Plates.* By Charles Johnson and Hilary Jenkinson. Oxford: Clarendon Press, 1915. 250 p. and 44 plates.

044. *The Later Court Hands in England: From the Fifteenth to the Seventeenth Century.* By Hilary Jenkinson. 1927. Reprint. Cambridge: Cambridge University Press, 1962. 200p. + plates.

Beginning researchers will want to examine these two works on the paleography of English historical documents from the Norman Conquest through the early modern era. Their coverage is detailed particularly in the earlier Johnson and Jenkinson volume. Introductory texts explain the history and methods of historical English handwritings. This material is followed by a large number of facsimiles of documents along with annotated transcriptions. A very detailed Italian textbook on paleography and diplomatic is Jole Mazzoleni, *Paleografia e Diplomatica e Scienze Ausiliarie* (Naples: Libreria Scientifica, 1970). L. C. Hector, *The Handwriting of English Documents* (London: Edward Arnold, 1966) is a smaller but still useful and more affordable version of Johnson and Jenkinson, as is C. E. Wright, *English Vernacular Hands from the Twelfth to the Fifteenth Centuries* (Oxford: Oxford Paleographical Handbooks, 1959).

045. *A Formula Book of English Official Historical Documents, Part I: Diplomatic Documents* and *Part II: Ministerial and Judicial Records.* Edited by Hubert Hall. 1908–1909. Reprint. New York: Burt Franklin, 1969. 170p. and 229p. ISBN 0-8337-1544-5.

This two-volume work is a collection of examples of the format and phrasings used in the major official English historical documents. Actual primary documents have been transcribed along with introductions and notations. Chronologically the documents range from Anglo-Saxon times to the nineteenth century, although medieval documents predominate. While only English documents, most of which are written in Latin, appear in this collection, it is still an excellent place for any beginning student of the Middle Ages to start learning about the structure and format of official documents. Many similar works exist for other countries. The first volume consists of "diplomatic documents" such as royal charters, warrants, writs, confirmations, letters, and proclamations by which the government communicated its orders and policies. In the second volume, the documents transcribed are the various ministerial and judicial inquisitions by which the government gathered fiscal, military, and legal information and resources. There is a very informative essay on the study of diplomatic in Hubert Hall's *Studies in English Official Historical Documents* (1908. Reprint. New York: Burt Franklin, 1969).

046. *Guide to Seals in the Public Record Office.* London: Her Majesty's Stationery Office, 1954. 67p.

Sigillography, the study of the seals used to authenticate official documents, is a highly technical subject within medieval studies on which little has been written in English. This short study is an admirable and lucid introduction to that subject for beginners. It focuses on the types of seals found in the Public Record Office of Great Britain while including some discussion of foreign seals and private seals. Although this study does not have a bibliography, references to further reading can be culled from its footnotes.

047. *Handbook of Greek and Latin Palaeography.* By Edward Maunde Thompson. London: Kegan Paul, Trench, Trubner & Co., 1906. 361p. Index.

Most students of history will never need to read handwritten manuscripts from the classical period of Greek and Roman history. But for those who do need to decipher the mysteries of ancient scripts, this older work is a useful introduction. Its scope is actually both ancient and medieval Greek and Latin hands. Many similar works, however, exist for the medieval and early modern periods.

The techniques and implements of writing are first described, and then various chapters discuss the different forms of Greek and Latin writing. A helpful but very dated bibliography identifies collections of facsimiles of documents.

048. *Heraldry, Flags, and Seals: A Select Bibliography, With Annotations, Covering the Period 1920 to 1945.* By S. Trehearne Cope. London: Association of Special Libraries and Information Bureaux, 1948. 146p. Index.

Although dated, the 445 annotated entries for books and articles in this bibliography are a useful introduction for students. The listings for seals are particularly helpful, as little is writtten about sigillography in the English language. A detailed subject index allows the user to find all materials of potential interest.

049. *Illustrated Introduction to Latin Epigraphy.* By Arthur E. Gordon. Berkeley: University of California Press, 1983. 264p. Index. ISBN 0-520-03898-3.

Monumental inscriptions are an incredibly important source of historical information for Greco-Roman classical civilization, which declines in significance, however, by the early medieval period. This volume consists of a short introduction that describes the nature of these inscriptions, their subject matter, and their format, and it supplies a bibliographic essay on the literature of epigraphy. A selection of 100 Latin inscriptions dating from the sixth century B.C. to A.D. 525 makes up the remainder of the book. E. G. Turner's *Greek Manuscripts of the Ancient World* (Oxford: Oxford University Press, and Princeton, NJ: Princeton University Press, 1971) performs a similar function for Greek sources. While *Illustrated Introduction to Latin Epigraphy* is an excellent starting place for the beginning student, still useful and more detailed is John Edwin Sandys, *Latin Epigraphy: An Introduction to the Study of Latin Inscriptions,* 2d ed. (1927. Reprint. Cambridge: Cambridge University Press, 1969).

050. *The Record Interpreter: A Collection of Abbreviations, Latin Words and Names Used in English Historical Manuscripts and Records.* 2d ed. Compiled by Charles Trice Martin. 1910. Reprint. Dorking, Surrey, England: Kohler & Coombes, 1976. 464p.

Old documents from the Middle Ages and the early modern periods are usually written in a Latin that is idiosyncratic and frequently abbreviated. Martin's book is a guide to deciphering and understanding these peculiarities. It contains a series of alphabetical lists:

abbreviations of Latin words, abbreviations of French words, a glossary of medieval Latin, and the Latin forms of various place-names, bishoprics, surnames, and Christian names used in England. A more detailed Italian work is *Lexicon Abbreviaturarum: Dizionario di Abbreviature Latine et Italiane,* 5th ed., by Adriano Cappelli (Milan: Hoepli, 1954), which is easily accessible to students with an elementary knowledge of Latin. Its entries include a facsimile of a handwritten abbreviation as well as printed versions of the abbreviations and their extended forms. There is an English translation of the introduction of Cappelli's book: *The Elements of Abbreviation in Medieval Latin Paleography* (Lawrence, KS: University Press of Kansas, 1982).

051. *Two Select Bibliographies of Mediaeval Historical Study: I. A Classified List of Works Relating to the Study of English Paleography and Diplomatic. II. A Classified List of Works Relating to English Manorial and Agrarian History from the Earliest Times to the Year 1660.* Edited by Margaret F. Moore. London, 1912. Reprint. New York: Burt Franklin, 1967. 185p. Index. ISBN 0-8337-2452-5.

The 428 items listed in the paleography and diplomatic section are what continues to make this older volume valuable to students of medieval history. Although it was originally published in 1912, this bibliography remains helpful because the study of paleography and diplomatic have not changed dramatically since the beginning of the twentieth century. While the focus of this book is the British Isles, the paleography section also deals with other Western European nations. There is an accompanying index for titles, authors, and subjects.

2.
Bibliographies

Once a subject of research has been decided on, a logical next step is to compile a bibliography of books, articles, and any other sources relevant to that topic. One approach is to mine the bibliographies and footnotes of other books, articles, or theses on the same general topic. This method will provide many useful items, but it would be foolish to rely on this method alone. Recent and relevant publications will be missed. Furthermore, it is unlikely that one researcher was trying to answer the same questions as another researcher, and older but relevant works will be overlooked when a researcher simply relies on the footnotes and bibliographies of other scholars. Only the use of a systematic approach will assure a reasonably complete list. That means methodically working through the appropriate bibliographies and indexes that have been painstakingly prepared by scholars and librarians for the use of other scholars and librarians.

This chapter looks at bibliographies and bibliographic guides of value and interest to historical research. A bibliography is an organized list of books, articles, or other materials that focus on some topic, sometimes a fairly general one, such as European history, or a specific one, like Iceland in the Middle Ages. The individual entries may also provide further brief information in the form of annotations. Bibliographic guides do more. They tend to be more heavily annotated and contain additional introductory and explanatory information to guide the researcher's choice. Another type of bibliographic listing is the periodical index, but that will be discussed later in a separate chapter.

The variety and number of bibliographies and bibliographic guides that are available are very large, and more are being added all the time. This, in turn, has made further bibliographies necessary. Discovering what bibliographies are available and what new ones are being published is the purpose of bibliographies about bibliographies. Librarians have to try to keep track of tens of thousands of new books as they are published every year. National bibliographies cite books published in a particular country. Those that keep track of the appearance of new books are current national bibliographies; those attempting to list books published in the past are retrospective national bibliographies. Most bibliographies, however, deal with defined topics, citing relevant books and articles wherever published. The subjects may be as extensive as all modern history or as specific as the works written about a single county or town. They list works on their subject as far back as useful scholarship exists. In this way they are retrospective, although some bibliographies list only recent works, which makes them "current awareness" or simply "current" bibliographies. This type of bibliography is usually published in a serial form, generally appearing annually.

The items listed in this chapter begin with a section of useful bibliographies citing reference works. These are followed by a section that looks at national bibliographies, with an emphasis on books published in the United States and Britain. The third section deals with general historical bibliography. This is followed by sections dealing with important national or regional bibliographies, some of the more significant bibliographies for chronological periods, and finally with a selection of bibliographies on important subfields of history.

Bibliographies of Reference Works

052. *American Reference Books Annual.* Edited by Bohdan S. Wynar. Littleton, CO: Libraries Unlimited, 1970–. ISSN 0065-9959. Annual.

For up-to-date reviews that describe and evaluate new reference works, this publication is an excellent source and can be used to supplement Sheehy's *Guide to Reference Books* [*see* 055]. Each volume covers the previous year's new publications. The reviews average 250 words in length, are signed, and include references to reviews of the same work in other publications. They are arranged by subject, e.g., fine arts, political science, area studies, and, of course, history. Many books of interest to historians appear in sections other than that for history. Each volume includes an author/subject/title index. Cumulative indexes are published for every five years.

053. *Bibliographic Index: A Cumulative Bibliography of Bibliographies.* New York: H. W. Wilson, Vol. 1–. 1937–. ISSN 0006-1255.

Published in April, August, and December; the last part is a bound cumulative annual. New bibliographies appear constantly. The purpose of this publication is to provide a current listing of them. Originally *Bibliographic Index* appeared every three years, but in 1969 it started to appear annually. It is organized by detailed subject categories. The types of items listed include not only separate published bibliographies but also bibliographies that appear as parts of books, pamphlets, and journals. A bibliography has to contain 50 or more entries for inclusion. The listing focuses on works in English, Germanic languages, and Romance languages.

054. *Essay and General Literature Index.* New York: H. W. Wilson, 1900–. Published twice yearly; the second part is an annual cumulation that later is incorporated into a five-year cumulation. ISSN 0014-083X.

Unlike most other Wilson indexes, this one is not concerned with periodicals. Instead, it indexes collections of articles appearing in books on subjects in the humanities and social sciences. Such collective books include festschriften, for example, collections of essays published in honor of a famous scholar. Individual entries appear alphabetically, where appropriate, under the headings of authors, subject, and occasionally title. There is a separate listing by author or editor and title of the books indexed in each volume. This often neglected index is an excellent source for discovering high-quality, scholarly contributions.

055. *Guide to Reference Books.* 10th ed. Edited by Eugene Sheehy. Chicago: American Library Association, 1986. 1,560p. Index. ISBN 0-8389-0390-8.

Probably the best general bibliography for locating reference materials on all subjects is the *Guide to Reference Books.* It used to be known as "Winchell," after an earlier editor, and now is often simply referred to as "Sheehy," its present editor. Five broad sections divide the volume: general reference works, humanities, social sciences, history and area studies, and pure and applied sciences. These sections are further divided by subject, disciplines, or geographical areas, such as newspapers, philosophy, law, the Americas, and chemistry. Within these divisions, more specialized categories, appropriate to that context, are used. Individual entries are given an alphanumeric designation followed by the bibliographic citation and a descriptive and evaluative annotation. There is a large author, title, name, and subject index. All library researchers, particularly

students of history, will frequently find this work very helpful. A
similar publication, devoted solely to Canada, is *Canadian Reference
Sources: A Selective Guide*, edited by Dorothy E. Ryder (Ottawa:
Canadian Library Association).

056. *Sources of Information in the Social Sciences: A Guide to the Literature*. 3d ed. Edited by William H. Webb et al. Chicago: American
Library Association, 1986. 777p. Index. ISBN 0-8389-0405-X.

Many historians use methodologies and interpretive insights first
developed in one of the social sciences. Therefore, they will find this
bibliography to be a useful and reasonably up-to-date resource. Besides
general social science, the disciplines covered in this guide are geography, economics and business administration, sociology,
anthropology, psychology, education, political science, and even history. Each individual discipline's section is divided into two parts.
First, a subject specialist discusses the core or representative
monographic literature. Next comes an annotated listing of important
reference works: bibliographies, dictionaries, and handbooks. Individual entries are all assigned an alphanumeric designation. There is
a detailed index as well as much cross-referencing throughout the text.

057. *Walford's Guide to Reference Material*, Vol. 1 *Science and
Technology*, Vol. 2 *Social and Historical Sciences, Philosophy & Religion*,
and Vol. 3 *Generalia, Language & Literature, the Arts*. 4th ed. Edited by
A. J. Walford. London: Library Association, 1980–1987. ISBNs
0-85365-611-8, 0-85365-564-2, and 0-85365-836-6.

Usually referred to just as "Walford," this work is the British
counterpart of Sheehy's *Guide to Reference Works* [*see* 055]. An emphasis is placed on listing reference books that are recent and in
English. The first volume contains 4,000 annotated entries, with
references to another 1,000 works. There are 5,000 entries in the
second volume, with a further 2,000 works mentioned in the annotations. More than 7,000 works appear in the entries of volume three
along with an additional 2,000 works referred to in the annotations.
The annotations describe the work and evaluate its usefulness.
There is a separate index for each volume. In the first two volumes
subjects, authors, and titles are indexed but in the third volume only
authors and titles. While Sheehy and Walford overlap considerably
in their listings, they also complement each other, as Walford lists
more British and European items.

058. *A World Bibliography of Bibliographies and of Bibliographic
Catalogues, Calendars, Abstracts, Digests, Indexes, and the Like*. 4th ed.

By Theodore Besterman. Lausanne, Switzerland: Societas Biblio-
graphica, 1965–1966. 5 vols. Index.

059. *A World Bibliography of Bibliographies, 1964–74; A List of Works
Represented by Library of Congress Print Catalog Cards. A Decennial
Supplement to Theodore Besterman, A World Bibliography of Bibliographies.* By Alice F. Toomey. Totowa, NJ: Rowman and Littlefield,
1977. 2 vols. ISBN 0-87471-999-2.

Together these two massive works respectively list 117,000 and
18,000 separately published bibliographies and lists of manuscripts
and patents published through 1974. Many of these can be used in
historical research. The first set is truly international in scope, while
the supplement is limited to those items for which Library of Congress catalog cards were printed and includes new editions and
reprints of works listed by Besterman. Entries are organized under
various subject headings and subheadings such as "Bolivar, Simon,"
"Mormons," or "Toulouse, battle of." The fifth volume of
Besterman's work is an index to authors, titles, libraries and archives, and patents. This work is definitely worth consulting to
determine whether a bibliography exists. Theodore Besterman's
four-volume *History and Geography: A Bibliography of Bibliographies*
(Totowa, NJ: Rowman & Littlefield, 1972) is a reprint of the relevant
material from his larger work.

National Bibliographies and Library Catalogs

Guides

060. *An Annotated Guide to Current National Bibliographies.* By Barbara
L. Bell. Alexandria, VA: Chadwyck-Healey, 1986. 407p. ISBN
0-85964-123-6.

Current national bibliographies are regular listings of new publications about a particular country or published in that country. The
British National Bibliography and the U.S. *National Union Catalog* are
classic examples of the national bibliography, but most countries
have also begun to publish similar publications. These publications
provide a publishing history for the sponsoring nation and so can be
valuable to historians. Barbara Bell's guide supplies a selective listing of these publications. Entries for individual countries provide
the title of the relevant bibliography, its compiler(s), the scope and
coverage, contents, the cataloging and classification system used,

information on individual entries, organization, indexes, currency, availability, and notes on other unique aspects of the publication. There is also a separate, selective bibliography of writings on national bibliographies. Another similar work, although limited to Third World nations, is G. E. Gorman and J. J. Mills, *Guide to Current National Bibliographies in the Third World*, 2d ed. (London: H. Zell, 1987).

061. *Retrospective National Bibliographies: An International Directory.* Edited by Marcelle Beaudiquez. Munich and New York: K. G. Saur, 1986. 189p. Index. ISBN 3-598-20399-3.

Historians frequently use the books of earlier eras as primary sources, and retrospective national bibliographies allow them to locate those types of books. The purpose of this work is to provide an inventory of available retrospective national bibliographies from throughout the world, excluding Eastern bloc nations. Because not every country possesses a formal retrospective national bibliography, the types of materials listed by this work are not limited to retrospective bibliographies. They also include bibliographies that contain both materials published in a particular country and materials about that particular country, plus catalogs of special and national libraries that perform the function of supplying a retrospective bibliography. These items are organized alphabetically by country and within each country in chronological order of their publication. The section on each country begins with a brief history of publishing there, and the individual entries include a bibliographic citation along with a descriptive annotation. There is a brief author-title index.

United States

062. *American Bibliography; A Chronological Dictionary of all Books, Pamphlets and Periodical Publications Printed in the United States of America from the Genesis of Printing in 1639 down to the Year 1800; with Bibliographical and Biographical Notes.* By Charles Evans. Chicago: By the author, and Worcester, MA: American Antiquarian Society, 1903–1959. Reprint 1941–1967. 14 vols. Index. ISBN 0-8446-1175-1.

063. *Supplement to Charles Evans' American Bibliography.* By Roger Pattrell Bristol. Charlottesville, VA: University Press of Virginia, 1970. 636p. ISBN 0-8139-0287-8.

064. *National Index of American Imprints through 1800: The Short-Title Evans.* By Clifford Kenyon Shipton and James E. Mooney. Worcester, MA: American Antiquarian Society, 1969. 2 vols.

Charles Evans is one of the giants of historical bibliography in the United States. His bibliography provides a chronological listing of almost 36,000 books from the beginning of North American printing in 1639 through 1800. Besides being available at those libraries that own original copies of these books, they are also on the microcard and microfiche collection *Early American Imprints 1639–1800* [*see* 674 and 675]. Originally Evans planned to go to 1820, but he had completed only about half of the year 1800 at the time of his death. The works of Bristol and Shipton and Mooney supplement and amplify that of Evans. Of related interest is J. Sabin's *Bibliotheca Americana* and its associated titles [*see* 071].

065. *American Bibliography; A Preliminary Checklist for 1801–1819*. By Ralph Robert Shaw and Richard H. Shoemaker. New York: Scarecrow Press, 1958–1966. 22 vols. ISBN 0-8108-1607-5.

066. *A Checklist of American Imprints for 1820–1829*. By Richard H. Shoemaker. New York: Scarecrow Press, 1964–1971. 10 vols. *Title Index*. By M. Frances Cooper. Metuchen, NJ: Scarecrow Press, 1972. 556p.

067. *A Checklist of American Imprints for 1830–*. Metuchen, NJ: Scarecrow Press. 1972–. Vol. 1– (in progress).

068. *Bibliotheca Americana: A Catalogue of American Publications, including Reprints and Original Works, from 1820 to 1861*. By Orville Augustus Roorbach. New York: Roorbach, 1852–1861. Reprint 1939. 4 vols.

069. *The American Catalogue of Books (Original and Reprints), Published in the United States from Jan. 1861 to Jan. 1871, with Date of Publication, Size, Price, and Publisher's Name*. By James Kelly. New York: Wiley, 1866–1871. Reprint 1938. 2 vols.

070. *American Catalogue founded by F. Leypoldt, 1876–1910*. New York: Publishers Weekly, 1880–1911. Reprint 1941. 8 vols. in 13 parts. Title varies.

The modern work of historical bibliography for the United States begun by Charles Evans has been continued by that of Shaw, Shoemaker, and others. Again books are listed chronologically by year of publication. But much of the nineteenth century remains to be completed. In the meantime, the works of Roorbach, Kelly, and Leypoldt provide adequate guides to publications.

071. *Bibliotheca Americana: A Dictionary of Books Relating to America, from its Discovery to the Present Time*. By Joseph Sabin, and continued

by Wilberforce Eames and R. W. C. Vail. New York: Joseph Sabin, 1868–1892; New York: Bibliographical Society of America, 1928–1936. 28 vols.

This classic bibliography, often known simply as "Sabin," contains 106,413 numbered items as well as mentioning many others in its notes. Its purpose is to list by author all books concerned with America, including in some cases the libraries where they can be found. The books listed do not necessarily have to have been published in the United States. An aid for using Sabin is provided by J. E. Molnar's *Author-Title Index to Joseph Sabin's 'Dictionary of Books Relating to America'* (New York: Scarecrow, 1975. 3 vols.). A modern revision of Sabin's work can be found in L. S. Thompson's *The New Sabin: Books Described by Joseph Sabin and His Successors, Newly Described Again on the Basis of Examination of the Originals, and Fully Indexed by Title, Subject, Joint Authors, and Institutions and Agencies* (Troy, NY: Whitson, 1974– [in progress], 8 vols.) and *European Americana: A Chronological Guide to Works Printed in Europe Relating to the Americas 1493–1776* edited by J. Alden and D. C. Landis (New York: Readex, 1980– [in progress]).

072. *Books in Print.* New York: Bowker, 1948–. Annual. ISSN 0068-0214.

For determining the current availability for purchase of a book, this massive set is the best source and can be found in most libraries and bookstores. It was originally subtitled *An Author-Title-Series Index to the Publishers' Trade List Annual,* but that practice stopped in 1972. It is now published in separate alphabetically arranged sets for authors, titles, and subjects; another volume lists publishers and their addresses. Many other countries have similar publications: for Great Britain there is *Whitaker's Books in Print: The Reference Catalogue of Current Literature* (1874–), and for France *Les Livres Disponibles* (1977–). Also useful are the publications *Books in Series 1876–1949* (New York: Bowker, 1982. 3 vols.) and *Books in Series in the United States* (New York: Bowker, 1977–). Other current listings of English-language publications in the United States and other parts of the world are *Cumulative Books Index, A World List of Books in the English Language* (New York: H. W. Wilson, 1933–) and the *American Book Publishing Record* (New York: Bowker, 1960–). Retrospective cumulations of *American Book Publishing Record* and the *United States Catalog; Books in Print* (New York: H. W. Wilson, 1899–1928. Four editions) take the listings back to 1876, where they overlap with the *American Catalogue* (1876–1910) [see 070].

073. *National Union Catalog, pre-1956 Imprints. A Cumulative Author List Representing Library of Congress Printed Cards and Titles Reported by Other American Libraries.* [London]: Mansell, 1968–1980. 685 vols. and *Supplement.* [London]: Mansell, 1980–1981. Vols. 686–754.

Generally referred to as the NUC. More than 13 million books, pamphlets, maps, atlases, and music held by the Library of Congress and other research libraries in the United States are listed in this massive publication. Individual items are listed alphabetically by personal or corporate author, usually as a Library of Congress catalog card. Entries also supply a list of other libraries owning that item. Materials from all over the world, from the beginning of printing and in myriad languages, appear on these pages. It is a good source for discovering and locating books and other materials. The *National Union Catalog: A Cumulative Author List* continues the coverage of the pre-1956 imprints volumes. Published on paper monthly with quarterly, yearly, and quinquennial cumulations until 1983, when the set began to appear on microfiche, these newer volumes are not as useful to historical research as the pre-1956 volumes. They are, however, the closest thing the U.S. has to a current national bibliography.

United Kingdom

074. *The British Library General Catalogue of Printed Books to 1975.* London: Bingley; London: K. G. Saur, 1980–1987. 360 vols. ISBN 0-86291-006-4.

This set is the British version of the *National Union Catalog, pre-1956 Imprints,* and it cumulates and supersedes the previous *British Museum, Department of Printed Books, General Catalogue of Printed Books, Photolithographic Edition to 1955* and its various supplements. The new set has been supplemented for acquisitions through 1985. Books are basically listed under personal or corporate author, although there are some subject entries. For most historical questions, the older catalog is quite adequate and probably will be more readily available given the high price of the new catalog. There is also the separate *Subject Index of the Modern Works Added to the Library, 1881–1900,* edited by G. K. Fortesque (London: British Museum, 1902–1903. 3 vols.), which has been continued at this point for books acquired through 1985.

075. *A Short Title Catalogue of Books Printed in England, Scotland and Ireland and of English Books Printed Abroad, 1475–1640.* 2d ed.

Compiled by Alfred W. Pollard and G. R. Redgrave. Rev. and enl. by W. A. Jackson, F. S. Ferguson, and Katherine F. Pantzer. Oxford: Oxford University Press, 1976–1986. 2 vols. ISBNs 0-19-721789-3 and 0-19-721790-7.

076. *Short Title Catalogue of Books Printed in England, Scotland, Ireland and British America, and of English Books Printed in Other Countries, 1641–1700.* 2d ed. Compiled by D. G. Wing and T. J. Crist. New York: Modern Language Association, 1972–1988. 3 vols. ISBN 0-87352-044-0.

077. *The Eighteenth Century: Guide to the Microfilm Collection.* Woodbridge, CT: Research Publications, 1984–.

078. *Eighteenth-Century British Books: An Author Union Catalogue.* Edited by F. J. G. Robinson. Folkestone, England: Dawson, 1981–1982. 5 vols.

079. *Nineteenth Century Short Title Catalogue. Series I. Phase I. 1801–1815.* Newcastle-upon-Tyne, England: Avero; Alexandria, VA: Chadwyck-Healey, 1984–. ISBN 0-907977-05-7.

These various sets are often indiscriminately referred to as STCs— Short Title Catalogues. They are guides to books published in England or in English from the beginning of printing to 1918. Individual works are listed under the name of their author and provide a bibliographic citation besides giving the locations of various British and American libraries that own copies. Most of the books listed for the sixteenth and seventeenth centuries can now be read on commercially published microfilms purchased by research libraries. Eventually many of the eighteenth- and nineteenth-century books will be available in the same format. The two earlier sets are frequently referred to as "Pollard and Redgrave" or "Wing." The earlier editions of their works are still worth consulting if the second editions are not available. Since the eighteenth- and nineteenth-century works are being compiled on computerized data bases and microfiche, they are available or will be for on-line searching.

General Historical Bibliographies

Bibliographies of Bibliographies

080. *Bibliographies in History,* Vol. 1: *An Index to Bibliographies in History Journals and Dissertations Covering the U.S. and Canada,* and Vol. 2: *An Index to Bibliographies in History Journals and Dissertations*

Covering All Countries of the World Except the U.S. and Canada. Santa Barbara, CA: ABC-CLIO, 1988. 459p. ISBN 0-87436-521-X.

Bibliographies in History provides an annotated bibliography of difficult-to-locate bibliographical items appearing in journals and dissertations. It is based on the data bases used to compile *America: History and Life* and *Historical Abstracts* [*see* 234 and 236]. Therefore, its coverage of literature in journals goes back to 1954 and of dissertations to 1974. In all, the two-volume set contains 5,000 entries. Volume I deals with 1,461 items on subjects about the U.S. and Canada. The rest of the world is covered by the second volume, which consists of 3,437 entries. Individual entries are numbered and supply the full bibliographic information. Most entries also include a helpful descriptive annotation and are signed by the author. Both volumes have their own separate author and subject indexes. This set is a convenient and up-to-date reference source that will be of interest to both specialists and beginning students.

081. *A Consumer's Guide to the Current Bibliography of Historical Literature: Antiquity, the Middle Ages, Modern Western Europe, North America, and Latin America.* Prepared by the Bibliography and Indexes Committee of the History Section of the Reference and Adult Services Division. Chicago: American Library Association, 1988. 53p. Index. ISBN 0-8389-7240-3.

Designed to meet the needs of people beginning library research in history, this publication discusses 29 indexes of interest to historians. It is divided into five main sections: antiquity, the Middle Ages, modern Western Europe, North America, and Latin America. This division is somewhat artificial, since publications in one section frequently contain material also appropriate to the scope of other sections. Individual titles are classified either as principal current indexes or as other current bibliographies and indexes. Entries for principal indexes are more detailed, but all entries supply a bibliographic citation and descriptive and evaluative information on scope, format, and coverage. This includes information on whether the publication has a computerized data base that can be searched on-line. There is a title index.

082. *Historical Bibliographies: A Systematic and Annotated Guide.* By Edith M. Coulter and Melanie Gerstenfeld. New York: Russell and Russell, 1935. Reprint 1965. 206p. Index.

First published in 1935, this 775-item work is badly dated. There is a brief section of general bibliographies. This is followed by the historical bibliographies, which begin with those concerned with general history. Next come sections dealing with broad chronological periods or individual countries. Individual entries are numbered and listed by the compiler, followed by the title and other bibliographic information. Citations to reviews of the various bibliographies are supplied along with a brief but evaluative and descriptive annotation. There is an index to authors, titles, and subjects. An up-to-date selective guide similar to Coulter and Gerstenfeld's would be useful for many students.

083. *Serial Bibliographies and Abstracts in History.* Compiled by David Henige. Westport, CT: Greenwood Press, 1986. 220p. Index. ISBN 0-313-25070-7.

This useful bibliography lists almost 900 abstracts, serial bibliographies, and bibliographic surveys published in journals. The emphasis is on bibliographies listing journal articles, and works solely devoted to listing books are excluded. History is defined in the broadest sense, so this work includes many mainly literary, economic, or social-science publications. Entries are numbered and arranged alphabetically by title. The annotations describe the bibliography's scope, size, and periodicity, with some evaluation of its quality. Cross-references are provided to other related items. This bibliography contains an impressive range of listings, although there are some surprising omissions. An older and more general version of the same type of publication is *Serial Bibliographies in the Humanities and Social Sciences* by Richard A. Gray and Dorothy Villmow (Ann Arbor, MI: Pierian Press, 1969), while the listings in *Serial Bibliographies for Medieval Studies* by Richard Rouse (Berkeley: University of California Press, 1969) go far beyond the scope indicated by the title in their interest to all historians.

Current Bibliographies

084. *Annual Bulletin of Historical Literature.* London: Historical Association, Vol. 1–. 1911–.

Intended for teachers and students in both secondary and higher education, librarians, and the general reader, this publication consists of bibliographic essays/chapters surveying and evaluating the significant publications, both books and journal articles, of the previous year. Each essay is authored by one or more experts in the field. After an essay on general works, most of the remaining chapters cover chronological periods in European history, e.g., "Ancient History" and "Eighteenth Century." There are also regional chapters for Africa, the Americas, and Asia and Oceania. As a result the publication has a definite European emphasis. The individual chapters are further subdivided into sections on various regions, nations, or topics. There is a name index for authors and a few titles of journals. A related publication is the annual *International Bibliography of Historical Sciences* (New York: K. G. Saur for the International Committee of Historical Sciences, 1947–), which is not very current and is difficult to use due to its arrangement and the many languages used in its compilation.

085. *Recently Published Articles.* Washington, DC: American Historical Association, Vol. 1–. 1976–. ISSN 0145-5311. Published three times a year, in the spring, summer, and autumn.

Although this particular publication first appeared separately in 1976, it was published as part of the *American Historical Review* from 1895 to 1975. Its purpose is to provide a current listing of a selection of new journal articles of interest to historians. No other publication matches it in its combination of currency and comprehensiveness. The scope of its interests is worldwide and covers all periods of history. Although periodicals in English predominate, 4,000 journals, including those in many other languages, are surveyed. It is divided into 20 sections, based on chronological period or geographical region, which are compiled by editors who are experts in that field of history. There are further chronological and geographical subdivisions within the sections, with the individual entries listed alphabetically by the name of the author. There is no index, because the organization functions as a subject index. *Recently Published Articles* ceased publication at the end of 1990.

Guides

086. *The American Historical Association's Guide to Historical Literature.* Edited by George Frederick Howe et al. New York: Macmillan, 1961. 962p. Index.

Designed to be "an inventory of the best historical literature extant at the time of compilation" (v.p.), this work serves as an introductory bibliography to guide further study in all fields of history. It contains approximately 20,000 entries organized into nine broad categories: introduction and general history, ancient history, the Middle Ages, Asia, modern Europe, the Americas, Africa, Australasia and Oceania, and recent history. These categories are further subdivided into 40 sections, which are assigned a letter or combination of letters.

Each section has an editor (or editors) who is an expert in the field to select the items to be included. The sections are further organized into various chronological divisions and topics. Individual entries are assigned an alphanumeric designation based on the section's letter and their order of appearance in the section. The various works are listed alphabetically by author with a bibliographic citation followed by a brief descriptive and evaluative annotation. There is an extensive author, title, and subject index. This work is quite dated, but a completely new edition to be published by Oxford University Press in two volumes is in preparation and is planned to appear in 1994.

087. *The Historian's Handbook: A Descriptive Guide to Reference Works.* By Helen J. Poulton and Marguerite S. Howland. Norman, OK: University of Oklahoma Press, 1972. 304p. Index. ISBN 0-8061-1009-0.

This work has stood for many years as the one-volume guide to the reference materials for the study of general history. Its scope is all periods of history and all geographical areas, although the emphasis remains on the U.S. and Western Europe. There are 11 chapters covering such topics as library organization, bibliographies, encyclopedias and dictionaries, serials and newspapers, legal sources, and government publications. Individual chapters are written as bibliographic essays; full citations to works appear in the footnotes. Separate indexes for title and subjects and authors allow the reader to locate readily both individual items and all those that are concerned with a common subject. Although this work remains useful, the continued publication of new reference works and the revolutionary expansion of computerized data bases and microforms have rendered it somewhat dated.

Specialized Historical Bibliographies: Regions and Countries

United States

General

088. *Bibliographies in American History: Guide to Materials for Research.* By Henry Putney Beers. New York: H. W. Wilson, 1942. 487p. Index.

089. *Bibliographies in American History, 1942–1978: Guide to Materials for Research.* By Henry Putney Beers. Woodbridge, CT: Research Publications, 1982. 2 vols. Index. ISBN 0-89235-038-5.

These two works by Henry Putney Beers provide a bibliography of bibliographies concerning American history published during or before 1978. The 1942 edition lists 7,500 titles, and the 1982 edition contains an additional 12,000 entries. Works listed include not just bibliographies published as separate works; there are also bibliographies that form parts of books, bibliographies appearing in journals, and government publications. Chapters are organized topically, and a large amount of space is devoted to bibliographies concerning individual states. Extensive indexes locate personal names, subjects, and places. The bibliographies listed in Prucha's *Handbook for Research in American History* [*see* 090] take up, to a large degree, where Beers left off.

090. *Handbook for Research in American History: A Guide to Bibliographies and Other Reference Works.* By Francis Paul Prucha. Lincoln, NE: University of Nebraska Press, 1987. 289p. Index. ISBN 0-8032-3682-4.

Prucha's *Handbook* is an excellent resource for all students of American history, both beginners and veterans, and it is available in paperback. Its 1,500 items are divided into two parts. Part I contains 800 items in 16 chapters, each dealing with a different type of material commonly found in research libraries or archives. The chapters range from "Libraries: Catalogs and Guides" to "Databases," with such topics as manuscripts, oral history, newspapers, and legal sources coming in between. Each chapter is a combination of a bibliographical essay and bibliographic listing that is sometimes lightly annotated. Individual items are assigned a reference number. The second part of the guide contains 700 items in 15 chapters, which list new and important bibliographies on such subjects in American history as "Foreign Policy," "Women," and "Economic History." Each chapter begins with a brief introduction followed by a lightly annotated bibliography. This section is designed to supplement Henry Putney Beers' two-volume *Bibliographies in American History* [*see* 088 and 089].

091. *Harvard Guide to American History.* Edited by Frank Freidel with Richard K. Showman. Cambridge: Harvard University Press, 1974. 2 vols. Index. ISBN 0-674-37560-2.

This classic bibliographic guide to American history is an excellent selective bibliography for books and articles published before 30

June 1970. The items selected are intended to be useful for general readers, students, and scholars. The guide is divided into two volumes. In the first there are 29 chapters organized into four sections: research methods and materials, biographies and personal records, comprehensive and area histories, and special subjects (e.g., immigration and ethnicity, education, and literature). The second volume consists of 27 chapters divided into five chronological sections: America to 1789; United States, 1789–1860; Civil War and Reconstruction; Rise of Industry and Empire; and Twentieth Century. Early chapters in the first volume begin with descriptive essays on methods and sources, followed by bibliographic listings. Most chapters, however, are simply classified bibliographies. There is a large index for personal and proper names in the second volume. A paperback edition containing both volumes in one is available. The time is approaching for the preparation of a new edition of this increasingly dated standard of historical reference.

092. *Writings on American History: A Subject Bibliography of Articles.* Edited by Cecilia Dadian. Millwood, NY: Kraus-Thomson for the American Historical Association, 1974–. Annual. The old series, published from 1903 to 1977, covered the years 1903–1961. There were no volumes published for 1941–1947. The years 1962–1973 are covered by separate cumulative sets.

Sponsored by the American Historical Association, *Writings on American History* originally listed books, essays in books, and articles in journals. The bulk of new publications became so great, however, that by 1977 the original series closed with the year 1961. Well before that time, scholars recognized that the situation was intolerable. So in 1974 the first volume of the new series of *Writings on American History* appeared, which limited its coverage to journal articles. Approximately 4,000 journals are surveyed annually for relevant articles, although ordinarily only about 500–600 journals will contain relevant items. Material from *Recently Published Articles* [see 085] forms the basis for each new *Writings on American History*, although many additional items are added. Entries are arranged in chronological, geographical, and topical sections, each with numerous subheadings. With the 1986–1987 volume, a more detailed subdivision of the geographical section was adopted. The volumes that fill the gap between 1961 and 1974 are *Writings on American History, 1962–73: A Subject Bibliography of Articles* edited by James J. Dougherty (Millwood, NY: KTO Press, 1976. 4 vols.) and *Writings on American History, 1962–1973: A Subject Bibliography of Books and Monographs* (White Plains, NY: Kraus International, 1985. 9 vols.).

The latter set is based on Library of Congress catalog cards, and each volume contains author and personal name indexes. *Writings in American History* ceased publication at the end of 1990.

Specialized by Regions or Chronological Period

093. *A Bibliography of American County Histories*. Compiled by P. William Filby. Baltimore, MD: Genealogical Publishing, 1985. 449p. ISBN 0-8063-1126-6.

Filby has attempted to provide a comprehensive listing of every significant county history published before the beginning of 1985. Whenever possible, he supplies full bibliographic information, including the number of pages and the existence of reprint editions. Only true county histories have been listed, so the various local biographical collections and atlases have been ignored. When four or five substantial histories exist for a county, commemorative works of fewer than 100 pages have been eliminated. The arrangement is alphabetical by state and within each state alphabetical by county. Works dealing with more than one county are listed in a "regional" section at the beginning of an individual state's listings. This work is more up-to-date and accessible than Marion J. Kaminkow's *United States Local Histories in the Library of Congress: A Bibliography* (Baltimore, MD: Magna Carta Book Company, 1975, 5 vols.) but is much less comprehensive and leaves out some important county histories.

094. *Bibliography of American Historical Societies (The United States and Canada)*. 2d ed. By Appleton Prentiss Griffin. 1907. Reprint. Detroit: Gale, 1966. 1,374p. Index. ISBN 0-87968-736-3.

Originally published in 1895 as part of the *Annual Report of the American Historical Association,* this bibliography was revised and updated through some of 1905 and again published as the second volume of the *Annual Report of the American Historical Association for the Year 1905* (Washington, DC: Government Printing Office, 1907). It lists more than 7,500 publications by the various national, state, and local historical societies in North America. The work has a section for national societies such as the American Historical Association and the National Geographic Society, as well as a state historical societies section. Individual entries provide bibliographic information and sometimes include descriptive or contents annotations. There are separate indexes for authors and subjects, biographies, and societies. This bibliography is a very useful source for printed primary documents.

095. *A Bibliography of United States-Latin American Relations since 1810.* Edited by David E. Trask, Michael C. Meyer, and Roger R. Trask. Lincoln: University of Nebraska Press, 1968. 441p. ISBN 0-8032-0185-0.

096. *Supplement to a Bibliography of United States-Latin American Relations since 1810.* Lincoln: University of Nebraska Press, 1979. 193p. ISBN 0-8032-3051-6.

These two volumes are the most comprehensive guide to the literature of U.S.-Latin American relations prior to the 1980s. They contain entries for approximately 15,000 books, articles, and dissertations. Following a chapter listing guides and other reference works, each volume is organized into two main sections, which are supplemented by several specialized chapters. The first approaches the topic by chronological periods, and the second focuses on individual countries.

097. *The Frontier Experience: A Reader's Guide to the Life and Literature of the American West.* Edited by John Tuska and Vicki Piekarski with Paul J. Blandings. Jefferson, NC: McFarland, 1984. 434p. Index. ISBN 0-89950-118-4.

The American West is a topic closely associated with romance and legend as well as history. Therefore, this bibliographic guide deals with both the history and the fiction of the West. Altogether, there are 23 chapters written by eight contributors in this book. Each chapter begins with an introductory essay followed by an annotated bibliography. The first 17 chapters deal with historical subjects such as native Americans, religion, and transportation and conclude with lists of suggested fiction and films on that topic. In the remaining five chapters, how the West was depicted in fiction, poetry, art, film, and television are discussed. There are separate name and title indexes. Although it is written for the general reader, anyone beginning to study the American West will find it worth consulting.

098. *Revolutionary America 1763–1789: A Bibliography.* Compiled by Ronald M. Gephart. Washington, DC: Government Printing Office, 1984. 2 vols. Index. ISBNs 0-8444-0359-8 and 0-8444-0379-2.

As an example of a bibliography covering an important subject, this work is excellent. It contains 20,000 titles published before the end of 1972, presented in almost 15,000 entries. The goal was to list all the important printed primary sources and secondary literature, including dissertations, festschriften, journal articles, and newspapers. Intended for a mixed audience of professional historians, educated laymen, librarians, and students, this work achieves that objective. The entries are organized into 12 chapters. These cover topics such as research and reference sources, general and local histories, the political history of various periods and regions during the years 1763–1789, the making of the Constitution, the economic, social, and intellectual history of the era, and biographical material. Individual entries are assigned a number and provide the standard bibliographical citation as well as a Library of Congress call number. About 40 percent of the entries have annotations—bibliographic and descriptive—averaging about 125 words. A large index consists of proper names and some broad subjects.

United Kingdom and Ireland

099. *Royal Historical Society Annual Bibliography of British and Irish History*. Brighton, England: Harvester Press, and New York: St. Martin's Press, 1975–. ISSN 0308-4558.

Starting its coverage with 1974, first published in 1975 under the editorship of Sir Geoffrey Elton, and now edited by D. M. Palliser, this publication provides bibliographic information on new publications quickly. It lists monographs, journal articles, collections of articles, edited documents, reference works, and any other relevant printed materials. The coverage, as the title indicates, is limited to British history, including British colonial and foreign policies. The chronological coverage extends from the Roman occupation to the present. Beginning with two chapters on auxiliary works and general works on British history, the bibliography is divided into various geographical and chronological periods, e.g., "England 450–1066" and "Scotland before the Union." Each of those sections is compiled by a different editor. Within the sections, the editors further classify entries under categories like "Religion," "Economic Affairs," and "Cultural and Intellectual." Individual entries are assigned an alphanumeric designation. This indicates the section where they are located and the order in which they were prepared, as that is the order in which they are printed. Author and subject indexes allow the reader to locate needed items. For those wishing to keep up with the bulk of the new research on British and Irish history, this annual publication is the place to look. *Writings on British History* (London: Institute of Historical Research and Royal Historical Society, 1937–) was originally intended to fill this bibliographic niche and was far more sophisticated. But like *Writings on American History* [*see* 092], it fell further behind in its currency and will be discontinued when it reaches 1974. *Writings on Irish History* (published in *Irish Historical Studies*, 1936–), however, has kept current.

100. *Texts and Calendars: An Analytical Guide to Serial Publications.* By E. L. C. Mullins. London: Royal Historical Society, 1958. Reprint 1978. 685p. Index. ISBN 0-8476-1347-X.

101. *Texts and Calendars II: An Analytical Guide to Serial Publications 1957–1982.* By E. L. C. Mullins. London: Royal Historical Society, 1983. 323p. Index. ISBN 0-86193-100-9.

These two very useful volumes provide annotated lists of the various printed collections of historical documents and calendars of documents published by government agencies and local record societies in England and Wales. Such bodies include the Public Record Office of Great Britain, the British Academy, the Hakluyt Society, and the South Wales and Monmouth Record Society. Individual entries are organized under the name of the group that published them, in the order they were published, and descriptively annotated. There is a detailed subject index at the end of each volume. For a listing of Scottish publications through 1985, there is *Scottish Texts and Calendars: An Analytical Guide to Serial Publications* by David and Wendy Stevenson (London: Royal Historical Society, 1987).

Latin America

102. *A Bibliography of Latin American Bibliographies.* By Arthur E. Gropp. Metuchen, NJ: Scarecrow, 1968. 515p.

103. *A Bibliography of Latin American Bibliographies Published in Periodicals.* By Arthur E. Gropp. Metuchen, NJ: Scarecrow, 1976. 2 vols.

These works are the starting point for Latin American bibliographic research. Gropp was the librarian at the Columbus Memorial Library at Washington, D.C. His first volume focused on monographs published through 1965 and was intended to update an earlier work from 1942 of the same title by Cecil Jones. Gropp retained 2,900 entries from Jones' work and added 4,000 new ones. He also began organizing the entries by subject categories and within those categories by country. There is a detailed index to personal names, corporate bodies, government offices, serial titles, and subject entries. Most helpful to historians are the 329 historical bibliographies and the 723 titles listed in the individual biography section. In 1976 Gropp added a further 1,000 bibliographies published in periodicals through 1965. Four supplements have been published. The latest, *A Bibliography of Latin American Bibliographies, 1980–1984: Social Sciences and Humanities* by Lionel V. Lorona (Metuchen, NJ: Scarecrow, 1987), covers both the monographic and periodical literature.

104. *Handbook of Latin American Studies.* Austin, TX: University of Texas Press, 1935–. Annual. ISSN 0072-9833.

Established in 1935, this is the standard bibliographic reference serial for Latin American studies. Since 1965 volumes for the humanities and the social sciences have been issued in alternating years. A cumulative author index for volumes 1–28 (1936–1966) was published in 1968. History is covered in the humanities volume, which is published in even-numbered years. The history section is organized by country or region beginning with Mexico and followed by Central America, the Caribbean, the Guianas, the Spanish border-lands, Spanish South America, and Brazil. Within each country or region, important books and articles are listed in alphabetical order within the historical periods: colonial, independence, or national. There is a list of journals and their abbreviations at the end of each discipline and a master list of journal titles at the end of each volume. The critical annotations by specialists make this a valuable bibliography even if it is not always current.

105. *Latin American Studies: A Basic Guide to the Sources.* 2d ed., revised and enlarged. Edited by Robert A. McNeil and Barbara G. Valk. Metuchen, NJ: Scarecrow, 1990. 470 p. ISBN 0-8108-2236-9.

Edited by the head of the Hispanic Division of the Bodleian Library, Oxford, and the editor of the *Hispanic American Periodicals Index* (HAPI), this guide is the most valuable introduction to research on Latin America in the social sciences and humanities. Thirty-seven chapters are arranged in six sections and describe the library and archival resources in Great Britain, the United States, Western Europe, and Latin America. There are helpful sections on bibliog-raphies, printed sources, non-print sources, and specialized information such as censuses, laws, and statistics. The book is designed to meet the research needs of students, scholars, and librarians. An excellent older guide, edited by Charles C. Griffin, is *Latin America: A Guide to the Historical Literature* (Austin: University of Texas Press, 1971). Broader in scope and without annotations but useful for updating Griffin are the three volumes edited by Robert L. Delorme: *Latin America: Social Science Information Sources, 1967–1979* (Santa Barbara, CA: ABC-CLIO, 1981), *Latin America, 1979–1983: A*

Social Science Bibliography (Santa Barbara, CA: ABC-CLIO, 1984), and *Latin America, 1983–1987: A Social Science Bibliography* (Westport, CT: Greenwood, 1988).

Other Regions and Nations
(alphabetical by title)

106. *The American Bibliography of Slavic and East European Studies.* Stanford, CA: American Association for the Advancement of Slavic Studies, 1956–. Annual. Each volume has an index. ISSN 0094-3770.

The purpose of this bibliography is to provide a comprehensive listing of research in Slavic studies in the U.S. and Canada. Slavic and East European studies are defined to include the U.S.S.R. and the various Eastern European countries, including East Germany, Greece, Cyprus, and the Baltic states. Material covered includes books, journal articles, essays in collective works, book reviews, dissertations, and review articles. Recently, the bibliography has listed publications for two years rather than one. Current European research on Slavic topics can be found in *The European Bibliography of Soviet, East European, and Slavonic Studies.*

107. *Asia: Reference Works: A Select Annotated Guide.* By G. Raymond Nunn. London: Mansell, 1980. 365p. Index. ISBN 0-7201-0921-3.

Asia, according to the definition used by this book, does not include the Middle East region west of Pakistan, Soviet Asia, or Oceania. More than 1,500 reference works are listed here. They are organized into geographical sections, with works for larger regions followed by those for individual countries: for example, a section for East Asia is followed by sections for China, Japan, Korea, and Mongolia. Within these sections, the reference books are organized by types of works—handbooks, directories, gazetteers. Individual entries are numbered, provide a detailed bibliographic citation, and include a descriptive annotation. There is an author-title index. This volume is very strong in its coverage of historical materials. Although limited to China, Ernst Wolff's *Chinese Studies: A Bibliographic Manual* (San Francisco, CA: Chinese Materials Center, 1981) is most useful. Another excellent regional bibliography compiled under the general editorship of J. D. Pearson is *South Asian Bibliography: A Handbook and Guide* (Atlantic Highlands, NJ: Humanities Press, 1979).

108. *Bibliographie annuelle de l'histoire de France du cinquieme siècle à 1958.* Paris: Comite français des sciences historiques and Centre national de la recherche scientifique, 1955–. Annual. ISSN 0067-7043.

Aiming to provide a comprehensive listing of new research in French history, unlike similar publications from other countries, this bibliography still remains reasonably current with only a one- to two-year delay. Its chronological scope goes from the fifth century A.D. to 1958 (originally 1939). Items listed include books, journal articles, essays in collective works, and conference proceedings. Although written in French, non-French publications are also listed in this work. Items are organized under the broad subject headings of general, political, institutional, economic and social, religious, imperial, cultural, and local history. Within the sections there are further chronological and topical subdivisions, depending on the nature of the material. Individual entries are numbered and provide a complete bibliographic citation. There are separate subject and author indexes. With a little effort and the use of a French dictionary, this bibliography can be accessible and very useful to non-French readers.

109. *Bibliography of Asian Studies.* Ann Arbor, MI: Association for Asian Studies, 1954–. Annual. Index. ISSN 0067-7159.

For the general subject of Asian studies written in Western languages, there is no better serial bibliography. Both new books and journal articles are listed. The basic organization of the individual items is by broad geographical regions, then by the individual countries, and finally by various subjects. The annual index is for authors. There are also the multivolume *Cumulative Bibliography of Asian Studies, 1941–1965* and the *Cumulative Bibliography of Asian Studies, 1966–1970* (Ann Arbor, MI: Association of Asian Studies, 1969 and 1973).

110. *International African Bibliography.* London: Mansell, 1971–. Vol. 1–. Quarterly. ISSN 0020-5877.

This publication continues the current bibliography that was published in the journal *Africa* from 1929 to 1970. Books, articles, and p~pers on all aspects of African studies are listed. These are organized by broad geographical regions and by subjects within those sections. A cumulative volume with an excellent index has been published: J. D. Pearson, ed., *International African Bibliography 1973–1978: Books, Articles, and Papers in African Studies* (London: Mansell, 1982) and further cumulations are planned. For a complementary bibliography covering journal articles published from 1973 to 1982 see *Africa since 1914: A Historical Bibliography* (Santa Barbara, CA: ABC-CLIO, 1985). An annual bibliography with a very similar scope is the new *Africa Bibliography* (Manchester: Manchester University Press, 1984–).

111. *Jahresberichte für deutsche Geschichte*. Berlin: Akademie Verlag, 1925–1953. Annual. 1954– . Biennial. ISSN 0075-286X.

For all aspects and periods of German history, this serial bibliography, published in German, is the most complete current listing. Originally it appeared annually but shifted to biennial publication in 1954. The individual entries are numbered and are organized under detailed chronological, geographical, and topical categories, which makes this bibliography quite easy to browse.

112. *Japanese History and Culture from Ancient to Modern Times: Seven Basic Bibliographies*. By John W. Dower. New York: Markus Wiener, 1986. 232p. ISBN 0-910129-20-7.

The seven selective bibliographies referred to by the title of this book can also be thought of as seven chapters or sections. Various chronological periods are dealt with in the first five chapters: prehistory to 1600, 1600 to 1945, foreign relations from 1868 to 1945, Japan and Asia from 1931 to 1945, and post-1945. These are followed by two brief chapters on bibliographies and research guides and on journals and other serials. The sources listed in these bibliographies are written in English and include surveys, monographs, journal articles, printed primary sources, government documents, and primary documents on microfilm. Items are listed within the chapters under various subheadings and then by their importance as judged by the author of the bibliography. Unfortunately, this volume does not have any sort of index. It is, however, up-to-date into 1986 and is available in paperback—all of which makes it an excellent place to begin research in Japanese history.

113. *The Middle East: Abstracts and Index*. Pittsburgh, PA: Northumberland Press, 1978–. Annual. ISSN 0162-776X.

While not focused on history, this current bibliography is still quite useful for locating new scholarship on this volatile region. It is also available on DIALOG. For retrospective coverage of journal articles on the Middle East see *Articles on the Middle East, 1947–1971: A Cumulation of the Bibliographies from the Middle East Journal*, edited by

Peter M. Rossi and Wayne E. White (Ann Arbor, MI: Pierian Press, 1980), in four volumes with detailed indexing.

114. *Russia and the Soviet Union; A Bibliographical Guide to Western Language Publications.* Edited by Paul L. Horecky. Chicago: University of Chicago Press, 1965. 473p. ISBN 0-226-35186-6.

This volume and *East Central Europe: A Guide to Basic Publications* (Chicago: University of Chicago Press, 1969) and *Southeastern Europe: A Guide to Basic Publications* (Chicago: University of Chicago Press, 1969), its companion volumes by the same editor, provide a selective bibliography of books and articles on these countries and regions published through the mid to late 1960s. Many of the works listed are in Western languages other than English, and each volume contains more than 3,000 bibliographic entries. The volume on Russia and the Soviet Union includes items on science and technology; the other two volumes confine their coverage to historical, socioeconomic, and cultural topics. Most of the materials listed in these volumes will be of interest to historians. Organization is by topical and regional chapters, each written by an expert on that subject or country. Individual entries are numbered and include both bibliographic information and a descriptive annotation. Each volume includes an author, subject, and title index. Stephan M. Horak has continued to update these works in his *Russia, the USSR, and Eastern Europe: A Bibliographic Guide to English Language Publications, 1964–1974* (Littleton, CO: Libraries Unlimited, 1978) and its supplements for the years 1975–1980 and 1981–1985 (Littleton, CO: Libraries Unlimited, 1982, 1987), which provide an annotated bibliography of important English-language publications.

115. *World Bibliographical Series.* Robert Neville, executive editor; John Horton, Ian Wallace, Ralph Lee Woodward, and Hans Wellisch, series editors. Oxford: Clio Press.

The number of titles in this series is approaching 100. Individual volumes focus on a single country and introduce its culture, history, place in the world, and unique qualities. There is an introductory essay and a reference map. The annotated bibliography is divided into appropriate topical chapters such as law, literature, foreign relations, and religion. Most volumes contain between 500 and 1,000 entries. Some are now in their second edition.

Specialized Historical Bibliographies:
Chronological Periods

116. *Introduction to Ancient History.* By Hermann Bengtson. Berkeley, CA: University of California Press, 1970. 213p. Index. ISBN 0-520-01723-4.

Ancient history has long lacked a good introductory bibliographic guide in English. This work is actually a translation of *Einführung in die alte Geschichte,* used by German university students. Nine chapters discuss various aspects of ancient history such as scope, chronology, geography, sources, monuments, epigraphy, numismatics, and other allied disciplines. Each chapter consists of a historiographical essay or essays with an accompanying bibliographic survey. Most of the works listed are German, although Chapter 9 is a select bibliography added for English-speaking students. Although this work is of some help, it is dated; and an introduction specifically written for English-speaking readers is needed.

117. *Guide to the Sources of Medieval History.* By R. C. Van Caenegem with F. L. Ganshof. Amsterdam: North-Holland Publishing Company, 1978. 428p. Index. ISBN 0-7204-0743-5.

118. *Medieval Studies: A Bibliographical Guide.* By Everett U. Crosby, C. Julian Bishko, and Robert L. Kellogg. New York: Garland, 1983. 1,131p. Index. ISBN 0-8240-9107-8.

Students and scholars of the Middle Ages are well served by these two bibliographic guides to research. R. C. Van Caenegem's work is a thoroughly revised translation and updating of his similar Dutch and German works. It is organized into 23 chapters divided into five sections. These are presented as bibliographic essays and include much discussion of the primary sources, with many bibliographic citations interspersed. The five sections of Van Caenegem's work deal with the types of sources used by medieval historians, libraries and archives, collections and bibliographies of published primary sources, reference works for studying medieval documents, and reference works for the auxiliary sciences of history. There is an index for authors and titles. In contrast, *Medieval Studies: A Bibliographical Guide* contains 9,000 entries for monographs, surveys, and translations published through 1980. The entries are organized into 141 geographical, chronological, and topical chapters. Individual entries consist of a bibliographic citation and are followed by a brief descriptive and evaluative annotation. There is an index of authors and editors and a separate and very brief index for topics. These two works should be among the first places for anyone doing research in the Middle Ages to consult, although not for the periodical literature. For the former standard bibliography, which was originally published in 1917 and last updated by the author in 1931, see the revised edition of Louis John Paetow's *A Guide to the Study of Medieval History* (New York: Appleton-Century-Crofts, 1959. Reprint 1980). This work has been further updated by Gray Cowan Boyce, *Literature of Medieval History, 1930–1975: A Supplement to Louis John Paetow's 'A Guide to the Study of Medieval History,'* 5 vols. (Millwood, NY: Kraus International Publications, 1980).

119. *International Medieval Bibliography*. Leeds, England: University of Leeds, 1967–. Published twice yearly. Index. ISSN 0020-7950.

Appearing in January and July, this excellent serial bibliography lists articles, notes, and essays but not books on medieval topics. The chronological scope is A.D. 450–1500. About 1,000 journals and some 100 festschriften and collections of essays are surveyed for relevant material for each issue. Those not containing any medieval items are marked by an asterisk. The organization is topical—e.g., administration, crusades, law, numismatics—with various geographical subdivisions. There are separate author and general indexes.

120. *Bibliographie internationale de l'humanisme et de la Renaissance*. Geneva: Federation international des sociétés et institute pour l'étude de la Renaissance, 1965–. Annual. ISSN 0067-7000.

Covering all aspects of the fifteenth and sixteenth centuries, this serial bibliography lists recent books and articles. Items are listed alphabetically by author, and there is a subject bibliography. A somewhat more specialized serial bibliography is the *Archive for Reformation History: Supplement; Literature Review/Archiv fur Reformationsgeschichte: Beiheft; Literaturbericht* (Gütersloher: Verlagshaus Gerd Mohn, 1904–). This annual publication lists books and articles dealing with the "long" sixteenth century, which extends into both the fifteenth and seventeenth centuries. Writing on the many aspects of the Reformation is predominant. It is organized under topical and geographical subheadings. The individual items are numbered and include a brief signed abstract. An excellent, recent, one-volume bibliography is Benjamin G. Kohl's *Renaissance Humanism, 1300–1550: A Bibliography of Materials in English* (New York: Garland, 1985), which has a wider scope than its title indicates. Older but still very useful for beginning researchers is Roland H. Bainton and Eric W. Gritsch's

Bibliography of the Continental Reformation: Materials Available in English, 2d ed. (Hamden, CT: Archon, 1972).

121. *The Eighteenth Century: A Current Bibliography.* New York: AMS Press, 1978–. New Series Vol. 1–. Annual. Index. ISSN 0161-0996.

This excellent interdisciplinary publication's coverage of the scholarly literature starts with the year 1975. It has been plagued by long delays in publication throughout its history. Books, journal articles, and essays in collective works are listed. All aspects of the eighteenth century—literary, artistic, historical, and intellectual— are covered. The geographic scope is international, with Western Europe and American topics dominating the listings. Most items listed are in English, although materials in other languages are included. Many of the books are reviewed, while others and some of the articles are briefly annotated. There is a personal name index that basically consists of authors and editors. This bibliography is the successor to the listing "English Literature 1660–1800," which appeared in the *Philological Quarterly* from 1926 to 1970. From 1970 to 1974 the listing was expanded and made interdisciplinary, although it was still published as part of the *Philological Quarterly.*

122. *Twentieth Century World History: A Select Bibliography.* By Freda Harcourt and Francis Robinson. New York: Barnes & Noble, 1979. 154p. ISBN 0-06-492680-X.

The world during the twentieth century and many of its important aspects form the scope of this helpful brief bibliography for students. The first 17 of the 27 chapters cover topics such as decolonization, fascism, technological innovation, and urbanization, and the remaining nine chapters deal with various regions or countries. Each chapter begins with a brief introduction followed by a listing of 10 to 40 important books on that topic. There is no index. Such brief introductory bibliographies are very useful, and forthcoming titles in the recent series "History and Related Disciplines: Select Bibliographies" under the general editorship of R. C. Richardson, published by Manchester University Press/St. Martin's Press, will be most welcome.

Specialized Historical Bibliographies: Subjects

123. *Afro-American Reference: An Annotated Bibliography of Selected Resources.* Edited by Nathaniel Davis. Westport, CT: Greenwood Press, 1985. 288p. Index. ISBN 0-313-24930-X.

The scope of this guide is all aspects of the Afro-American experience in the United States, but it also includes some items on the rest of the Americas. Most of the 642 items listed in this bibliography are reference works, although other works pertaining to Afro-American studies are included if they contain important bibliographies or other information. This work is organized by broad subject categories, starting with general works and proceeding to more specialized topics such as history, literature, family, and slavery. Individual entries are numbered and include the bibliographic citation, a descriptive annotation that evaluates the reference qualities of the work, and a listing of the Library of Congress subject headings for the work. There are separate author, title, and subject indexes. Although this guide is interdisciplinary, many works of interest to historians are scattered throughout its pages, and it is a good place to begin for anyone working in Afro-American history. For a more comprehensive work, see the *Dictionary Catalog of the Schomburg Collection of Negro Literature and History* (Boston: G. K. Hall, 1962–1976. 9 vols. with supplements) and its supplement, *Bibliographic Guide to Black Studies*.

124. *Bibliography of Mexican American History*. Compiled by Matt S. Meier. Westport, CT: Greenwood Press, 1984. 500p. Index. ISBN 0-313-23776-X.

This bibliography's intention is to provide a comprehensive listing of materials dealing with Mexican Americans from the Treaty of Guadalupe Hidalgo in 1848 to 1982. Some important works covering Mexican-American history before 1848 are also included. Its 4,500 entries include reference works, general histories, journal articles, government documents, essays in collective works, and dissertations and theses. Starting with a chapter on general works, there are five chapters dealing with chronological periods and three topical ones concerned with labor and immigration, civil rights and politics, and culture. When it is appropriate, the individual chapters contain sections for books, theses and dissertations, and periodicals. The separate entries are numbered and provide a bibliographic citation. Occasionally they are briefly annotated when the title of the item does not provide an adequate description of its contents. There are separate author and subject indexes.

125. *A Comprehensive Bibliography for the Study of American Minorities*. Compiled by Wayne Charles Miller et al. New York: New York University Press, 1976. 2 vols. Index. ISBN 0-8147-5373-6.

Consisting of 29,000 entries, this multidisciplinary bibliography covers the major and minor European groups along with generous consideration to African, Asian, Hispanic, and native Americans. Individual chapters are devoted to specific groups and begin with an introductory essay. There are detailed author and title indexes in the second volume.

126. *A Comprehensive Bibliography of American Constitutional and Legal History, 1896–1979.* By Kermit L. Hall. Millwood, NY: Kraus International, 1984. 5 vols. Index. ISBN 0-527-37408-3.

More than 18,000 books, essays, and journal articles from the disciplines of law, history, and related fields are listed in this impressive bibliography. To be included, at least one-third of the item's content had to be historical. Both primary and secondary works appear in the listings. The work is divided into seven broad chapters: general surveys and texts, institutions, constitutional doctrine, legal doctrine, biographical, chronological, and geographical. These chapters are further subdivided, and within those categories items are listed alphabetically by author. Individual entries are numbered and provide a detailed bibliographic citation. The fifth volume contains separate detailed author and subject indexes.

127. *The Craft of Public History: An Annotated Select Bibliography.* Edited by David F. Trask and Robert W. Pomeroy III. Westport, CT: Greenwood Press, 1983. 481p. Index. ISBN 0-313-23687-9.

According to the preface, "'public history' denotes the practice of history and history related disciplines in settings elsewhere than in educational institutions—schools, colleges, and universities," (p. xi), i.e., the history practiced in museums, historical societies, archives, libraries, businesses, and governments. The 1,700 items in this selective bibliography form the first introduction to this field to be published. They are arranged into 11 chapters. Each begins with an explanatory introduction followed by a classified annotated bibliography. Individual bibliographic entries are numbered. The annotations are basically descriptive, and the items selected tend to be methodological or "how-to-do-it" in nature. Topics covered by the various chapters include training for the practice of public history, archives, genealogy, historical editing, policy history, and oral history. An author index supplies a further aid to the reader. This excellent and wide-ranging bibliography is well worth consulting.

128. *Guide to Research on North American Indians.* By Arlene B. Hirschfelder, Mary Gloyne Byler, and Michael A. Dorris. Chicago:

American Library Association, 1983. 330p. Index. ISBN 0-8389-0353-3.

For those needing an introductory, one-volume bibliographic guide for research on North American Indians, this is a very helpful resource. It lists 1,100 of the most important books, articles, government publications, and other appropriate materials for beginning research on the various aspects of the subject and guiding further study. These materials are organized into 27 chapters dealing with more specialized aspects of the Indians' history, economy, society, and culture. Each chapter contains an introductory essay followed by listings of primary, secondary, and reference literature. Individual entries provide a bibliographic citation and a detailed descriptive and evaluative annotation. There are separate author-title and subject indexes. Those desiring more complete listings of the vast literature on North American Indians will still need to consult the various specialized bibliographies published by the Newberry Library's Center for the History of the American Indian (some of which are listed on pages 2–7 of the guide being discussed).

129. *A Guide to the Sources of United States Military History.* Edited by Robin Higham. Hamden, CT: Archon Books, 1975. 559p. ISBN 0-208-01499-3. With *Supplement I* (1981), 300p., ISBN 0-208-01750-X and *Supplement II* (1986), 332p., ISBN 0-208-02072-1.

This excellent set of bibliographies supplies a useful introduction to U.S. military history. The original volume consists of 19 chapters, each written by an expert. In the later volumes, the number of chapters has been expanded to 23. Some of the chapters are chronological, some topical. Each contains an introductory bibliographic and historiographic essay followed by a selected bibliography of approximately 300 items. The supplements that update the original volume are published every five years. Complementing this work is Susan K. Kinnell's *Military History of the United States: An Annotated Bibliography* (Santa Barbara, CA: ABC-CLIO, 1986) and Garland Publishing's excellent bibliographic series *Wars of the United States.* For British history see Higham's well-respected *A Guide to the Sources of British Military History* (Berkeley, CA: University of California Press, 1971), which provided the model for his American volumes. It also has a supplement, *British Military History: A Supplement to Robin Higham's Guide to the Sources,* edited by Gerald Jordan (New York: Garland, 1988).

130. *The History of Ideas: A Bibliographical Introduction,* Vol. I: *Classical Antiquity* and Vol. II: *Medieval and Early Modern Europe.* By

Jeremy L. Tobey. Santa Barbara, CA: ABC-CLIO, 1975 and 1977. 211p. and 319p. Index. ISBNs 0-87436-143-5 and 0-87436-239-3.

These two informative volumes deal with far more than the history of philosophy, as they also contain substantial material on science, religion, and aesthetics. The method of presentation is a bibliographic essay that discusses books, essays in collective volumes, and articles in scholarly journals. Full citations for the works discussed in the text are located in author-title indexes at the end of each volume.

131. *International Bibliography of the History of Religions/ Bibliographie International de l'Histoire des Religions.* Leiden, Netherlands: Brill, 1954–. Annual with cumulations. Index.

The scope of this serial bibliography is worldwide and all periods of history. Both books and articles are listed. Unfortunately, it has also fallen further and further behind in its coverage, due to inadequate resources. After a general chapter, the remaining chapters range from primitive religions through antiquity and then cover the major religions of Judaism, Christianity, Islam, Hinduism, Buddhism, Chinese religions, Japanese religions, and minor religions. Individual entries are listed by author, and there is an index for each volume. Religion usually forms an important subsection of current and retrospective general historical bibliographies. For a useful specialized bibliography of articles on American and Canadian religious history published between 1973 and 1980 there is *Religion and Society in North America: An Annotated Bibliography,* edited by Robert deV. Brunkow (Santa Barbara, CA: ABC-CLIO, 1983). Some individual denominations are covered by bibliographies or reference guides, e.g., John Tracy Ellis and Robert Trisco, *A Guide to American Catholic History,* 2d ed. (Santa Barbara, CA: ABC-CLIO, 1982).

132. *Introduction to Library Research in Women's Studies.* By Susan E. Searing. Boulder, CO: Westview Press, 1985. 257p. Index. ISBN 0-86531-267-2.

Women's studies are generally interdisciplinary, although much of the material found in this volume is of general interest to researchers in women's history. For students, there are chapters explaining research strategies, the library catalog, and interlibrary loan. This section is followed by a series of bibliographic chapters on the reference materials appropriate for women's studies, such as various general bibliographies, specialized subject bibliographies, biographical sources, and directories. The individual, annotated entries provide a bibliographic citation including both Dewey and Library of Congress call numbers. Annotations are descriptive and evaluative, particularly concerning the item's utility to women's studies. There are separate author, title, and subject indexes. Also useful are the following historical bibliographies: *Women in Western European History: A Select Chronological, Geographical, and Topical Bibliography*, Vol. 1: *From Antiquity to the French Revolution* and Vol. 2: *The Nineteenth and Twentieth Centuries*, edited by Linda Frey, Marsha Frey, and Joanne Schneider (Westport, CT: Greenwood Press, 1982 and 1984); *Women in American History: A Bibliography*, edited by Cynthia Harrison (Santa Barbara, CA: ABC-CLIO, 1979); and *Women and Feminism in American History: A Guide to Information Sources*, edited by Elizabeth Tingley and Donald F. Tingley (Detroit, MI: Gale, 1981).

133. *Isis: An International Review Devoted to the History of Science and Its Cultural Influences. Critical Bibliography*. Philadelphia: History of Science Society, 1913–. Annual. Index. ISSN 0021-1753.

At the end of every year the journal *Isis* publishes its *Critical Bibliography*, which basically lists new publications in the history of science. These listings are quite current, as they include items that have appeared through September. Items from before the current year are also included if they were missed originally. The types of materials appearing in this bibliography include books, essays in collective volumes, journal articles (some 500 journals are systematically surveyed), and book reviews. Each volume begins with two sections concerned with reference and survey publications of general interest in the history of science. The next two sections list items under the history of the various branches of science, e.g., zoology or meteorology, or by chronological periods. Occasionally items are given very brief annotations describing their contents. There is an index to personal and institutional names. For a cumulative index, see *Isis Cumulative Bibliography: A Bibliography of the History of Science formed from Isis Critical Bibliographies 1–90, 1913–1965*, edited by Magda Whitrow (London: Mansell, 1971–1984, 6 vols.), and *Isis Cumulative Bibliography, 1966–1975; A Bibliography of the History of Science Formed from Isis Critical Bibliographies 91–100 Indexing Literature Published from 1965 through 1974*, edited by John Neu (London: Mansell, 1980–1985, 2 vols. in progress). The history of medicine is dealt with by the National Library of Medicine's annual *Bibliography of the History of Medicine* (1964–) and the Wellcome Institute of the History of Medicine's quarterly *Current Work in the History of Medicine* (1954–). The journal *Technology and Culture* publishes an annual *Current Bibliography of the History of Technology* (1962–).

134. *Jewish Reference Sources: A Selective, Annotated Bibliographic Guide.* By Charles Cutter and Micha Falk Oppenheim. New York: Garland, 1982. 180p. Index. ISBN 0-8240-9347-X.

Designed for both laymen and students, this guide provides a selective listing of 487 reference works and monographs published through May 1982 and important for the interdisciplinary field of Jewish studies. Its geographical scope is international. The entries are divided into broad categories of general and subject reference and further subdivided into more specialized classifications with many cross-references. Most of the items selected are written in English. Individual entries include a bibliographic citation and a descriptive annotation along with the frequent listings of other related titles. There are separate author and title indexes. This work contains many items of interest to persons doing research into religious and Jewish history. Another helpful guide is Jeffrey Gurock's *American Jewish History: A Bibliographical Guide* (n.p.: B'nai B'rith, 1983). See also Abraham J. Edelheit and Hershel Edelheit's *Bibliography on Holocaust Literature* (Boulder, CO: Westview, 1986), which lists 9,000 items in English on this important topic.

135. *Oral History: A Reference Guide and Annotated Bibliography.* By Patricia Pate Havlice. Jefferson, NC: McFarland, 1985. 140p. Index. ISBN 0-89950-138-9.

For those beginning research using the techniques of oral history or even those who are seasoned practitioners, this guide is an excellent resource. Oral history is a relatively new methodology used by historians that first came to prominence after World War II. This bibliography lists the 773 books, dissertations, and articles that have appeared on the topic of oral history from the 1950s to late 1983. After 15 other oral-history bibliographies, the remaining entries appear under the name of the author, or if there is no author are listed under title. Each entry includes both bibliographic information and a brief descriptive summary. There is an index of titles and subjects.

136. *The Psychohistorian's Handbook.* By Henry Lawton. New York: Psychohistory Press, 1988. 241p. ISBN 0-914434-27-6.

Psychohistory is one of the more technical subfields of history. It is also one of the most controversial. For students and scholars interested in learning more about or beginning research in psychohistory, this book is a must. It consists of 11 chapters covering such topics as psychoanalytic theory, psychohistorical methodology, psychobiography, and teaching psychohistory. Each chapter includes a narrative or descriptive essay interspersed with sections of annotated bibliography to guide further study and research. The author is a practitioner of psychohistory and a staunch defender of its scholarly validity.

137. *Social History of the United States: A Guide to Information Sources.* By Donald F. Tingley. Detroit: Gale, 1979. 260p. Index. ISBN 0-8103-1366-9.

138. *U.S. Cultural History: A Guide to Information Sources.* By Philip I. Mitterling. Detroit: Gale, 1980. 581p. Index. ISBN 0-8103-1369-3.

Both of these volumes are part of the Gale Research Company's "American Government and History Information Guide Series." This series includes other volumes on educational, military, religious, and urban history along with many other topics. Each volume is basically a selective bibliography in which the individual entries are given brief, descriptive annotations. They are excellent resources for beginning researchers. There are the usual chapters on reference works and general survey publications and other chapters organized by the subcategories appropriate to the individual subject. Separate author, title, and subject indexes are provided.

3.

Book Review Indexes

Since the historical literature on many topics is vast, making qualitative decisions as to which are the best books to read on a particular subject is often influenced by how well those books were received by the critics. Prior to 1970, locating reviews of historical monographs was a difficult task largely confined to searching book review sections of major historical journals. That has become a good deal easier in recent decades with the development of new historical indexes like *America: History and Life,* expanded coverage of historical journals in Wilson indexes like *Humanities Index,* and the publication of several retrospective indexes to book reviews in scholarly journals. Standard book review indexes like *Book Review Digest* and *Book Review Index* have increased their coverage of historical reviews, and sophisticated on-line and compact-disc versions of many periodical and newspaper indexes have made it easy to locate reviews of current books.

General

139. *Book Review Digest.* New York: H. W. Wilson, 1905–. Monthly except for February and July with annual cumulations. ISSN 0006-7326.

This title (commonly abbreviated as BRD) is the oldest and best known of the general reviewing indexes. It provides excerpts of and citations to reviews of current fiction and nonfiction. Reviews are selected from 95 periodicals in the humanities, social sciences, and general sciences from titles published in the U.S., Canada, and the United Kingdom. Most major historical journals are included, and coverage was expanded in 1989. To qualify for inclusion, a book must be published or distributed in the U.S. or Canada. A work of fiction must have received reviews in at least four periodicals, and a work of nonfiction must have been reviewed at least twice. All of the reviews must have appeared within 18 months after publication. Reviews are listed alphabetically under the author's last name. There is also a subject and title index. A cumulative *Author/Title Index 1905–1974* was published in 1976. On-line access is available beginning with January 1983 through Wilsonline, and a compact-disc version on Wilsondisc provides similar coverage since January 1983.

140. *Book Review Index.* Detroit: Gale Research, 1965–. Six bimonthly issues with annual cumulations. ISSN 0524-0581.

Often referred to as BRI, this index provides broad access to book reviews in the social sciences, humanities, and sciences. Begun as a monthly in 1965, publication was briefly suspended from 1969 to 1972. A retrospective index for those years was published in 1975. BRI includes citations to reviews of any type of book that has been or is about to be published and that is at least 50 pages long. All reviews in 470 indexed journals are cited, including contents notes and collection recommendations. Entries are arranged alphabetically by the name of the author of the book. The information included in an individual entry includes author, title, source, date, and page on which the review appears. There is a title index. Unlike BRD [*see* 139], there is no subject indexing. The 1987 cumulation of BRI listed 123,000 reviews of 68,000 titles. A *Master Cumulation, 1965–1984* was published in 1985, providing title access to 1.6 million citations. On-line access has been available through DIALOG File 137 since 1969; the file is updated three times yearly.

141. *Books in Print with Book Reviews Plus.* New York: Bowker Electronic Publishing. Compact disc. 6 updates a year.

The compact-disc version of *Books in Print* was first published several years ago. Since that time an upgraded version including book reviews has been developed and is now available in many academic and public libraries. *Books in Print with Book Reviews Plus* includes the complete data base of some 850,000 books currently in print plus more than 50,000 unabridged book reviews from *Booklist, Choice, Library Journal, Publishers Weekly,* and *Reference and Research Book News,* among others. Each review includes publication title, date, and byline when listed. Approximately 25,000 book reviews are added each year. This is an excellent source for current book reviews from libraries and publishers' reviewing journals.

142. *Canadian Book Review Annual*. Toronto: Simon & Pierre, 1975–. Annual. ISSN 0383-770X.

This is primarily an evaluative guide to English-language trade books. Every year it publishes reviews of from 200 to 500 words by subject specialists of approximately 500 Canadian titles. The French-Canadian equivalent, *Livres et Auteurs Quebeçois,* has ceased publication.

143. *General Periodicals Index on InfoTrac* (Academic Library Edition). Foster City, CA: Information Access Co., 1988–.

This compact-disc index has appeared under a variety of titles and formats. Originally issued on videodisk in 1984, it assumed its current structure and format in 1988. It provides access to reviews in more than 20 major historical journals plus reviews from the *New York Times Book Review* and *Times Literary Supplement.* Coverage for most historical journals begins in 1987. Uniquely, the indexers have added grades of A to F for the books, based on the reviewers' comments. Monthly updates are available, making it an excellent source for current book reviews.

144. *National Library Service Cumulative Book Reviews Index, 1905–1974.* Princeton, NJ: NLS, 1975. 6 vols.

This publication supplies a cumulative index to the book reviews appearing in *Book Review Digest* (1905–1974), *Library Journal* (1907–1974), *Saturday Review* (1924–1974), and *Choice* (1964–1974). The titles listed for the *Book Review Digest* refer to its digests and not the complete review. More than one million reviews are given author and title access by this index.

Humanities

145. *Arts and Humanities Citation Index.* Philadelphia: Institute for Scientific Information, 1976–. Quarterly with annual and quinquennial cumulations. ISSN 0162-8445.

A major but often neglected source for reviews. Each annual cumulation includes approximately 50,000 book review citations. The easiest method for finding these book reviews is to check in the "Citation" section of the index under the author of the book's last name; e.g., looking under Din, GC will locate reviews of Gilbert C. Din, *The Imperial Osages* (1983). Using this method will locate five reviews in the 1984 annual cumulation and six more in the 1985 cumulation. A subject approach using the "Permuterm" section of the index is also possible, but it is far more cumbersome. [For additional information on this index *see* 226.]

146. *Combined Retrospective Index to Book Reviews in Humanities Journals, 1802–1974*. Edited by Evan I. Farber. Woodbridge, CT: Research Publications, 1983–1984. 10 vols. ISBN 0-89235-061-X.

This helpful compilation provides one of the best sources for retrospective book reviews. Reviews are drawn from 150 humanities journals, including some that were founded before 1850, such as the *American Oriental Society Journal, Dublin Review, Edinburgh Review, North American Review, Punch,* and *Spectator.* The first nine volumes provide access to more than 500,000 reviews arranged in alphabetical order by the name of the author of the book. When known, the names of the authors of the reviews have been included. The final volume is an alphabetical list of books reviewed by title and provides cross-references to the author entries.

147. *Humanities Index.* New York: H. W. Wilson, 1974–. Quarterly, with annual cumulations. ISSN 0095-5981.

This easy-to-use and readily available publication indexes book reviews from 345 periodicals, including 76 major historical periodicals published in the U.S., Great Britain, and Canada. These book review citations follow the main body of the index in a separate alphabetical listing. Reviews of less than one page or for books more than five years old are excluded. The volume for 1987–1988 listed 3,400 reviews. Originally this index formed part of the *Social Sciences and Humanities Index* (1965–1974), which formerly had been titled the *International Index* (1907–1965). Neither of these indexes included book reviews [*see* 229].

148. *An Index to Book Reviews in the Humanities.* Williamston, MI: Philip Thomson, 1960–. Annual. ISSN 0073-5892.

Initially this publication was a selective index of book reviews in the humanities. With Volume 12 (1974), however, it began to index all the reviews published in the journals it covered. Limited to books in English, it includes about 400 reviews arranged alphabetically by author. Reviewers' names are listed when known, and periodical titles are coded to a master list. Coverage of history is spotty. More attention is given to interdisciplinary period journals like *Victorian Studies* and *Eighteenth-Century Studies.*

Social Sciences

149. *Combined Retrospective Index to Book Reviews in Scholarly Journals, 1886–1974.* Edited by Evan I. Farber. Arlington, VA: Carrollton Press, 1979–1982. 15 vols. ISBN 0-8408-0157-2.

A spin-off from earlier CRIS indexes to the journal literature of history, sociology, and political science, this cumulation provides access to more than a million reviews in 458 scholarly journals in these fields. The first 12 volumes provide author access, and the last three provide title access. Citations include an abbreviated journal title, volume number, year, issue number, and page. Unlike the *CRIS Index to Book Reviews in Humanities Journals* [*see* 146], no reviewers' names are listed in this index. It is, however, a very useful guide to reviews published in national, regional, and state historical journals.

150. *Social Sciences Citation Index.* Philadelphia: Institute for Scientific Information, 1969–. Quarterly, with annual and quinquennial cumulations. ISSN 0091-3707.

Organized exactly like its sister index, the *Arts and Humanities Citation Index* [*see* 145], this publication's historical coverage includes approximately 50 periodicals with an emphasis on the history and philosophy of science and the history of social science. Each annual cumulation includes about 35,000 book review citations. There is some overlap in the coverage of the two citation indexes. Reviews can be located quickly by checking under the author's name in the "Citation" section of the index. On-line versions are available as Social SCISEARCH on BRS or on DIALOG File 439. The BRS edition is updated weekly, and DIALOG is updated monthly. A compact-disc version was released in the summer of 1989.

History

151. *America: History and Life,* Part B: *Index to Book Reviews.* Santa Barbara, CA: ABC-CLIO, 1964–. Semiannual. ISSN 0097-6172.

This is the best source for book reviews in American and Canadian history. Although the index began in late 1964, book reviews were not included until Volume 11 for 1974. From Volume 11 to Volume 25 in 1988, book review citations appeared in Part B, which was issued twice a year. Beginning with Volume 26 (1989), the entire index was redesigned, and book reviews are now included in each of the first four issues. Issue 5 provides a cumulative subject and author index and a book title index. On-line coverage begins with 1980 on DIALOG File 38. Over the past several years, reviews have averaged 4,000 annually.

Newspapers

152. *National Newspaper Index on InfoTrac.* Foster City, CA: Information Access Corp., 1988–.

Earlier versions of this index were available on microfilm (1979–). The compact-disc format was introduced in 1988 and provides coverage of the most recent three years of reviews in the *New York Times, Wall Street Journal, Christian Science Monitor, Los Angeles Times,* and *Washington Post.* Reviews are graded from A to F by the IAC staff and appear under title in the A–Z sequence of the index. On-line coverage is available through DIALOG File 111.

153. *New York Times Index.* New York: NYT Co., 1913–. Semimonthly with quarterly and annual cumulations. ISSN 0147-538X.

Book reviews have always formed an important part of this index since its creation. Retrospective volumes produced for the period 1851–1912 include book reviews written after 1862 under the heading "book reviews and books" or simply "reviews." Currently they are listed alphabetically by title under the subject heading "book reviews." Authors appear in the main A–Z sequence of the index with cross-references to the book review section. The volume of titles reviewed has remained consistent over the years. The 1913 index listed 2,045 reviews, and the 1987 index lists 2,151. A five-volume cumulation, the *New York Times Book Review Index, 1896–1970* was published by Arno Press in 1973. It provides author, title, and subject access to more than 100,000 reviews.

154. *Newspaper Abstracts on Disc.* Ann Arbor, MI: UMI, 1987–. Updated bimonthly.

This sophisticated new compact-disc system provides access to reviews in the *Atlanta Constitution* (1985–), the *Boston Globe* (1985–), the *Chicago Tribune* (1985–), the *Christian Science Monitor* (1985–), the *Los Angeles Times* (1985–), the *New York Times* (1987–), the *Wall Street*

Journal (1985–), and the *Washington Post* (1989–). There are no plans to restrict its coverage to any set period of years. Sophisticated Boolean searching capacity provides multiple author, title, and subject access. On-line coverage is available on DIALOG File 603 for the years 1984–1988 and on File 484 since 1989.

155. *The Times Index.* Reading, England: Research Publications, 1973–. Monthly with annual cumulations. ISSN 0260-0668.

This publication provides access to book reviews in *The Times, Sunday Times, Times Literary Supplement, Times Educational Supplement, Times Education Supplement: Scotland,* and *Times Higher Education Supplement.* Earlier versions of this index, the *Annual Index* (1906–1913), the *Official Index* (1914–1957), and the *Index to the Times* (1957–1972) did not cover the various auxiliary publications of *The Times.* Coverage of book reviews in a special section, "Books Reviewed and Noticed," appeared for the first time in the 1955 edition. In recent editions reviews appear under the heading "Books (Titles and Reviews)" in alphabetical order by title. Author entries with citations also appear in the main alphabetical index. More than 3,100 reviews were listed in the 1987 annual cumulation.

Book Trade and Library Association Publications

While virtually every country has specialized book trade or library association publications featuring advance reviews or notes of new books, the following selections are the most helpful sources for reviews of new history books.

156. *Booklist.* Chicago: American Library Association, 1905–. Bimonthly except July–August. ISSN 0006-7385.

Geared principally to small and medium-size libraries, *Booklist* contains approximately 400 reviews of history books each year. The reviews are written by staff writers, and only recommended titles are listed. Books are often reviewed from galley proofs. *Booklist's* major competitor for this market, *Library Journal,* publishes less than half the number of history reviews. Its semiannual combined author-title indexes appear in the 15 February and August issues. Canadian publications that perform a similar function are *Books in Canada* (Toronto: Canadian Review of Books, 1971–) and *Quill and Quire* (Toronto: Key Publishers, 1935–). For Great Britain there is

British Book News (London: The British Book Council, 1940–). French books are covered by *Bulletin Critique de Livre Français* (Paris: Association pour la Diffusion de la Pensée Française, 1945–), which has an English-language edition, *New French Books.*

157. *Choice.* Middletown, CT: Association of College and Research Libraries, 1964–. Eleven times a year. ISSN 0009-4978.

This review periodical is by far the most important source of reviews for academic libraries in the U.S. Of the 6,159 reviews published in 1988, 911 were for new history books. All reviews are written and signed (since September 1984) by American and Canadian academics. They are often critical and comparative. Cumulative annual author and title indexes are printed in the July–August issue.

4.
Periodical Guides and Core Journals

The scholarly historical journal appeared in the nineteenth century and quickly became a significant part of historical literature. Most journals publish articles, which generally are specialized studies about as long as a chapter in a book, and book reviews. During the twentieth century the number of journals grew, and there was a narrowing of their specialization. Now there are thousands of journals published throughout the world. This chapter begins by listing important sources for finding out about historical journals. Next it lists and describes a selection of journals commonly found in college and university libraries. This list is intended to be representative rather than comprehensive.

Periodical Guides

158. *Historical Journals: A Handbook for Writers and Reviewers.* By Dale R. Steiner. Santa Barbara, CA: ABC-CLIO, 1981. ISBN 0-87436-312-8.

Historical Journals is basically a writer's and a book reviewer's guide to journals of interest to historians. It is not comprehensive, as it lists only 350 titles published in the United States and Canada. But notwithstanding the smaller number of journals listed, Steiner's book also contains a significant number of journals not listed by Fyfe [see 160]. Furthermore, since it is specifically oriented toward writers and reviewers, its entries provide more specific publication information: type of manuscript style required by each journal, preferred length of manuscripts, length of time needed to consider a manuscript, and proportion of manuscripts accepted for publication. There are also two chapters at the beginning of the book that provide guidelines and advice on preparing an article for submission and writing book reviews. There are more comprehensive publications that provide almost identical information. All disciplines are served by the *Directory of Publishing Opportunities in Journals and Periodicals*, 5th ed., (Chicago: Marquis Academic Media, 1981). The humanities are comprehensively covered by the *MLA Directory of Periodicals: A Guide to Journals and Series in Languages and Literatures*, 1986–1987 edition (New York: Modern Language Association of America). Steiner's volume has the virtues of being specifically historical in its focus and readily affordable for a personal library.

159. *Historical Periodicals Directory.* Edited by Eric H. Boehm, Barbara H. Pope, and Marie S. Ensign. Santa Barbara, CA: ABC-CLIO, 1981–1986. 5 vols. ISBN 0-87436-022-6.

Volume One: *USA and Canada.*
Volume Two: *Europe: West, North, Central, and South.*
Volume Three: *Europe: East and Southeast.*
Volume Four: *Latin America and West Indies.*
Volume Five: *Australia and New Zealand and Cumulative Subject and Geographical Index to Vols. 1–5.*

International in its coverage, this directory lists well over 6,000 periodicals dealing with history from around the world. The publications included may be issued at regular or irregular intervals, but at least 30 percent of their contents must be devoted to history. Many local genealogical publications are included. Volumes are organized geographically, and within each volume entries are listed alphabetically by title under the country where they are published. Each entry is numbered and gives the title, publisher, address, in-house indexing, language(s) of the publication, past titles, coverage in indexing and abstracting services, and ISSN number. The final volume includes a geographical and subject index to the whole set. It supersedes Eric Boehm and Lalit Adolphus's *Historical Periodicals: An Annotated World List of Historical and Related Serial Publications* (1961).

160. *History Journals and Serials: An Analytical Guide.* By Janet Fyfe. Westport, CT: Greenwood Press, 1986. ISBN 0-313-23999-1.

This volume is an annotated listing of almost 700 English-language journals specializing in history from all over the world. Its purposes are basically to help librarians select journals for their collections and to aid historians in deciding which journals they might be interested in submitting manuscripts to or reading. Virtually all important historical periodicals are listed. Each entry supplies information about location, indexing, scope, and format for each title. The journals are arranged under broad subject or geographical headings. Indexes for geographical location, title, publisher, and subject greatly assist the reader.

Core Journals

161. *Agricultural History*, 1927–. Quarterly. Berkeley: University of California Press. ISSN 0002-1482.

Sponsored by the Agricultural History Society, this journal has a scope that encompasses all periods and geographical areas. At the same time the majority of articles published in it deal with American history. Special-topic issues appear frequently. A normal issue contains four to seven articles, while a special-topic issue can have more than 20 articles. About 25 books are reviewed in an average issue. Also the first issue of each volume includes a feature, "Significant Books on Agricultural History," discussing the previous year's publications. A table of contents for the entire volume is supplied in the fourth issue along with an index of authors, titles, and subjects and a list of books reviewed. The British equivalent of this journal is called the *Agricultural History Review* and is published twice yearly.

162. *American Historical Review*, 1895–. 5 issues a year. Washington, DC: American Historical Association. ISSN 0002-8762.

All periods and all geographical areas fall within the scope of this journal as befits the diverse interests of the members of its parent organization, the American Historical Association. It has the widest circulation of any academic historical journal in North America. Each issue contains about five articles, notes and comments, review articles, and about 200 signed book reviews arranged into broad categories of time period and area. Authors of books under review are allowed to respond to their critics. The scholarly standards of this publication are of the highest order. A detailed author, title, and subject index is printed in the fifth issue of each volume. It should be noted that every nation that is historically conscious to even a moderate degree will have a general historical journal similar to the *American Historical Review*. The *English Historical Review* [see 175] performs that role for the United Kingdom, France has its *Revue Historique*, and Germany produces *Historische Zeitschrift*.

163. *American Journal of Legal History*, 1957–. Quarterly. Philadelphia: Temple University. ISSN 0002-9319.

The focus of this journal is the history of American and English law. There are usually three to five articles in an individual issue along with occasional short notes. Between 8 and 15 signed book reviews are normally published in each issue. There is a simple index of authors and titles in the fourth issue of each volume. The equivalent British publication is called the *Journal of Legal History*, and in l983 an excellent new American journal, *Law and History Review*, began to appear twice yearly.

164. *American Quarterly*, 1949–. Quarterly. Philadelphia: American Studies Association. ISSN 0003-0678.

Although this is an interdisciplinary journal devoted to American Studies, it has a strong emphasis on the historical approach to social and cultural topics. Furthermore, the articles published tend to be interesting and provocative as well as soundly researched and entertaining. Each issue has 4 to 8 articles, with occasional theme issues. There are 6 to 8 long, signed book reviews in most issues.

165. *The Americas: A Quarterly Review of Inter-American Cultural History*, 1944–. Quarterly. West Bethesda, MD: Academy of American Franciscan History. ISSN 0003-1615.

Ranking just behind the *Hispanic American Historical Review* [*see* 178] in importance among Latin American history journals, this journal has for many years been edited by Antonine S. Tibesar, O.F.M. Four to 5 articles and 12 to 15 book reviews are published in each issue. High-quality articles, timely reviews, and an excellent section, "Inter-American Notes," characterize this veteran journal.

166. *Bulletin of the Institute of Historical Research.* [*See* 181]

167. *Business History Review*, 1926–. Quarterly. Cambridge: Harvard Graduate School of Business. ISSN 0007-6805.

Called the *Bulletin of the Business History Society* from l926 until l953, this publication is the foremost journal specializing in business history in the English language. Its scope is international, with the modern period in the United States and Europe tending to predominate. Each issue contains three or four articles and one archival essay that discusses the resources for business history in a selected repository. Several review articles are published every year, and every issue contains about 30 signed book reviews. The fourth issue contains a simple index for the whole volume. *Business History* is the British journal that corresponds to *Business History Review*.

168. *Canadian Historical Review*, 1920–. Quarterly. Toronto: University of Toronto Press. ISSN 0008-3755.

The focus of this journal is Canadian history with no restrictions as to era, subject, or region. As such, it is the Canadian equivalent of the *Journal of American History*. An issue usually contains three or four articles along with a section of notes and comments that include news items. There is also a "List of Recent Publications on Canadian History." Thirty-five to forty signed book reviews appear in each issue. The fourth issue of a volume includes a simple index. It should not be confused with the *Canadian Journal of History*, which publishes articles on all aspects of history.

169. *Church History*, 1935–. Quarterly. Wallingford, PA: American Society of Church History. ISSN 0009-6407.

The history of Christianity in all times and places forms the scope of this journal. It is the premier religious history periodical in North America. There are usually five articles in each issue, with occasional review articles. Thirty to 60 books are given substantial signed reviews in each issue, and there are another 10 books mentioned in shorter book notes. The simple index appearing in issue four lists articles and book reviews alphabetically by author. *The Journal of Ecclesiastical History* is the well-edited English periodical concerned with general church history. It is important to remember that most major and even many minor church denominations publish their own historical journals and that these are generally very scholarly and objective publications.

170. *Civil War History: A Journal of the Middle Period*, 1955–. Quarterly. Kent, OH: Kent State University Press. ISSN 0009-8078.

This journal has a considerably broader scope than its title might suggest. It not only deals with the Civil War years but also has an interest in topics ranging from the events of the 1840s through the 1870s and all aspects of history, not just military. Each issue contains 4 to 5 articles. The number of signed book reviews varies from as few as 4 to as many as 15. There is a detailed author, title, and subject index in the fourth issue of every volume.

171. *The Classical Journal*, 1905–. Quarterly. Tallahassee, FL: Classical Association of the Middle West and South. ISSN 0009-8353.

Classical Studies is a field blessed with many distinguished journals, of which *Classical Journal* is the best known in the United States. Since the focus of this journal is the classics, its contents are multi-disciplinary, although history figures prominently. Each issue contains 4 to 9 articles. There is a special section called "Forum," which consists of about 4 short articles dealing with the teaching of the classics at the high-school and college level. The book review section is comparatively skimpy, with only 1 to 6 signed reviews being standard. A simple index is compiled for every 2 volumes. The Classical Association in Great Britain publishes a similar although more sophisticated journal called *Classical Quarterly*, which is actually published only twice a year and contains only articles. *Classical Review*, a companion publication, supplies the other 2 parts of the quarterly and also publishes more than 50 signed reviews plus another 50 short notices in each issue.

172. *Current History*, 1914–. 9 issues a year. Philadelphia: Current History. ISSN 0011-3530.

The purpose of this long-running periodical is to provide assessments from experts concerning the current political, economic, and military situations in various foreign countries. Individual issues are arranged around a geographical or national theme and contain 7 to 8 articles. The books reviewed in each issue also relate to its subject theme. There is no index.

173. *Diplomatic History: The Journal of the Society for Historians of American Foreign Relations*, 1977–. Quarterly. Wilmington, DE: Scholarly Resources. ISSN 0145-2096.

American foreign relations in all of its aspects—diplomatic, cultural, and intellectual—form the special interest of this periodical. Each issue includes 4 or 5 articles, and there are occasional review essays. The second or Spring issue of each volume includes a section, "Doctoral Dissertations in U.S. Foreign Affairs," that is a classified listing of recent dissertations relevant to the readership of *Diplomatic History*. It does not publish book reviews, and there is no index.

174. *Eighteenth-Century Studies*, 1967–. Quarterly. Northfield, MN: American Society for Eighteenth-Century Studies. ISSN 0013-2586.

Like most other journals dealing with the eighteenth century, this one is interdisciplinary, although the basic orientation is historical. Generally an issue will contain 4 articles and 15 to 20 signed book reviews. It is not indexed by its editors. There is a British counterpart, titled the *British Journal for Eighteenth Century Studies*.

175. *English Historical Review*, 1886–. Quarterly. Oxford: Longmans. ISSN 0013-8266.

The oldest English-language periodical devoted solely to history, the *English Historical Review* has maintained the highest standards of scholarship throughout its more than 100 years of publication. Its historical interests are the medieval and modern periods for all geographical areas and subjects. British and European topics are preponderant. Each issue contains 3 to 4 articles and 1 to 3 shorter "Notes and Documents." There are 15 to 20 longer signed book reviews and more than 100 signed short book notices. The July issue includes the valuable "Notices of Periodical and Occasional Publications," which lists, with brief summaries and occasional evaluative comments, historical articles from some 80 periodicals published during the previous year. The notices are arranged geographically. There is a simple annual index at the end of each volume. A general and more detailed index for the years 1956–85 was published in 1986.

176. *Ethnohistory*, 1954–. Quarterly. Durham, NC: Duke University Press. ISSN 0014-1801.

This unique journal is sponsored by the American Society for Ethnohistory. Basically it is an interdisciplinary publication that integrates the disciplines of history and anthropology. There is a strong emphasis on subjects dealing with contacts between European and non-European cultures, and most articles concern themselves with non-Western cultures, particularly the Indians of North and South America. Each issue contains 5 to 7 articles and 15 to 25 signed book reviews. There is no in-house index. This journal has had a difficult time maintaining its production schedule, especially during the early 1980s, but things now seem to have stabilized.

177. *French Historical Studies*, 1958–. 2 issues a year. Columbus, OH: Society for French Historical Studies. ISSN 0016-1071.

All periods and aspects of French history fall within the scope of this scholarly journal. There are four to five articles in most issues, with occasional short notes. There are no book reviews. Instead, each issue has a section, "Recent Books on French History," that is a classified bibliography. News items of interest to French historians are also listed. It is not indexed by the editors. *French History*, which began publishing in the 1980s, is the British equivalent.

178. *Hispanic American Historical Review,* 1918–. Quarterly. Durham, NC: Duke University Press. ISSN 0018-2168.

The grandfather of all journals on Latin American history, *HAHR* continues to publish lengthy, scholarly articles on all periods and aspects of Latin American history. The editorial office, currently at the University of Florida, shifts several times in a decade. Each issue contains 3 or 4 articles and about 50 signed book reviews, plus occasional interviews with noted scholars. The fourth issue of each volume includes an index of articles, authors, books reviewed, and reviewers. Several cumulative indexes have been published, the most recent having appeared in the February 1986 issue and indexing volumes 56–65 (1976–85).

179. *The Historian: A Journal of History,* 1938–. Quarterly. Allentown, PA: Phi Alpha Theta. ISSN 0018-2370.

As the official journal of Phi Alpha Theta, the academic honor society for history, *The Historian* naturally makes the history of all areas, all periods, and all subjects its province. However, subjects dealing with American history appear more frequently than any other area. Each issue has 5 to 6 articles, and there is an occasional review article. An extensive section of 50 to 60 book reviews appears in each issue. News items of interest to members of Phi Alpha Theta are also published. There is no index for individual volumes, although simple five-year cumulative indexes are regularly compiled.

180. *Historical Journal,* 1928–. Quarterly. Cambridge: Cambridge University Press. ISSN 0018-246x.

This journal covers all areas of historical study from the fifteenth century to the present, although its contents are largely concerned with British and European topics. It was originally entitled *The Cambridge Historical Journal,* from 1923 to 1958. This well-edited and highly scholarly journal typically contains seven to eight long articles, two to four communications (shorter articles), one to three review articles or historiographical reviews, and several signed book reviews. The fourth part of each volume includes a simple index.

181. *Historical Research,* 1923–. 3 issues a year. Oxford: Basil Blackwell. ISSN 0020-2894.

The year 1987 marked a change for the venerable journal *Bulletin of the Institute of Historical Research.* It became simply *Historical Research* and started publishing three issues a year instead of two. Apart from a change in the cover design, little else is different other than that selected papers from the Anglo-American Conference of Historians will be published in the June issue. The scope will remain British and European history from the Middle Ages to the present. Typically an issue consists of four to six articles and a "Notes and Documents" section, which publishes short contributions on methodology and archives or significant documents with scholarly notes and commentary. There are no book reviews, and the journal has no in-house index.

182. *History and Theory: Studies in the Philosophy of History*, 1960–. Quarterly. Middleton, CT: Wesleyan University. ISSN 0018-2656.

The purpose of *History and Theory* is to provide a forum for debate, discussion, and research into "what is history?" Historiography, methodology, and philosophy of history are some of the broad subjects appearing in this periodical. There are no restrictions on time periods or geographical areas. Each issue consists of three or four articles and four to six review articles that usually focus on only one book. There is also a section called "Books in Summary," in which eight to ten books are briefly noted. The third issue of each volume contains the index for the first three issues of the year. The fourth number of each volume is called a "Beiheft" and consists of either a monographic or bibliographic study of some topic within the interests of *History and Theory*.

183. *History of Education Quarterly*, 1961–. Quarterly. Bloomington, IN: History of Education Society. ISSN US-00-182680.

All aspects of education at all levels in all countries and all periods fall within the scope of this impressive journal. There are more contributions dealing with American history than anything else. Separate issues contain articles, review essays, and book reviews, although the proportions can vary greatly. In the past, review essays appear to have been favored, but the new editors are using more single book reviews of 600 to 1,000 words. Occasionally issues will include "forums," which are debates among scholars, and "retrospectives," which are historiographical overviews. There is no in-house indexing.

184. *The History Teacher*, 1967–. Quarterly. Long Beach, CA: Society for History Education. ISSN 0018-2745.

This interesting and useful journal is unique in that its concern is with good teaching and that it not be run by education specialists.

As a result, the prose is readable and the ideas presented are realistic and intellectually sound. Each issue contains 5 to 7 articles. They are divided into 3 categories. The first is the "Craft of Teaching," which consists of methods or how-to articles. Articles in the section "State of the Profession" are concerned with the role of teachers or the role of history in education. "Historiography" contains articles that discuss ideas and interpretations in various historical writings. Basically, most issues of concern to history teachers from the upper elementary grades through college level form the focus of this journal. Its "Reviews" section is divided into "Media," commenting on movies and audiovisuals; "Textbooks and Readers," which provides useful evaluations of current materials; and "Books," which reviews historical monographs. There are 20 to 30 reviews in each issue. An index at the end of the volume supplies the locations for authors, titles, reviewers, and a few broad subjects.

185. *History: The Journal of the Historical Association,* 1912–. 3 issues a year. London: Historical Association. ISSN 0018-2648.

The Historical Association is an English organization consisting primarily of history teachers in secondary and higher education but also including anyone with a strong interest in history. Therefore, the scope of its journal takes in all periods, areas, and subjects with the exception of classical antiquity. British and European topics predominate, reflecting the interests of contributors and readers. Because of its broad-based readership, there is a strong emphasis on well-written articles of wide interest. Each issue contains three articles and one or two review articles. There is also an "Editorial Notes" section containing news items and announcements of publications. The large number of book reviews and short notices (150–200 per issue) are particularly useful. There is no annual index. Other journals published by the Historical Association are *The Historian,* which is a sort of newsletter and popular magazine, and *Teaching History,* the British equivalent of *The History Teacher* [see 184].

186. *Isis: An International Review Devoted to the History of Science and Its Cultural Influences,* 1912–. 5 issues a year. Philadelphia: History of Science Society. ISSN 0021-1753.

All fields and periods in the history of science are covered by *Isis.* It is also the oldest and most widely read of the journals specializing in this subject. The contents of this journal are evenly balanced in terms of the subjects of the articles published. Each issue contains two to four articles and one or two review essays. Other occasional features include "Critiques and Contentions," "Documents," and "Notes and Correspondence." Professional news items are printed also, and each issue contains approximately 50 signed book reviews. The fourth issue of the year has an index. The fifth issue in each volume is an annual critical bibliography for the history of science, a feature that makes this journal particularly valuable to researchers. *Annals of Science* is a bimonthly journal from Great Britain that is most similar to *Isis* in its scope.

187. *Journal of African History*, 1960–. 3 issues a year. Cambridge: Cambridge University Press. ISSN 0021-8537.

This journal attempts to cover all parts of Africa and all periods of its history, although it publishes a disproportionate number of articles on the colonial period and on economic topics. Occasionally it publishes special issues focusing on a particular theme. Each issue includes approximately 7 articles, and review articles appear several times each year. There are roughly 20 signed and titled book reviews in each issue as well as some signed book notes. The end of each volume has a "Contents List and Index." In Volume 27 (1986) the journal switched from 4 issues a year to 3, due to a decline in the number of submissions.

188. *Journal of American History*, 1914–. Quarterly. Bloomington, IN: Organization of American Historians. ISSN 0021-8723.

Formerly known as the *Mississippi Valley Historical Review* (1914–64), the *Journal of American History* is the largest scholarly periodical to take general American history as its focus. Three to four articles appear in each issue and usually one historiographical piece called a "Perspective." There are occasional review essays and research notes and comments. Other useful features are classified listings of recent articles and dissertations. The fourth (March) issue of each volume includes an excellent detailed index to authors, titles, and subjects.

189. *Journal of Asian Studies*, 1941–. Quarterly. Ann Arbor, MI: Association for Asian Studies. ISSN 0021-9118.

Originally titled *Far Eastern Quarterly*, this journal is the leading academic periodical specializing in Asian studies. Its scope is all of Asian history and culture all periods. Three articles and a review article are standard for most issues. Abstracts of the articles appear at the front of the issue. There are about 50 signed book reviews in every issue, and news items are printed in the section called

"Editor's Note." A simple index is provided in the fourth issue of each volume.

190. *Journal of Black Studies,* 1970–. Quarterly. Beverly Hills, CA: Sage Publications. ISSN 0192-513X.

Although this is an interdisciplinary journal, articles on historical topics or using a historical approach predominate. All geographical areas and all periods of time fall within the scope of this journal. Each issue contains five to seven articles, and occasionally there is a review article. Signed book reviews sometimes appear, although they are not a regular feature. A simple author/title index is provided in the fourth issue of each volume.

191. *Journal of British Studies,* 1961–. Quarterly. Chicago: University of Chicago Press. ISSN 0021-9371.

With the appearance of Volume 24 (1985), the *Journal of British Studies* shifted from a semiannual to a quarterly publication schedule. It is sponsored by the North American Conference on British Studies along with another quarterly journal, *Albion.* Both journals take British history, dealing with all subjects and all periods as their focus. Neither is a truly interdisciplinary "studies" periodical. Each issue of the *Journal of British Studies* publishes three or four articles and two to four review articles. These review articles are another feature that was added in 1985. There is usually at least one theme issue published each year. The fourth issue includes an alphabetical listing of articles, review articles, and books reviewed by author.

192. *Journal of Contemporary History,* 1966–. Quarterly. London: Sage Publications. ISSN 0022-0094.

Contemporary history is defined by this journal as the twentieth century with occasional forays into the nineteenth. Although there is a heavy concentration on British and European topics, articles on other parts of the world often do appear. Special theme issues are frequently published. Typically, an issue consists of approximately eight articles. They are well researched and usually well written. There are no book reviews, although a list of books received is published. An annual index appears in issue four of each volume, and Volume 21, no. 4 (1986) contained a cumulative author-subject index for Volumes 1–21.

193. *Journal of Economic History,* 1941–. Quarterly. Iowa City, IA: Economic History Association. ISSN 0022-0507.

Although this journal is international in its scope, inevitably it publishes a larger portion of articles dealing with United States history than with any other country or region. Individual issues contain 7 to 12 articles. Shorter "Notes and Discussion" pieces and review articles appear frequently. The second issue of the year (June) publishes papers from the annual meeting of the Economic History Association. It also provides summaries of recent dissertations on economic history. There are approximately 50 signed book reviews in each issue. The fourth issue of the year includes a simple index. There is a British journal called the *Economic History Review* that has the same international scope, although it publishes more articles on United Kingdom topics. It does, however, contain two unique features of particular interest to researchers. The first issue of each volume has a "Review of Periodical Literature" that gives an evaluative discussion of selected periodical literature from two years earlier. Then in the fourth issue, a "List of Publications on the Economic and Social History of Great Britain and Ireland" appears; it is a classified list of books and articles from the previous year.

194. *Journal of Interdisciplinary History*, 1970–. Quarterly. Cambridge, MA: M.I.T. Press. ISSN 0022-1953.

The purpose of this innovative journal is to link the findings and methods of other disciplines to the advancement of historical knowledge. All geographical areas and historical periods fall within its scope. Special theme issues are common. Normally an individual issue of the journal will contain 4 long articles, a research note, a review article, and about 30 signed book reviews. However, if it is a theme issue, it could have about 10 articles. The fourth issue of each volume contains a complete table of contents, but there is no index.

195. *Journal of Latin American Studies*, 1969–. 3 issues a year. Cambridge: Cambridge University Press. ISSN 0022-216X.

Published under the sponsorship of the various institutes and centers of Latin American studies in Great Britain, this journal concentrates on the study of Latin American social sciences (including history). A typical issue includes 7 or 8 articles, a review article, and approximately 40 signed book reviews. Currently edited at the Institute of Latin American Studies, University of London, the publication features articles on history and political science. A cumulative index for volumes 1–15 (1969–83) was published in 1986.

196. *Journal of Library History*. [See 208]

197. *Journal of Modern History*, 1929–. Quarterly. Chicago: University of Chicago Press. ISSN 0022-2801.

The focus of this excellent journal is European history from the Renaissance to the present. It maintains a good balance in the topics that it publishes. There are occasional theme issues. A typical issue includes 2 or 3 articles and 2 or 3 review articles. In addition there are 30 to 40 signed book reviews in each issue. The fourth issue has an index to articles, books reviewed, and authors for the entire volume.

198. *Journal of Near Eastern Studies*, 1884–. Quarterly. Chicago: University of Chicago Press. ISSN 0022-2968.

The history of the ancient and medieval Near East is well served by this impressive but somewhat technical journal. Subjects dealing with archaeology and ancient languages appear frequently. Each issue contains four or five articles and about ten signed book reviews. It will also publish contributions in German and French as well as English.

199. *Journal of Negro History*, 1916–. Quarterly. Washington, DC: Association for the Study of Negro Life and History. ISSN 0022-2922.

Although black history for all periods and places is the scope of this journal, it primarily publishes articles dealing with the United States. Each issue contains 4 to 6 articles. Documents are also published 2 or 3 times in each volume. The number of signed book reviews ranges from 10 to 25 per issue. A section called "Notes and Announcements" prints news items of interest to black-history specialists. Until 1970 there was a detailed index at the end of each volume, but that practice has been abandoned.

200. *Journal of Psychohistory: A Quarterly Journal of Childhood and Psychohistory*, 1973–. Quarterly. New York: Association for Psychohistory. ISSN 0145-3378.

Formerly entitled *History of Childhood Quarterly* (1973–76), this journal has broadened its scope to include the application of psychoanalytical methods to any appropriate historical setting, not just childhood. An average issue will have four to seven articles, one or two review articles, and three to ten signed book reviews. There is a simple index for the volume in the fourth issue, which lists articles and books reviewed.

201. *Journal of Social History*, 1967–. Quarterly. Pittsburgh: Carnegie-Mellon University. ISSN 0022-4529.

As the most prestigious journal specializing in this type of history in the United States, this publication has a scope necessarily broad and unrestricted by time period or geographical area. Contributions focusing on the United States predominate. Each issue contains 5 to 7 articles, 1 or 2 review essays, and 25 to 30 signed book reviews. Issue number four (Summer) of each volume contains a simple author-title index for the articles and review essays but not the book reviews. There is a similar British journal called *Social History* (3 issues a year) that has a much stronger British and European focus.

202. *Journal of Southern History*, 1935–. Quarterly. Athens, GA: Southern Historical Association. ISSN 0022-4642.

One of the oldest and best of the regional historical journals in the United States, it specializes in all periods and aspects of the South's history. An individual issue will contain 3 or 4 articles, with occasional review articles. There is an extensive book review section of about 50 reviews per issue along with some shorter book notes. News items and notices of interest to members of the Southern Historical Association are also printed. The fourth issue of the year includes a detailed index of authors, titles, and subjects. The second issue of each year contains a useful classified survey of recent periodical literature on Southern history.

203. *Journal of Sport History*, 1974–. 3 issues a year. Chicago: North American Society for Sport History. ISSN 0094-1700.

The history of sport in all countries and all time periods forms the focus of this well-produced journal. Coverage of subjects from within the traditional area of Western civilization is quite balanced, although there is a definite but understandable lack of articles dealing with traditional Asia and Africa. A normal issue will consist of 3 or 4 articles, with an occasional review article. Seven to 12 signed book reviews are published in each issue. A useful section called "Recent Dissertations" is published in the second (Summer) issue of the journal and lists relevant new dissertations. Each issue contains another valuable feature: a "Journals Survey" listing articles on sport history appearing in other journals. There is no in-house index.

204. *Journal of the History of Ideas: An International Quarterly Devoted to Intellectual History*, 1940–. Quarterly. Rochester, NY: University of Rochester. ISSN 0022-5037.

As the leading English-language journal for intellectual history, the *Journal of the History of Ideas* maintains the expected standards of rigorous and sometimes rarefied scholarship. Each issue publishes six to eight articles and one to three shorter notes. Several review articles are published in each volume, although there are no book reviews. There is a list of books received. A simple index of authors and broad subjects appears in the last issue of each volume.

205. *Journal of Urban History*, 1974–. Quarterly. Birmingham, AL: Center for Urban Affairs. ISSN 0096-1442.

All periods and all geographical areas fall within the scope of this periodical devoted to the history of cities and urban studies. The bulk of the contributions deal with American history. Each issue normally contains three articles, one interview, and about three signed book reviews. The growing interest in urban history is further reflected by the existence of the British *Urban History Yearbook* and the Canadian *Urban History Review* (3 issues a year).

206. *Labor History*, 1960–. Quarterly. New York: Tamiment Institute. ISSN 0023-656X.

The focus of this journal is the history of labor, both organized and unorganized, during all periods of American history. It also publishes comparative studies when appropriate. Each issue has 4 or 5 articles. Notes and documents are frequently published, and review essays appear on occasion. The fourth (Fall) issue of each volume contains the useful features "Annual Bibliography of American Labor History," which is a classified listing of new publications, and "Recent Dissertations in American and European Labor History," which lists new dissertations along with an author-produced abstract of from 175 to 200 words. There are between 15 and 30 signed book reviews in each issue. The fourth issue also includes a simple index for the volume that separately lists articles, books reviewed, contributors, and book reviewers.

207. *Latin American Research Review*, 1965–. 3 issues a year. Albuquerque, NM: Latin American Institute. ISSN 0023-8791.

The Latin American Studies Association (U.S.) publishes the *LARR* from editorial offices shifted among the various major United States centers for Latin American studies. Each issue includes four to five articles, several research reports, and eight to ten review essays in which five to seven books are discussed. Articles tend to be interdisciplinary but research based.

208. *Libraries & Culture*, 1966–. Quarterly. Austin, TX: University of Texas Press. ISSN 0894-8631.

Originally titled *The Journal of Library History: Philosophy & Comparative Librarianship* (ISSN 0275-3650), in l987 this journal assumed its present title. Its interdisciplinary and international focus is the interaction of books, libraries, culture, and society throughout history. Special issues focusing on a theme or publishing the proceedings of conferences appear frequently. Normally an individual issue contains 3 to 6 articles and 1 to 3 shorter notes. Regular issues will have 15 to 20 signed reviews. The fourth (Fall) issue of each volume contains a detailed author, title, and subject index. *Library History* is a similar British journal.

209. *Oral History Review,* 1966–. Annual. Denton, TX: Oral History Association. ISSN 0094-0798.

As the oldest and largest-circulation journal devoted to oral history, this publication takes all aspects, geographical areas, and time periods as its scope. At the same time, topics dealing with American history appear most frequently. A normal issue publishes 4 articles, 2 or 3 review articles, and another 20 signed book reviews. Notices and news items of interest to specialists in oral history are also printed. The British equivalent is a twice-yearly publication called *Oral History.*

210. *Pacific Historical Review,* 1932–. Quarterly. Berkeley, CA: Pacific Coast Branch, American Historical Association. ISSN 0030-8684.

Articles on the West, the Pacific Coast region, and U.S. foreign policy and expansionism predominate in the contents of this journal. But it is more than a regional journal. It also publishes articles on historiography and methodology, and its area of specialization is broad enough to be of general interest to other American historians. Three or 4 articles appear in each issue, and 1 or 2 items normally appear in the "Notes and Documents" section. Occasional review essays and historiographical essays are published. About 30 signed book reviews appear in each issue. The fourth (November) issue of each year contains a detailed author, title, and subject index.

211. *Past & Present: A Journal of Historical Studies,* 1952–. Quarterly. Oxford: Past and Present Society. ISSN 0031-2746.

As one of the most stimulating and readable of all historical journals, *Past & Present* tries hard to make all historical periods and geographical areas part of its focus. Articles on British and European topics still dominate its pages, as might be expected from a periodical based in England. From six to nine articles tends to be the range of material contained in each issue. Furthermore, this journal has a policy of publishing articles that are often considerably longer than normal. Frequently debates concerning controversial articles will develop and produce lively exchanges. There are no regular book reviews, although sometimes review articles are published. A classified list of the contents of issue numbers 1–100 is available (each issue is numbered separately), and an alphabetical listing by author of the contents of each year's issues is sent out with the fourth (November) issue.

212. *Renaissance Quarterly*, 1947–. Quarterly. New York: Renaissance Society of America. ISSN 0034-4338.

Devoted to the study of the European Renaissance between the years 1399 and 1660, this highly respected journal has a broader chronological range than *Sixteenth Century Journal* [*see* 215], while the range of subjects covered is narrower since intellectual, cultural, and literary studies are preponderant. Three articles are usually published in each issue along with about 40 signed book reviews. It also contains a useful section of news items and announcements. There is no index.

213. *Reviews in American History*, 1973–. Quarterly. Baltimore, MD: Johns Hopkins University Press. ISSN 0048-7511.

Instead of publishing articles, the purpose of this unique journal is the publication of review articles. These lengthy reviews can discuss a single book or a group of related books. Several retrospective bibliographic surveys also appear in each issue. There are normally 25 to 30 essays in an issue. *Reviews in European History* began at the same time as this journal but failed due to lack of interest.

214. *Signs: Journal of Women in Culture and Society*, 1975–. Quarterly. Chicago: University of Chicago Press. ISSN 0097-9740.

This scholarly journal is devoted to the interdisciplinary study of women. Although it contains articles dealing with nonhistorical topics, historical articles and book reviews are quite common. Each volume has a simple contents index. *Feminist Studies* is similar in its approach and scope.

215. *The Sixteenth Century Journal: A Journal for Renaissance and Reformation Students and Scholars*, 1972–. Quarterly. Kirksville, MO: Sixteenth Century Journal Publishers. ISSN 0361-0160.

All aspects of the sixteenth century fall within the scope of this interesting journal, although the approach is always historical even

when a literary or theological topic is being discussed. The coverage
of subjects is well balanced. Each issue has 5 to 7 long articles and 25
to 45 signed book reviews. A detailed author, title, and subject index
is printed in the fourth issue of each volume. Very similar in scope
is the highly thought of international annual *Archive for Reformation
History/Archiv fur Reformationsgeschichte*, publishing English and
German articles under the sponsorship of the American Society for
Reformation Research.

216. *Slavic Review: American Quarterly of Soviet and East European
Studies*, 1941–. Quarterly. Stanford, CA: American Association for
the Advancement of Slavic Studies. ISSN 0037-6779.

From 1941 to 1961 this journal was known as the *American Slavic and
East European Review*. There are 3 or 4 articles in each issue. The
journal also publishes short items called "Discussions" that function
as notes or comments. Review articles appear occasionally. The book
review section is large, with about 75 signed reviews per issue. There
is a simple volume index divided into lists of contributors (authors
of articles and reviews) and books reviewed (listed by author). *Slavic
Review* is the foremost American academic journal dealing with
Eastern European and Russian topics. The British counterpart is the
older *Slavonic and East European Review,* also a quarterly.

217. *Speculum: A Journal of Medieval Studies*, 1926–. Quarterly.
Cambridge, MA: Medieval Academy of America. ISSN 0038-7134.

This highly academic journal is the oldest and most widely read
periodical specializing in medieval history in the English language.
The number of articles in a single issue ranges from 4 to 6, with
review articles appearing on occasion. Shorter "Notes and Documents" items also appear frequently. There is a large book review
section containing about 60 signed reviews and from 20 to 60 shorter
notices. A simple annual volume index lists first the articles by their
authors and then book reviews.

218. *Western Historical Quarterly*, 1970–. Quarterly. Logan, UT:
Western Historical Association. ISSN 0043-3810.

This is the foremost academic journal focusing on the regional history of the American West. An average issue contains 3 articles and
about 30 signed book reviews. The third (July) issue publishes a
classified list of recent dissertations. Other regular features appearing in each issue are lists of new books, recent articles, and news
items of interest to historians of the West. Each volume includes a

simple list of authors, reviewers, articles, books reviewed, and broad subjects.

219. *William and Mary Quarterly: A Magazine of Early American History and Culture*, 1892–. Quarterly. Williamsburg, VA: Institute of Early American History and Culture. ISSN 0043-5597.

This well-edited and readable journal specializes in U.S. history from its colonial beginnings through the early republic. It was originally titled the *William and Mary College Quarterly Historical Magazine* until 1944. An individual issue will contain 3 to 5 articles and 1 to 3 shorter notes or documents. There are 15 to 20 signed book reviews in each issue. The fourth issue (October) includes an extensive index of authors, titles, and subjects for the volume.

5.

Periodical Indexes and Abstracts

During the first half of this century, the indexing of historical periodical literature was extremely limited. Historians were largely limited to the bibliographies at the backs of monographs or published separately. The appearance of the first genuine historical periodical indexes, i.e., *America: History and Life* and *Historical Abstracts*, in the 1950s and 1960s, along with expanded coverage by the Wilson Indexes, ushered in a revolution in historical bibliography. By the 1970s sophisticated citation indexes like the *Social Science Citation Index*, plus their on-line versions, allowed for the first computerized searching of historical data bases. These data bases expanded during the 1980s. New ones were added along with the development of compact-disc versions of the index, providing rapid searching at no per search cost. The 1990s will no doubt bring even broader coverage of the periodical literature in a variety of formats and the first full-text compact-disc systems.

Guides

220. *The Index and Abstract Directory: An International Guide to Services and Serials Coverage.* Premier edition. Birmingham, AL: EBSCO Publishing, 1989. 2,177p. ISBN 0-913956-42-2.

This recently published directory provides the most complete guide to indexing and abstracting services. Section 1 lists some 30,000 indexed periodicals with brief histories of the title, frequencies, editors, addresses, and prices. Also listed are all indexing and abstracting services that cover that title. These are arranged by subject from "Aeronautics" to "Zoology." Section 2 is an alphabetical list of some 700 indexing and abstracting services. Uniquely, this section lists all periodicals indexed or abstracted by each of these services. There is also an alphabetical title index, an index/abstract services by subject classification index, and an ISSN index. Other, less comprehensive guides to indexing and abstracting services include: *The Serials Directory: An International Reference Book*, also published annually by EBSCO; *Ulrich's International Periodicals Directory* (which now includes irregular serials and annuals), published annually by R. R. Bowker; and the *Librarian's Guide to Serials*, published annually by the Faxon Company.

General

221. *Canadian Periodical Index.* Toronto: Info Globe, 1938–. Monthly with bound annual cumulations. ISSN 0008-4719.

Appearing under different titles (the *Canadian Index* and the *Canadian Index to Periodicals and Documentary Films*) and various publishers (the Windsor Public Library, the University of Toronto Library, the Canadian Library Association, and the National Library of Canada), this publication has remained the first index of choice for most Canadian libraries. Acquired by Info Globe, the electronic-publishing division of the Toronto *Globe and Mail*, in December of 1986, it provides subject indexing to 380 general-interest and academic periodicals (both French and English). While the majority of these are Canadian periodicals, it also indexes 18 U.S. titles. A book review section lists books by author and title. Retrospective coverage from 1920 is provided by the *Canadian Periodical Index 1920–1937: An Author and Subject Index*, edited by Grace Heggie et al. (Toronto: Canadian Library Association, 1988). An alternative general-interest Canadian index, the *Canadian Magazine Index* (Toronto: Micromedia, ISSN 0828-8777), was launched in 1985. Issued monthly, it provides coverage of more than 400 Canadian periodicals and 18 U.S. titles.

222. *General Periodicals Index on InfoTrac.* Foster City, CA: Information Access Company, 1984–. Monthly cumulative updates. The Academic Library Edition on CD-ROM became available for the first time in 1988.

The appearance of InfoTrac on videodisc in 1984 ushered in the first wave of nonprint, non-on-line periodical indexes. Since that time InfoTrac systems have become extremely popular in U.S. academic libraries and some larger public libraries. In 1988 the Information Access Company shifted to the more flexible compact-disc format.

The Academic Library Edition of the General Periodicals Index provides indexing for 1,100 publications in the social sciences, humanities, business, management, economics, and current affairs. Coverage includes index citations from the current year cumulated with citations from the previous three years. Also included is indexing to the current year of the *Wall Street Journal* and the latest 60 days of the *New York Times*. An InfoTrac Backfile Database on a separate disc provides an additional four years of retrospective data. However, coverage of many history and other social-science periodicals does not begin until 1987. A Public Library Edition of InfoTrac is also available, as are various scaled-down versions such as the *Academic Index* and the *Magazine Index*. Because of its easy subject searching (some Boolean functions are in the planning stages), rapid access, and attachment to printers, this has become the general index of choice for many students.

223. *Periodical Abstracts Ondisc*. Ann Arbor, MI: UMI. 1988–. Cumulative bimonthly updates.

Available only on CD-ROM, this is a general reference index to 450 current periodicals, including all titles indexed in the *Reader's Guide* [*see* 225]. It initially indexed only five history journals: *American History Illustrated, Current History, History Today, Journal of American History*, and *Journal of Contemporary History*. In 1990 indexing back to 1988 was added for five additional titles: *American Historical Review, Journal of Latin American Studies, Journal of Modern History, Journal of Negro History*, and *Reviews in American History*. All citations include abstracts. Sophisticated software allows a variety of searching techniques not possible in print indexes or currently on InfoTrac [*see* 222]. These include the use of Boolean operators, proximity operators, truncation, sideways searching, and the capability to combine, modify, and reuse search sets. A word index, listing all single words appearing in the data bases, can be accessed for reference and search selection. Although the utility of this index is limited by its newness, it is clearly the wave of the future for general periodical indexes. Full-text coverage of some of these titles began in 1990.

224. *Reader's Guide Abstracts*. New York: H. W. Wilson, microfiche, 1984–. CD-ROM, 1984–. Print, 1988–. The microfiche is issued in eight cumulative issues, the CD-ROM is updated quarterly, and the print edition is issued ten times a year with two semiannual bound cumulations. ISSN 0899-1443.

This is a selective abstracting service covering all the periodicals indexed in the *Reader's Guide* [*see* 225]. Selection is based on the substantive nature of the article, its currency and topicality, its reference value, and its relevancy to school and college curricula. It currently abstracts some 25,000 articles annually. Abstracts are lengthy (100-plus words) and descriptive.

225. *Reader's Guide to Periodical Literature.* New York: H. W. Wilson, 1900–. Semimonthly in Sept., Oct., Dec., Mar., and Apr. and monthly in Jan., Feb., May, June, July, Aug., and Nov., with a bound annual cumulation. ISSN 0034-0464.

Three years after the founding of the H. W. Wilson Company in Minneapolis, Halsey Wilson issued the first *Reader's Guide* [*RG*], in 1901, initially as a supplement to the *Cumulative Book Index.* The infant publication indexed just seven periodicals. When the first five-year cumulation was issued in 1905, it was organized in a dictionary arrangement with uniform subject headings. Since that time, the *RG* has remained the standard guide to general English-language periodicals published in the U.S. Now indexing 195 titles, *RG* provides a cumulative author-subject index to mainstream general-interest periodicals. The entries are arranged alphabetically, and citations to book reviews follow the main body of the index. Like all other Wilson indexes, *RG* uses its own subject authority file. Numerous *see* and *see also* references guide the reader to appropriate or additional subject entries. The titles indexed are frequently revised on the basis of recommendations from the Committee on Wilson Indexes of the Reference and Adult Services Division of the American Library Association and the polling of subscribers. *Maclean's* [Canada] remains the only non-U.S. title to be indexed. On-line access (from January 1983–) is available through Wilsonline, and a CD-ROM version is available through Wilsondisc.

Humanities

226. *Arts and Humanities Citation Index* [*A&HCI*]. Philadelphia: Institute for Scientific Information, 1976–. Triannual, with bound cumulations. ISSN 0162-8445.

The introduction of the *Science Citation Index* in 1961 greatly expanded the search capacities of traditional subject indexes. The *A&HCI*, like its science counterpart and the *Social Sciences Citation Index* [*see* 232], provides a variety of access points and search strategies for its users. It consists of four parts: the citation index, the source index, the corporate index, and the permuterm index. The source index is most similar to traditional indexes and is really an author index to the literature of a particular year. However, search possibilities can be expanded, as all references or footnotes are also listed with brief bibliographical information. This expanded form of searching is referred to as "cycling" or "treeing." The citation index allows the user to search previously published works relevant to a particular topic and to locate current articles on that topic. A permuterm subject index provides access via title words and enrichment terms (supplied for esoteric titles). A corporate index, divided into geographical and organizational sections, provides access to literature produced by institutions and organizations. Covering all of the arts and humanities from archaeology to religion, the *A&HCI* indexes 1,256 journals comprehensively and 812 selectively. These journals are edited in 44 countries in a variety of languages. More than 200 history journals are indexed, making *A&HCI* the next-most-important index after either *America: History and Life* or *Historical Abstracts* [see 234 and 236]. A five-year cumulation for the years 1975–1979 was published in 1987. On-line coverage from 1980 is available through BRS and on DIALOG File 439, with weekly and biweekly updates. In 1989 this file exceeded 1.2 million bibliographic records.

227. *British Humanities Index*. London: Library Association Publishing, 1962–. Quarterly, with bound annual cumulations. ISSN 0007-0815.

This is an alphabetically arranged subject index to primarily British journals in the fields of politics, archaeology, architecture, language, history, music, economics, philosophy, art, folklore, and books and publishing. Its predecessors, the *Athenaeum Subject Index* (1915–1918) and the *Subject Index to Periodicals* (1919–1961) indexed as many as 500 British and American periodicals. When the *Subject Index* ceased publication in 1961, it was succeeded by the *British Humanities Index* [BHI] and the *British Technology Index*. Unlike the *Humanities Index* [see 229], this publication does not integrate authors and subjects in the main index, although there is a special author index in the annual cumulation. *BHI* currently indexes 344 titles, mostly British but including occasional titles from Australia and New Zealand. Fifty-four new titles were added in 1987, including many history titles, e.g., *British Journal for Eighteenth Century Studies*, *Bulletin of Latin American Research*, *Mediterranean History Review*, and *Parliamentary History*. *BHI* also indexes articles from *The Times* [London] and the *Times Literary Supplement*.

228. *Hispanic American Periodicals Index* [*HAPI*]. Los Angeles: UCLA Latin American Center Publications, 1974–. Annual. ISSN 0270-8558.

This is a general index to the humanities and social-science literature of Latin America. Currently indexing more than 250 periodicals, with its primary focus on titles published in Hispanic America, it has broadened its scope in recent years to include coverage of Hispanic groups in the U.S. There are separate author and subject indexes. The latter uses a controlled vocabulary that was issued in the form of a thesaurus in 1983. Articles indexed are written in English, Spanish, Portuguese, and other Western European languages. The use of volunteer indexers has resulted in considerable delays in publication. The Seminar on the Acquisition of Latin American Library Materials [SALALM] serves as an adviser. A retrospective volume covering the years 1970–1974 was published in three volumes in 1984. Earlier coverage is available in the *Index to Latin American Periodical Literature, 1929–1960* and supplements for 1961–1965 and 1966–1970, all published by G. K. Hall.

229. *Humanities Index*. New York: H. W. Wilson, 1974–. Quarterly, with bound annual cumulations. ISSN 0095-5981.

This publication is an alphabetically arranged integrated author and subject index to 347 periodicals in the humanities, including 76 history titles. The focus of the index, which was originally published as a supplement to the *Reader's Guide* [*see* 225] in 1907, is on English-language periodicals. After a gentlemen's agreement between H. W. Wilson and R. R. Bowker, Bowker agreed to get out of the index business if Wilson would get out of the directory business. When Bowker's *Annual Library Index* ceased publication in 1910, the *International Index* was established by Wilson. It indexed 19 titles from *Reader's Guide* along with an additional 55 social-science and humanities titles. Books were also indexed until 1914. The name was changed in 1965 to the *Social Sciences and Humanities Index*, and in 1974 the two broad subjects were separated into two indexes. Since that time the coverage of the humanities has more than doubled. Like other Wilson indexes, *Humanities Index* receives suggestions from the American Library Association Committee on Wilson Indexes. In recent years many new history journals have been added, including *Journal of Ecclesiastical History, Journal of Family History, Journal of Urban History*, and *Reviews in American History*. In 1988 coverage was extended to state historical journals like the *Southwestern Historical Quarterly* and the *Virginia Magazine of History and Biography*. An on-line version of this index has been available through Wilsonline since February 1984 and a CD-ROM version is available through Wilsondisc, also since 1984.

Social Sciences

230. *Public Affairs Information Service (PAIS) Bulletin*. New York: PAIS, 1915–. Biweekly, with quarterly and bound annual cumulations. ISSN 0898-2201.

231. *PAIS Foreign Language Index*. New York: PAIS, 1972–. Quarterly, with bound annual cumulations. ISSN 0896-792X.

PAIS is a nonprofit association of libraries, founded in 1914 and chartered in New York for the purpose of indexing library materials in the field of public policy and public affairs. A year later the first *PAIS Bulletin* was issued. The *Bulletin* is a subject index to the current English-language literature in disciplines ranging from the humanities to the sciences, with political and social issues as its principal focus. It provides selective indexing to more than 800 periodicals and more than 6,000 other publications. Its content reflects the recent acquisitions at the Economic and Public Affairs Division of the New York Public Library. The *PAIS Foreign Language Index* provides similar indexing coverage for 400 journals and a variety of other publications in French, German, Italian, Spanish, and Portuguese. *PAIS* uses its own subject headings, and a thesaurus is available. An author index is provided only in the annual cumulations. On-line coverage is available through BRS and on DIALOG File 49 as *PAIS International*. Coverage includes the *Bulletin* since 1976 and the *Foreign Language Index* since 1972. The file is updated monthly. *PAIS on CD-ROM* was issued in 1988, providing a similar coverage but with quarterly updates. A *Cumulative Subject Index to the P.A.I.S. Annual Bulletin, 1915–1974* was published in 15 volumes by Carrollton Press in 1977–1978.

232. *Social Sciences Citation Index [SSCI]*. Philadelphia: Institute for Scientific Information, 1972–. Three issues a year, with bound annual cumulations. ISSN 0091-3707.

This index is an international interdisciplinary index to the literature of the social sciences. It currently provides comprehensive indexing to 1,429 periodicals and selective indexing to an additional 1,215. Of these only 47 are history journals, including 21 general historical titles, 13 focusing on the history and philosophy of science, and 13 dealing with the history of the social sciences. The organization and search strategies parallel the *Arts and Humanities Citation Index [see 226]*. The *SSCI* indexed selected books in the social sciences until 1982. The 1988 annual cumulation included references to 55,162 articles, 34,232 book reviews, and large numbers of citations to notes, editorials, abstracts of meetings, reviews, and discussions. Multiyear cumulations are available for the following years: 1966–1970, 1971–1974, 1975–1980, and 1981–1985. Frequently searched on-line, *SSCI* has been available on BRS with weekly updates since 1972, and as File 7 on DIALOG with monthly updates. In 1989 the file contained more than 2.4 million bibliographic records. A CD-ROM version was issued in July 1989 with coverage from 1987–.

233. *Social Sciences Index*. New York: H. W. Wilson, 1974–. Quarterly, with bound annual cumulations. ISSN 0094-4920.

This is a general social-sciences index providing broad coverage of anthropology, economics, geography, international relations, law and criminology, political science, psychiatry, psychology, social work, and sociology. It has recently expanded its coverage to include 353 English-language periodicals based on recommendations from the American Library Association Committee on Wilson Indexes. It was preceded by the *International Index*, 1910–1964, and the *Social Sciences and Humanities Index*, 1965–1974. Since its separation from the latter, its journal coverage has more than doubled. Like other Wilson indexes it is an alphabetically arranged, integrated author-subject index using Wilson's own subject headings. While less useful to historians than the *Humanities Index* [see 229], it does provide indexing for such titles as *Economic History Review, Ethnohistory, Explorations in Economic History, Journal of Economic History, Journal of Latin American Studies, Journal of Social History*, the *Latin American Research Review*, and *Social History*, among others. Coverage is particularly strong in the fields of area studies, ethnic studies, feminist studies, and urban studies. On-line access has been available through Wilsonline since February 1983, with twice-weekly updates. A CD-ROM version is available from Wilson-disc with similar coverage but updated quarterly. A British social-sciences index, *ASSIA: Applied Social Sciences Index & Abstracts* (London: Library Association, ISSN 0950-2238) was launched in 1987. This bimonthly abstracting service provides selective coverage of more than 500 English-language journals, with a primary focus on contemporary social forces.

History

234. *America: History and Life*. Santa Barbara, CA: ABC-CLIO, 1964–. Five issues a year. Issues 1–4 contain abstracts and citations for

articles, book reviews, and dissertations. Issue 5 is the annual index. ISSN 0002-7065.

Founded in 1964 and considerably expanded and improved since then, this is the index of first choice for the history of the U.S. and Canada. Each volume provides abstracts and citations to more than 7,000 articles appearing in more than 2,000 journals published in more than 40 languages. Some 700 of these journals are published in the U.S. and Canada, including the journals of state and local historical societies, the social sciences, the humanities, and other major journals. Until 1989 the index was organized into four parts. Part A—"Article Abstracts and Citations," with subject and author indexes—was issued three times a year. Part B—"Index to Book Reviews"—included book reviews from 130 key journals and was issued twice a year [see 151]. Part C— "American History Bibliography"—combined citations for articles, books, and dissertations and organized them by subject. It was issued once a year. Part D—"Annual Index"—included an author index, book-title index, subject index, and book reviewer index for Parts A, B, and C. This somewhat confusing arrangement was eliminated in 1989, and the index will now more closely resemble *Historical Abstracts* [see 236], with four issues of abstracts and citations and a fifth issue containing the annual index. Subject indexing has always been a strong point of ABC-CLIO's indexes as a result of the publisher's use of the Subject Profile Index (SPIndex) system of rotated descriptors. Five-year cumulations have been published for the first 25 volumes, and retrospective Volume "0" provides 6,154 abstracts for the years 1954–1963. The complete file is available for on-line searching on DIALOG File 38.

235. *C.R.I.S. The Combined Retrospective Index to Journals in History, 1838–1974.* Washington, DC: Carrollton Press, 1977–1978. 11 vols. ISBN 0-8480-0175-0.

Called the "great leap backward in retrospective indexing of social sciences literature," this historical set was one of three sets to provide subject and author access to 400,000 articles in 530 journals in history, political science, and sociology. Historical coverage to 1974 is drawn from 243 English-language periodicals covering all periods and areas of history. The first nine volumes are arranged by subject and keyword, and the last two are organized alphabetically by author. The appearance of this set has greatly expanded retrospective searching of historical periodicals.

236. *Historical Abstracts.* Santa Barbara, CA: ABC-CLIO, 1955–. Part A: *Modern History Abstracts 1450–1914.* ISSN 0363-2717. Part B:

Twentieth Century Abstracts 1914–Present. ISSN 0363-2725. Each is published four times a year, with the fourth issue the annual index.

Founded by Eric and Inge Boehm in Vienna in 1955, this index first moved to Munich and finally to California in 1960. It is now the most important index for history for the period after 1450 for all the countries in the world excluding the U.S. and Canada, which are covered in *America: History and Life* [*see* 234]. *Historical Abstracts* currently includes abstracts and annotations of articles from 2,100 journals published in 80 countries in 40 languages. The index covered only the years 1775 to 1945 until 1971, when it was expanded to include 1775 to the present. In 1973, coverage was further expanded to include 1450 to the present. Retrospective coverage of articles published from 1954 to 1978 is provided in Volumes 26–30. Bibliographic entries for books do not begin until 1980 (for books published in 1979). These changes have led to a rather peculiar system of numbering for the volumes and requires the potential user's close attention. The strength of this index, in addition to its comprehensive coverage, is the use of the Subject Profile Index system (SPIndex), which provides multiple access points. Five-year cumulations are available for volumes 1–35. An index to the retrospective volumes was published in 1988. Volumes 19 forward can be searched on DIALOG File 39.

6.

Guides to Newspapers, Newspaper Collections, and Newspaper Indexes

There scarcely can be a graduate student studying modern history who has not spent endless hours toiling over microfilm reels of nineteenth- and twentieth-century newspapers. Until recently this task was rendered more laborious by the lack of many newspaper indexes. Students in American history had access to only the *New York Times Index* and only for after 1913. For British history there were *Palmer's Index to the Times* and, for after 1906, the *Official Index to the Times*. Researchers were forced to travel long distances to major newspaper collections. In recent decades the situation has changed dramatically. Microfilmed newspaper collections are now widely available or can be borrowed through interlibrary loan. Most major newspapers in the United States are now indexed, as are a modest number of major European papers. Collective newspaper indexes are available on-line and on compact disc, while the first major newsbanks are supplying full-text coverage from the late 1970s. Other helpful developments include the retrospective indexing of the *New York Times* back to 1851 and the publication of the extremely valuable *Personal Name Index to the New York Times Index*. Retrospective microfilming of newspaper collections is ongoing in many countries.

Guides to Newspapers: General

237. *The Newspaper Press in Britain: An Annotated Bibliography.* Edited by David Linton and Ray Boston. London and New York: Mansell Publishing, 1987. 361p. Index. ISBN 0-7201-1792-5.

Listing more than 2,900 books, articles, and theses about the British press, this bibliography is the most comprehensive guide available to British newspaper research. Entries are critically annotated and often provide biographical information on journalists and brief histories of newspapers. Appendix 1 gives a helpful chronology of British newspaper history.

238. *Newspapers: A Reference Guide.* By Richard Schwarzlose. New York: Greenwood Press, 1987. 415p. Index. ISBN 0-313-23613-5.

Written by a professor of journalism at Northwestern University, this work is in essay form and describes 1,700 key sources for information on newspapers. Its principal focus is on English-language sources dealing with U.S. topics. The most helpful sections for historians contemplating extended newspaper research are Chapter 1 on the histories of newspapers, Chapters 2 through 4 on newspaper personalities, and Chapter 9 on reference works and periodicals about newspapers. Appendixes 1 and 2 provide a selected chronology of newspapers and list major research collections.

Directories

239. *Editor and Publisher International Yearbook.* New York: Editor and Publisher Co., 1921–. Annual. ISSN 0424-4923.

This comprehensive directory of U.S. newspapers and Canadian, British, and other foreign newspapers divides its U.S. coverage into dailies and weeklies arranged in alphabetical order by state and city. Canadian newspapers are treated in a special section, and the British are included in the foreign section. One unique feature of this directory is its listing of the "Top One Hundred Daily Newspapers in the U.S." according to their circulation. There is also a special section on newspaper syndicates or group-controlled newspapers.

240. *Gale Directory of Publications: An Annual Guide to Newspapers, Magazines, Journals and Related Publications and Broadcast Media.* 2 vols. Detroit: Gale Research, 1869–. Annual. Indexes. ISSN 0892-1636.

Since taking over and renaming the venerable *Ayer Directory of Publications,* Gale has expanded the coverage of newspapers and magazines and added a second volume of indexes, maps, and statistics. The 1989 edition (121st) lists 25,000 publications, making it the best guide to U.S. newspapers, including dailies and weeklies. A basic listing includes masthead title, address, date established, frequency, subscription information, circulation, and ownership. Arrangement is alphabetical by state and then by cities within the individual state. Earlier editions also can be used with great profit for historical research. In 1989 Gale launched a new publication, called *Gale International Directory of Publications,* which provides country-by-country coverage of more than 4,800 newspapers and general-interest magazines published in more than 100 countries.

241. *Willings Press Guide.* East Grinstead, West Sussex, U.K.: 1874–. Annual. ISSN 0000-0213.

More than a British equivalent of the old *Ayer's Directory,* this guide also provides selective coverage of international newspapers. The 115th edition, published in 1989, lists more than 11,000 U.K. newspapers, periodicals, and annuals. Basic listings supply title, date established, price, editors, and addresses. There is a classified subject index to publications. A special section in pink provides a comprehensive U.K. newspaper index arranged by place of publication, with dates of frequency and average circulation.

242. *Working Press of the Nation.* 5 vols. Chicago: National Research Bureau, 1945–. Annual. Index. ISSN 0084-1323.

This five-volume annual publication provides U.S. coverage of newspapers, magazines, radio and television, feature writers and photographers, and international publications of U.S. companies and agencies. Volume 1 is the *Newspaper Directory.* Arranged alphabetically by state and city, it provides information similar to that in *Gale Directory* [*see* 240] but uniquely adds an index of editorial personnel by subject and an index of papers by metro areas. There are also special sections for religious, black, and foreign-language newspapers published in the U.S.

National Union Lists of Newspapers

United States

243. *American Newspapers, 1821–1936: A Union List of Files Available in the United States and Canada.* Edited by Winifred Gregory. New York: Bibliographical Society of America, 1937. 791p. ISBN 0-527-02250-0.

A monumental achievement for its time, this was the most complete list of U.S. and Canadian newspapers for the nineteenth and early twentieth centuries. Since microfilming was uncommon at that time, the list largely represents bound files of newspapers. Its arrangement is alphabetical by state and then by city within individual states. Canadian newspapers are listed in a similar fashion following the U.S. section. Information provided includes titles, frequencies, dates, and libraries holding copies, which is indicated by National Union Catalog [see 073] symbols. Major holders of foreign newspapers are briefly noted in a concluding chapter.

244. *History and Bibliography of American Newspapers, 1690–1820.* By Clarence S. Brigham. Worcester, MA: American Antiquarian Society, 1947. Reprint. Westport, CT: Greenwood Press, 1976. 2 vols. ISBN 0-8371-86773.

Brigham began compiling data for these volumes in 1913 and published his findings in various installments of the *Proceedings of the American Antiquarian Society,* the last of which appeared in 1927. The present set is a revision of those installments with corrections and additions. It identifies 2,120 newspapers published during the period of 1690–1820; New York has the most (138), followed by Philadelphia (107) and Boston (73). Major collections of these early newspapers are described: the American Antiquarian Society (1,496 titles), the Library of Congress (936), and Harvard University (736). Unlike the brief entries in *American Newspapers, 1821–1936* [see 243], this work provides lengthy descriptions of each newspaper and notes early publishers and editors. Institutions holding runs of these papers are noted by brief title rather than symbols. Private collections are also listed. The complete file of titles listed by Brigham is currently being microfilmed by Readex. (*See* Chapter 14)

245. *Newspapers in Microform: United States, 1948–1983.* 2 vols. Washington, D.C.: Library of Congress, 1984. ISSN 0097-9627.

In 1948 the Library of Congress established a Microfilming Clearing House to serve as a central source of information about the microfilming of newspapers. The current cumulation includes titles reported to the Library of Congress through 1983. Despite the slightly misleading title, this is a comprehensive union list of all newspapers that have been microfilmed from the colonial period to 1983. Arranged alphabetically first by state and then by city, its entries note library holdings by National Union Catalog symbol. Pending the completion of the *United States Newspaper Project,* this work is the most complete guide to holdings of U.S. newspapers and the place of first reference for historians. Basic information provided for each paper includes title, duration of publication, prior titles (continues), and successor titles (continued by). The Library of Congress continues to collect information on microfilmed titles, but no update has been published recently.

246. *Newspapers in Microform: Foreign Countries 1948–1983.* Washington, DC: Library of Congress, 1984. 504p. ISSN 0192-1231.

This is a bibliography of all microfilm holdings of foreign newspapers (including Canadian and British) reported to the Library of Congress as of 1983. All major U.S., Canadian, and British repositories are included, as are many other national and university libraries. As with the above entry, the title of this publication is somewhat misleading, for newspapers dating back to the eighteenth century are included in its listings. Like the volumes for the United States, arrangement is alphabetical by country and then by city except for Canadian newspapers, which are subdivided into provinces first. Locations of microfilms are based on standard symbols listed in the latest edition of *Symbols of American Libraries.* For foreign institutions, symbols are based on a format previously used for Canada. "Ca" has been used as the first element of all Canadian institutions and "Uk" for all British institutions.

247. *United States Newspaper Project: National Union List.* 3d ed. Dublin, OH: OCLC, 1989. Microfiche. ISBN 0-555653-074-9.

This ongoing project is designed to identify all newspapers published in the United States and its trust territories, list the repositories that collect those newspapers, and list the holdings of those repositories. With sponsorship from the National Endowment for the Humanities, the Organization of American Historians, the Library of Congress, and the Council on Library Resources, this work will form an on-line union catalog of U.S. newspaper resources. An additional objective is to preserve, through microfilming and other means, newspaper files considered significant for research. The most recent cumulative installment of microfiche provides bibliographic information on more than 77,000 newspapers dating from 1690 to the 1980s. Some 26 states, 2 territories, and the Library of Congress have completed entering their holdings, as have the American Antiquarian Society, the New York Public Library, the State Historical Society of Wisconsin, and the Center for Research Libraries. There are a number of access points in the microfiche. Its arrangement is

alphabetical by the masthead title of the newspaper. Other indexes include place of publication, language, beginning dates,
and intended audience. When completed, this work should be the
definitive guide to U.S. newspapers. Unfortunately, some of the
data entries are rather complex and so will require reference to the
accompanying guides. Until it is completed, researchers will still
need to consult *Newspapers in Microform* [*see* 245].

Canada

248. *Union List of Canadian Newspapers*. Ottawa: National Library of
Canada, 1988. Microfiche. ISSN 0840-5832.

This microfiche collection issued by the National Library of Canada
provides the most complete listing to date of Canadian newspapers.
The goals of this publication are to serve as the definitive tool for
locating Canadian newspapers, to provide sufficient publication
information for reference purposes, and to aid the interlibrary lending of newspaper resources. The union list consists of a sequentially
numbered register and two indexes: a name/title index and a
geographical index that lists the entries alphabetically by province
and by city within the province. Newspaper holdings for more than
700 Canadian libraries are included.

Great Britain

249. *Bibliography of British Newspapers*. London: British Library,
1975–. Vol. 1: *Wiltshire*, edited by R. K. Bluhm, 1975; Vol. 2: *Kent*,
edited by Winifred Bergess, Barbara Riddell, and John Whyman,
1982; Vol. 3: *Durham and Northumberland*, edited by F. W. D.
Manders, 1982; Vol. 4: *Nottinghamshire*, edited by Michael Brook,
1987; and Vol. 5: *Derbyshire*, edited by Anne Mellors and Jean
Radford, 1987.

These are the first volumes of an ongoing project to provide a
comprehensive listing of British newspapers, national and local. It
includes those no longer published along with details of the location
of files in Great Britain and elsewhere. Published histories of
newspapers or bibliographic descriptions are also noted. Initiated
by the Library Association, the project has now been taken over by
the British Library. The bibliography is being published in parts
covering each county. Although it is planned to be completed in 20
years, it may take longer.

Australia

250. *Newspapers in Australian Libraries: A Union List.* 4th ed. Canberra: National Library of Australia, 1985. ISBN 0-642-99300-9. 2 vols.

This is the fourth edition of a union list that was first published in 1959. It is divided into two sections. Section 1 describes overseas newspapers held by Australian libraries; Section 2 describes Australian newspapers and their Australian holders. The arrangement is alphabetical, first by country and then by city or town.

Guides to Major Newspaper Collections (arranged in order of significance)

United States

Library of Congress
Serial and Government Publications Division
Washington, DC 20540

The Library of Congress owns the largest collection of newspapers in the world. In addition to its collection of U.S. newspapers, it has extensive foreign holdings from every part of the globe. An early 1980s estimate of its holdings noted 850,000 unbound issues, 75,000 bound volumes, 270,000 microfilm reels, and 12,000 microprint cards. The Library of Congress publishes various guides to its collections, and its holdings are listed in the *United States Newspaper Project* [*see* 247] and in *Newspapers in Microform* [*see* 245].

251. *African Newspapers in the Library of Congress.* 2d ed. Compiled by John Pluge, Jr. Washington, DC: Library of Congress, 1984. 144p. ISBN 0-8444-0457-8.

The Library of Congress has extensive holdings in African newspapers both in paper and microform. This second edition lists 931 titles, 322 of which have been added since the 1977 edition. The guide is arranged in alphabetical order by country and then within the individual country by city. Information provided includes title, date established, frequency, language, and holdings. There is also a title index.

252. *Arab-World Newspapers in the Library of Congress.* Compiled by George Dimitri Selim. Washington, DC: Library of Congress, 1980. 85p. ISSN 0196-3562.

This is a detailed listing of newspapers held by the Library of Congress that are published in the Arab countries in either Arabic or Latin scripts and those published outside of the Arab region in Arabic script. The list is arranged alphabetically, first by language and then by country, city, and title. Arabic titles are transliterated. All newspapers listed are on microfilm except those marked with asterisks.

253. *Chinese Newspapers in the Library of Congress: A Bibliography.* Compiled by Han-chu Huan and Hseo-chin Jen. Washington, DC: Library of Congress, 1985. 205p. ISBN 0-8444-0481-0.

The collection of Chinese-language newspapers in the Library of Congress is possibly the largest outside of China. Some 1,200 titles are listed in this bibliography, ranging from the 1870s to the present. The entries are arranged in alphabetical order, with the titles romanized according to the modified Wade-Giles system. Two indexes list newspapers by location and by strokes of the first character of each title.

254. *Newspapers Received Currently in the Library of Congress.* Compiled by the Serial and Government Publications Division. Washington, DC: Library of Congress, 1972–. Biannual. ISSN 0093-6464.

The revised and updated eleventh edition was published in 1988 and lists 363 U.S. and 1,115 foreign newspapers that are received and retained on a permanent basis, along with the 124 U.S. and 46 foreign newspapers that are retained only on a current basis. The guide is divided into U.S. and foreign sections, each with its own title index. Within these sections the arrangement is alphabetical by state and then city in the U.S. section and by country and city in the foreign section.

State Historical Society of Wisconsin Library
Newspaper and Periodicals Section
816 State St.
Madison, WI 53706

The State Historical Society of Wisconsin owns the second-largest collection of general newspapers in the United States. In addition to extensive U.S. newspaper holdings from every state, the society owns one of the largest collections of Canadian newspapers outside of Canada. Besides holdings listed in the *United States Newspaper Project* [*see* 247] and *Newspapers in Microform* [*see* 245], it publishes periodic guides to its collections.

255. *Native American Periodicals and Newspapers, 1828–1982. Bibliography, Publishing Record, and Holdings.* Edited by James P. Danky and compiled by Maureen E. Hady. Westport, CT: Greenwood Press, 1984. 532p. Indexes. ISBN 0-313-23773-5.

This guide provides lists of almost 1,200 native American periodicals in 146 North American libraries. Titles include literary, political, cultural, and historical journals as well as general newspapers and feature magazines published in cities and on reservations. Entries are arranged alphabetically by title, with additional access by geographic, editor, publisher, subject, subtitle, and chronological index. Microfilm availability and holdings of U.S. and Canadian libraries are indicated.

256. *Women's Periodicals and Newspapers from the 18th Century to 1981. A Union List of the Holdings of Madison, Wisconsin, Libraries.* Edited by James P. Danky et al. Boston: G. K. Hall, 1982. 390p. Index. ISBN 0-8161-8107-1.

This index provides access to one of the largest collections of women's periodicals in North America: almost 1,500 literary, political, and historical journals, and general newspapers and feature magazines. Entries are arranged alphabetically by title, with additional access by geographic, editor, publisher, subject, subtitle, and chronological indexes. Microfilm availability and holdings outside of the Madison libraries are indicated.

Center for Research Libraries
6050 South Kenwood Ave.
Chicago, IL 60637

From its founding in 1949 as the Midwest Inter-Library Center, the CRL has grown to include more than 100 participating libraries and research institutes in North America. Its newspaper holdings number more than 3,000 titles, with particular strengths in black newspapers, Civilian Conservation Corps newspapers, ethnic newspapers, special-interest newspapers, and underground-press titles. The center owns fairly long runs of more than 100 U.S. titles and 150 foreign ones. Recent acquisitions are noted in the bimonthly newsletter *Focus.* Most holdings are cataloged and have been reported to the *United States Newspaper Project* [*see* 247].

257. *CRL Microfiche Catalog*. Chicago, IL: CRL, 1982 and *1989 Microfiche Catalog Supplement*. Chicago, IL: CRL, 1989. 133 fiche.

The basic guide to the CRL's holdings is the 1982 *CRL Microfiche Catalog*, referred to as the "Book Catalog," and its cumulative supplements. The 1989 supplement contains 142,389 bibliographic records arranged by title. Most of the newspapers in the collection are also listed. Another helpful source for information in this library is its *Center for Research Libraries Handbook*, which is published irregularly. The 1987 edition contains a special section devoted to newspaper holdings.

Canada

National Library of Canada
Reference and Information Services Division
395 Wellington St.
Ottawa, Ontario, Canada K1A 0N4

The National Library of Canada was created in 1953 to relieve the Library of Parliament of the responsibility of serving as Canada's national library. Since that time the National Library has grown to be the largest library in Canada, with collections exceeding 8 million volumes. It owns the largest collection of Canadian newspapers in the world. Current holdings include 80,000 reels of microfilm and 300 current subscriptions to Canadian papers, along with nearly 100 subscriptions to ethnic papers published in Canada. Virtually all of the National Library's holdings have been reported in the latest *Union List of Canadian Newspapers* [*see* 248].

Great Britain

British Library
Humanities and Social Sciences Division
Great Russell St.
London WC1B, United Kingdom

The British Library was founded in 1973 under the British Library Act. It combines the former library departments of the British Museum, the National Central Library, the British National Bibliography Ltd., and the National Lending Library for Science and Technology. The Public Services Division of the Humanities and Social Sciences Section administers the *British Library Newspaper Library* (address: Colindale Ave., London NW9 5HE). The *Newspaper*

Library's collections consist of half a million bound volumes and 160,000 reels of microfilm of daily and weekly newspapers. These include English, Irish, Scottish, and Welsh provincial newspapers from 1690; London dailies and weeklies from 1601; Commonwealth titles from former colonial territories; 4,000 volumes of nineteenth-century South Asian newspapers transferred from the India Office Library in 1986; and a representative collection from the rest of the world. The Burney Collection of London Newspapers 1603–1800, the Thomason Collection of Civil War Newspapers, and the newspapers printed in Oriental scripts are held at the main library on Great Russell Street. A good introduction to the value of these collections for historical research is provided by John Westmancoat, *Newspapers* (British Library Reference Division, 1985). Alan Day's *The British Library: A Guide to Its Structure, Publications, Collections and Services* (London: Library Association, 1988) is also informative.

258. *Catalog of the Newspaper Library, Colindale.* London: British Museum Publications, for the British Library Board, 1975. 8 vols. ISBN 0-714-10352-7.

The Newspaper Library at Colindale in north London opened in 1932 as part of the British Museum. In 1973 it became part of the British Library. With collections of bound newspapers now exceeding 20 miles in length and stacked from floor to ceiling, it includes thousands of reels of microfilm and is one of the two largest collections of newspapers in the world. The "ready access" collections at Colindale focus on the period since the 1830s. This 8-volume guide describes the holdings at Colindale through 1971. Volumes 1–4 are arranged by geographical location, while volumes 5–8 list newspapers by title. Recent news from Colindale is announced in the *British Library Newspaper Library Newsletter* (No. 1–. 1980–).

259. *Keyword Index to Serials Titles.* British Library Document Supply Centre, Boston Spa, Wetherby, West Yorkshire, United Kingdom LS23 7BQ. Annual on microfiche.

The Document Supply Centre is the largest library in the world devoted to the supply of documents by loan, photocopy, and microform and is the national center for interlibrary lending within the United Kingdom and overseas. The *Keyword Index to Serials Titles* is published annually in January, and replacement sets are issued every quarter. The October 1988 issue lists some 345,000 serials, including selected newspapers, from the various divisions of the British Library and from Cambridge University Library. North

American scholars can use these holdings through their interlibrary loan departments.

Others

260. *Subject Collections: A Guide to Special Book Collections and Subject Emphases as Reported by University, College, Public, and Special Libraries and Museums in the United States and Canada.* 6th ed. Compiled by Lee Ash and William G. Miller. New York: R. R. Bowker, 1985. 2 vols. Index. ISBN 0-8352-1917-8.

Most of the important North American newspaper collections are listed here under the heading "Newspapers." Inverted subject headings like "Newspapers, Armenian" guide the researcher to important collections on specialized topics.

Guides to Indexed Newspapers

261. *Checklist of Indexes to Canadian Newspapers.* By Sandra Burrows and Franceen Gaudet. Ottawa: National Library of Canada, 1987. 148p. Index. ISBN 0-660-53735-4.

This first comprehensive list of indexes to Canadian newspapers is based on a survey of 4,000 institutions across Canada including libraries, newspaper offices, archives, and genealogical and historical societies. The indexes come in a variety of formats, from index cards to clippings files and obituary lists. Some 300 institutions were indexing newspapers in 1986. Data is in French and English and is organized alphabetically by province and city or town. Masthead title and geographic indexes provide additional access.

262. *Lathrop Report on Newspaper Indexes: An Illustrated Guide to Published and Unpublished Newspaper Indexes in the United States and Canada.* By Norman Lathrop and Mary Lou Lathrop. Wooster, OH: Norman Lathrop Enterprises, 1979. Looseleaf. Indexes. ISBN 0-910868-10-7.

Although intended as a continuation, only one volume of this guide was ever published. It describes some 500 newspaper indexes (excluding clippings files). There are alphabetical and geographical indexes that list compilers of indexes, a chronological index that lists the names of newspapers by first date of publication or earliest date of indexing, and a brief subject index. It is unfortunate that this project was not carried forward.

263. *Newspaper Indexes: A Location and Subject Guide for Researchers.* By Anita Cheek Milner. Metuchen, NJ: Scarecrow Press, 1977–1983. 3 vols. Indexes. ISBN 0-8108-1493-5.

What began as a thesis project for Milner culminated in the most detailed guide to indexed newspapers and clippings files for U.S. newspapers. Its greatest strength is in identifying local newspaper indexes maintained by a wide variety of public, college, and society libraries. Arrangement is generally alphabetical by state and then by county. There are also small sections on indexes to U.S. foreign-language newspapers, church publications, and some foreign newspapers. Indexed papers are coded to Library of Congress symbols. All repositories are listed in the second section of each volume with addresses and descriptions of services available. While it is somewhat dated, in the absence of a more sophisticated guide, this work remains the most comprehensive guide to indexed U.S. newspapers.

Newspaper Indexes: Individual Papers

United States (prior to 1900)

264. *Arkansas Gazette Index: An Arkansas Index.* Russellville, AR: Arkansas Tech University Library, 1970s–.

One of the more innovative local indexing projects is the ongoing *Arkansas Gazette Index.* This newspaper was founded in 1819 at Post of Arkansas. Two years later it moved to Little Rock, where it remains today as part of the Gannett chain. Two new volumes are currently appearing each year, one in the retrospective series and one in the current. The index is a selective subject index to Arkansas news and personalities appearing in the newspaper. So far 20 volumes have been published in the retrospective series covering the period of 1819 to 1893, and 24 volumes have been produced in the current series covering from 1964 to the present.

265. *New York Daily Tribune Index, 1875–1906.* New York: The Tribune Association. 1876–1907. 32 volumes. Reprinted as the *New York Tribune Index* on three reels of microfilm by UMI.

The *New York Tribune* was founded in 1841 by Horace Greeley and came to be one of the most important of the nineteenth-century New York dailies. It later merged with the *New York Herald* to become the *Herald-Tribune* in 1924, which ceased publication in 1966. A brief annual subject index was issued for the years 1875 to 1906. Because of the scarceness of this index, it was reprinted by UMI on microfilm.

266. *New York Times Index.* New York: New York Times Company, 1913–. Semimonthly, with quarterly and annual cumulations. ISSN 0147-538X.

The United States' most important newspaper index was launched in 1913 with monthly issues and with quarterly but no annual cumulations. In 1930 annual cumulations were added, and in 1948 it assumed its current format, semimonthly with quarterly and annual cumulations. A detailed subject index giving exact references to dates, pages, and columns, with numerous cross-references, it offers the most detailed indexing of any newspaper in the world and is frequently consulted for ready reference. The index is a guide to the Late City Edition, not the National Edition sold in many parts of the country. Articles are coded for length.

267. *New York Times Index. Prior Series. Sept. 1851–1912.* New York: R. R. Bowker, 1966–1976. 15 vols.

In 1976 Bowker completed a 15-volume set of retrospective indexes to the *New York Times* resulting in a complete run of indexing for the *Times* from its inception in September 1851. The first volume, covering the years 1851 to 1858, is a facsimile reprint of the original handwritten volume. The rest of the volumes were based on in-house files except for the years 1905 to 1912, which represent new indexing.

268. *New York Times Obituaries Indexes.* Vol. 1: 1858–1968. Vol. 2: 1969–1978. New York: New York Times, 1970 and 1980. 1,136p. and 131p. ISBN 0-88736-381-4.

These two volumes of obituaries are particularly helpful for historians. The first contains more than 350,000 entries, and the second added 40,000 more. The second also reprints in full 50 obituaries of prominent individuals for those years.

269. *Personal Name Index to the New York Times Index. 1851–1974.* Compiled by Byron A. Falk and Valerie R. Falk. Succasunna, NJ: Roxbury Data Interface, 1976–1983. 22 vols. 1975–1984 Supplement.

Verdi, Nevada: Roxbury Data Interface, 1986–1988. 4 vols. ISBN 0-89902-084-4.

This impressive set does much to unlock the riches of the *New York Times* by providing an alphabetical listing of more than 3 million names appearing in the *New York Times Index*. Listings provide complete names and years, but the page references are to the *New York Times Index*, not the newspaper itself. Since the prior series of the *New York Times Index* [*see* 267] was not complete for the years 1905–1912 when this project began, there are few references to those years. The 1975–1984 supplement continues the indexing through 1984 and includes the names missed from the prior series.

270. *Sun (Baltimore) and Evening Sun Index, 1891–1951.* Ann Arbor, MI: UMI, n.d. 209 reels of microfilm.

UMI is now distributing a retrospective index to the Baltimore *Sun* and *Evening Sun* that was originally produced by Bell & Howell. The *Sun* was founded in 1837 and the *Evening Sun* in 1910. This retrospective subject index to one of the most important American dailies provides researchers with additional access to information on the first half of the twentieth century. It is based on typed index cards maintained by the newspapers and by the Enoch Pratt Free Library of Baltimore.

271. *Virginia Gazette Index, 1736–1780.* By Lester J. Cappon and Stella F. Duff. Williamsburg, VA: Institute of Early American History and Culture, 1950. 2 vols. 0-910776-00-8.

The *Virginia Gazette* was actually the name of five colonial weeklies published in Williamsburg between 1736 and 1780. The last of these moved to Richmond in April 1780. The index is arranged alphabetically with some subject headings. The first *Gazette* was the second newspaper to be published in the South.

272. *Washington Star-News Index, 1852–1973.* Ann Arbor, MI: UMI, n.d.

The *Washington Star* was founded in 1852 as an evening daily and included the *Sunday Star*. In 1972 it merged with the *Washington Daily News*. A valuable source for its coverage of congressional news, it ceased publication in early 1981. From 1852 to 1906 the indexing is uneven: some years have no index, notably the period of the Civil War. Beginning in 1906, there is a comprehensive index to 1973.

United States (since 1900)

No new indexes of newspapers were begun in the first half of the twentieth century. Then in 1959 Dow Jones began producing the *Wall Street Journal Index*, starting with the year 1958. It was issued monthly, with an annual cumulation. Later, UMI provided retrospective coverage to 1955. In 1960 the *Christian Science Monitor* began issuing a monthly index to the *Monitor*, with semi-annual and annual cumulations. This index was taken over by UMI, and retrospective coverage was provided to 1945. In 1972 the Bell & Howell Company of Wooster, Ohio, launched the first of its newspaper indexes. Beginning with four newspapers—the *Chicago Tribune*, the *Los Angeles Times*, the *New Orleans Times-Picayune*, and the *Washington Post*—the company now dominates newspaper indexing through its subsidiaries UMI and Data Courier. The indexes themselves are produced by Data Courier in Louisville, Kentucky. Generally they are published in eight softbound monthly installments, with four quarterly cumulations and a hardbound annual. The quality of the indexing has improved dramatically in recent years. All indexes are strictly subject based. In earlier issues personalities and subjects appeared in separate sections. The following indexes were being produced in 1989:

273. *Atlanta Constitution and Journal Index*, 1982–. There was an *Atlanta Constitution Index: A Georgia Index* published from 1971 to 1979 by Georgia State University, but it was limited to state coverage.

274. *Boston Globe Index*, 1983–.

275. *Chicago Tribune Index*, 1972–.

276. *Christian Science Monitor Index*, 1945–.

277. *Denver Post Index*, 1976–.

278. *Detroit News Index*, 1976–.

279. *Houston Post Index*, 1976–.

280. *Los Angeles Times Index*, 1972–.

281. *Nashville Banner and Tennessean Index on Microfiche*, 1980–. This is produced on a quarterly basis by the Nashville Public Library but distributed by UMI.

282. *St. Louis Post-Dispatch Index*, 1975–.

283. *San Francisco Chronicle Index*, 1976–. [See 288]

284. *Times-Picayune (New Orleans) Index*, 1972–.

285. *USA Today Index*, 1982–.

286. *Washington Post Index*, 1971–. While this was one of the original Bell & Howell indexes produced from 1971 to 1981, a second index, called the *Official Index to the Washington Post*, was published by Research Publications from 1979 to 1988. UMI reacquired the indexing rights in 1989.

287. *Washington Times Index*, 1986–.

288. *San Francisco Newspapers Index. San Francisco Chronicle Index*. Bellevue, WA: Commercial Microfilming Service, 1986.

Compiled from files maintained by the California State Library, the *San Francisco Newspapers Index* covers the period 1904–1949. It indexes the *San Francisco Call* (1904–1913), the *San Francisco Examiner* (1913–1928), and the *San Francisco Chronicle* (1913–1949). The *San Francisco Newspaper Index* is continued by the *San Francisco Chronicle Index*, which covers the period 1950–1980 [for coverage after 1980 *see* 283]. The *San Francisco Newspaper Index* consists of 699 microfiches containing 1.8 million citations on approximately 922,000 cards. The *Chronicle Index* adds 277 microfiches with 720,000 citations from 363,000 cards. Subject headings are listed on the first four fiches, although they are not always used in the index. Citations include the month, day, year, page, and column for each entry.

289. *Wall Street Journal Index*. New York: Dow Jones, 1955–. Monthly, with annual cumulations. ISSN 0083-7075.

The *Wall Street Journal Index* is produced by Dow Jones and distributed by UMI. Since 1981 the annual cumulation has also provided indexing to *Barron's*. Unlike UMI-produced indexes, this index is divided into two sections: Corporate News (indexed by company name) and General News. Recent annuals have also included an almanac of the closing Dow Jones averages on Wall Street.

Canada

No commercial indexes to individual newspapers are currently being produced [*see* 301].

Great Britain

Indexes to *The Times* (London)

290. *Obituaries From the Times.* I: 1951–1960. II: 1961–1970. III: 1971–1975. Westport, CT and Reading, England: Newspaper Archive Developments (now Research Publications), 1975–1979.

This publication reprints approximately 4,000 obituaries that appeared in *The Times* and provides an index to all other obituaries and tributes that appeared during those years.

291. *Palmer's Index to the Times Newspaper.* (1790–June 1941). London: Palmer, 1868–1943. Reprint. New York: Kraus, 1965. Issued quarterly.

The first successful regular index to *The Times* was initiated by London bookseller Samuel Palmer in 1868. In 1891 he began retrospective indexing and eventually extended his index back to 1790. Neither he nor his successors were able to interest the newspaper in providing financial support for the index, and it ceased publication in 1941. Using *Palmer's Index* can be a difficult task for the beginner, as it indexes items under the first word of a heading rather than by subject. A useful guide to this style of indexing is Doreen Morrison's "Indexes to *The Times of London*," *The Serials Librarian*, Vol. 13 (September 1987): 89–104. *Palmer's Index* also indexed *The Times Literary Supplement* from 1907 to 1941 and *The Times Educational Supplement* from 1910 to 1941.

292. *The Times Index.* (1785–1790 and 1906–). Woodbridge, CT and Reading, England: Research Publications, 1906–. Monthly, with annual cumulations.

In competition with *Palmer's Index* [see 291], *The Times* decided to publish its own index in 1906, calling it the *Official Index to The Times.* Initially it appeared monthly, with an annual cumulation. In 1914 it shifted to quarterly publication. The title changed to the *Index to The Times* in 1957, and it also began bimonthly publication. It was renamed *The Times Index* in 1972 and switched back to quarterly volumes. At this time coverage of the *Sunday Times* (a separate paper), *The Times Literary Supplement, The Times Educational Supplement*, and *The Times Higher Educational Supplement* were added to the index. Yet another shift occurred in 1977 when the index returned to a monthly format, with an annual cumulation. Retrospective indexing for the period 1785–1790, which was not covered by *Palmer's Index*, was completed in 1978. Since 1982 Research Publications has published the index and improved its quality and consistency. Easy to work with, *The Times Index* uses a standard list of subject headings, which are frequently updated. Despite recent changes in ownership of both the paper and the index, it remains the index of record for the United Kingdom.

293. *The Times Literary Supplement Indexes*. I: 1902–1939. II: 1940–1980. III: 1981–1985. Woodbridge, CT: and Reading, England: Research Publications, 1980–. 6 vols. ISBN 0-907514-74X.

Since the original *Times Index* did not include indexing to *The Times Literary Supplement*, retrospective cumulative indexes have been published that serve as a guide to more than a million items that have appeared in this weekly publication. The indexes provide quick access to authors, books, subjects, translators, illustrators, poems, or periodicals discussed.

Other British Newspapers

294. *Guardian Index*. Ann Arbor, MI: UMI, 1986–. Monthly, with annual cumulations.

The Manchester Guardian was founded in 1819 by a group of Manchester Liberals. It has been published continuously since then. In 1919 the *Guardian Weekly* was introduced. *The Guardian* maintains an extensive staff of foreign correspondents and is noted for its objective coverage of the news. This new index covers both the daily and weekly editions and uses the standard UMI style.

Other Countries

295. *Le Monde Index*. Woodbridge, CT and Reading, England: Research Publications, 1987–. Monthly, with annual cumulations. (Indexes are available for 1944–1951, 1965–1968, and 1987–).

The influential Paris daily *Le Monde* was established in 1944, becoming the first independent postwar newspaper in France. Viewed as one of Europe's most intellectual papers, it publishes no photographs. The early volumes of the index were published by the paper beginning in 1965; retrospective indexing started with 1944. This index was subject based and gives a reference to the date of the issue only. Research Publications revived the indexing beginning with the year 1987 and plans to publish the current index and one retrospective volume each year until the retrospective coverage is complete. The new index follows the standard Research Publications format.

296. *El Pais Index.* Woodbridge, CT and Reading, England: Research Publications, 1988–. Annual, with coverage beginning in 1984.

Since its founding in 1976, six months after the death of the dictator Francisco Franco, the Madrid daily *El Pais* has gained a reputation as Spain's most important national newspaper. Its Sunday supplement provides excellent features on politics, culture, literature, and economics. A weekly international airmail edition is also published.

Newspaper Indexes: Collective

United States

297. *Black Newspaper Index.* Ann Arbor, MI: UMI, 1977–. Quarterly.

This subject-based index covers nine black newspapers in the United States: *Afro-American—Capitol Edition* (Washington, DC), *Amsterdam News* (New York), *Call and Post* (Cleveland), *Chicago Defender, Los Angeles Sentinel, Michigan Chronicle* (Detroit), *Muslim Journal* (Chicago), and the *Journal and Guide* (Norfolk, VA).

298. *National Newspaper Index.* Foster City, CA: Information Access Company, 1979–. Monthly, with updated cumulations. Microfilm for ROM Readers, 1979–; Compact Disc, 1988–.

The *National Newspaper Index* began in 1979 as a companion to the *Magazine Index.* Extremely innovative for its times, it was issued on microfilm suitable for loading on ROM (record output microform) readers. Initially it indexed the *Christian Science Monitor,* the *New York Times* (both the Late City and National editions), and the *Wall Street Journal* (both the Eastern and Western editions). Indexing for the *Los Angeles Times* and the *Washington Post* was added in 1982. The continuously cumulating index provided four years of indexing at the push of a button. After four years of cumulation, the first year was removed to microfiche. In July of 1988 the company IAC began issuing the index on compact disc on its InfoTrac system. This version covers the previous four years and is updated monthly. IAC uses modified Library of Congress subject headings. An on-line version is available on DIALOG File 111 and on BRS File NOOZ. The on-line version is updated within 24 hours of publication. The most current information first appears on DIALOG File 211 before being transferred to File 111.

299. *NewsBank Electronic Index.* New Canaan, CT: NewsBank, 1986–. Monthly, on compact disc.

This selective index covers more than 450 newspapers in the United States. Earlier print versions with accompanying texts on microfiche sets date back to 1970. Present coverage dates from 1982. Indexing is by broad subject headings and keyed to the accompanying microfiche collections, which are arranged in 14 broad subject categories.

300. *Newspaper Abstracts Ondisc.* Ann Arbor, MI: UMI, 1989–. Bimonthly cumulative updates on compact disc.

The most sophisticated of the new compact-disc newspaper indexes, this publication provides, at this time, indexing and brief abstracting of the following U.S. dailies: *Atlanta Constitution,* 1985–; *Boston Globe,* 1985–; *Chicago Tribune,* 1985–; *Christian Science Monitor,* 1985–; *Los Angeles Times,* 1985–; *New York Times,* 1987–; *Wall Street Journal,* 1985–; and the *Washington Post,* 1989–. A variety of search strategies is available, including Boolean searching, proximity operators, and truncation.

Canada

301. *Canadian News Index.* Toronto: Micromedia, 1977–. Monthly, with annual cumulations. ISSN 0225-7459.

The successor to the *Canadian Newspaper Index,* it currently provides selective indexing of the *Calgary Herald,* the *Halifax Chronicle Herald,* the *Toronto Globe and Mail,* the *Toronto Star,* the *Montreal Gazette, the Vancouver Sun,* and the *Winnipeg Free Press.* The index is divided into two sections: subject and personal name. Annotations are coded to indicate feature articles (F), regular columns (C), editorials (Ed), and noteworthy articles (N). All the indexed newspapers are held by the National Library of Canada and are available for interlibrary loan and photocopying.

Newspaper Indexes On-Line

302. *Courier Plus.* DIALOG Info. Services. File 484.

This is the newest entry in the newspaper on-line business. It replaces an earlier version, *Newspapers Abstracts Online* (1984–1988) on File 603. Newspaper indexing is provided for 25 major U.S. dailies from 1989 and for 300 magazines from 1988. Abstracts average about 25 words.

303. *Nexis.* Mead Data Central.

Nexis is one of the world's largest suppliers of full-text news and information sources. Coverage includes news, trade, and professional publications; news, publicity, business, and financial wire services; specialized newsletters; and hundreds of business, financial, and trade publications. Other components include a country information service, a health-care information service, an accounting information service, and the world's leading legal-research service. For many years Mead offered the New York Times *Information Bank* abstracts and index file as a separate service on file ABS. In 1989 the ABS file was merged into other Nexis files and renamed INFOBK. Coverage of the following newspapers is currently included: *Boston Globe* (Sept. 1988–), *Chicago Tribune* (Nov. 1988–), *Courier Journal* (Louisville) (Feb. 1988–), *Christian Science Monitor* (Jan. 1980–), *Los Angeles Times* (Jan. 1985–), *Newsday* (May 1988–), *New York Times* (June 1980–), *Washington Post* (Jan. 1977–), and abstracts from the *Wall Street Journal* (May 1973). Foreign-newspaper coverage includes the *Financial Times* (Jan. 1982), *Manchester Guardian Weekly* (Jan. 1981–), and the *Daily/Sunday Telegraph* (London) (Sept. 1988–). Wire service coverage includes the Associated Press, Asahi News Service, Reuters, Tass, and United Press International.

304. *National Newspaper Index.* DIALOG Info. Services. File 111. BRS Info. Technologies, File NOOZ. [*See* 298.]

Full-Text Newspapers On-Line and Newspaper Data Banks

United States

305. *Data Times.* Oklahoma City, OK.

Data Times, a division of DATATEK Corporation, offers a worldwide network of full-text newspaper and newswire information that spans 140 cities on four continents. Full-text coverage is available for the major U.S. and British newspapers as well as some of the lesser-known papers. Coverage varies, but for most papers it begins around 1985. *Data Times* users can also access Canadian newspapers from Infomart [*see* 308].

306. *VU/TEXT.* Philadelphia, PA.

VU/TEXT is owned by the Knight-Ridder newspaper chain, which also recently purchased DIALOG Info. Services. It is the largest U.S. data bank, offering full-text access to 41 U.S. dailies including most Knight-Ridder papers. Among the major papers covered are the *Arizona Republic, Boston Globe, Chicago Tribune, Detroit Free Press, Los Angeles Times, Philadelphia Daily News, Richmond News Leader, St. Louis Post-Dispatch, Seattle Post-Intelligencer,* and the *Washington Post. VU/TEXT* plans to add more papers. One of the interesting search strategies provided by *VU/TEXT* is the ability to do regional searches (all papers in the Northeast, the Southeast, the Central United States, or the West) or to search by the seven top circulation papers.

Canada

307. *Info Globe.* Toronto, Ontario.

This service provides full-text coverage of the *Toronto Globe and Mail* with back files to 1977. The full text is available on-line by 6 A.M. of the same day. It also provides coverage of *Canada Newswire,* a wire service data base carrying the full text of press releases, which is updated twice daily. *Info Globe* subscribers in Canada can also access the U.S. Dow Jones News/Retrieval service.

308. *Infomart Online.* Ottawa, Ontario.

Owned by Southam Newspapers, a major Canadian chain, Infomart provides full-text access to the *Ottawa Citizen, Financial Times of Canada, Montreal Gazette, Toronto Star, Windsor Star, Vancouver Sun,* and *Les Affaires.* The *Calgary Herald* and the *Edmonton Journal* will be added. Subscribers can also access the Canadian Press Wire Service and Canada News-Wire. Canadians can obtain full texts of U.S. dailies offered by *Data Times* [*see* 305] through *Infomart.*

Great Britain

309. *World Reporter.* Datasolve Ltd. London, United Kingdom.

World Reporter was launched in 1982 by Datasolve Ltd. in association with the British Broadcasting Corporation. In addition to summarizing the BBC World Broadcasts and External Services News, it provides full-text coverage of the following newspapers: *Financial Times* (1985–), *Washington Post* (1984–), *The Guardian* (1984–), and *Today* (1986–). Access is also available to the Associated Press Newswire (1983–) and the *Tass News Agency* (1986–). British researchers can also use the services of Nexis [*see* 303] through its London office.

Newspaper Research Collections on Microfilm

310. *Civil War Newspapers*. Ann Arbor, MI: UMI, n.d.

For students of the U.S. Civil War, this collection includes selective coverage of the war from 312 newspapers representing 29 states. It includes *Frank Leslie's Illustrated News*.

311. *Early American Newspapers*. New Canaan, CT: Readex, 1962–.

In 1962 Readex Microprint Corporation began publishing on microprint (six-by-nine-inch opaque cards) the more than 2,000 U.S. newspapers published prior to 1821, including all titles listed in Brigham's *History and Bibliography of American Newspapers* [*see* 244]. The project was completed in the late 1970s, and the collection became widely available in U.S. research libraries. In 1979 Readex decided to make the collection available on 35-mm reel microfilm, a project that is still ongoing. Some 250 titles have been filmed, and Readex is preparing a new guide to the collection. The disadvantage of the old microprint edition was that it required special readers and could not be photocopied. This publication is the most valuable collection of U.S. newspapers on microform. Another microfilm collection of newspapers from the eighteenth, nineteenth, and early twentieth century, consisting of 1,845 reels, is also titled *Early American Newspapers* (Ann Arbor, MI: UMI, n.d.).

312. *Early English Newspapers*. Woodbridge, CT and Reading, England: Research Publications (in progress).

The purpose of this project is to film the two largest collections of seventeenth- and eighteenth-century English newspapers: the Charles Burney Collection at the British Library and the John Nichols Collection at the Bodleian Library of Oxford. Some 640 titles on 2,114 reels had been filmed by 1989. A cumulative guide to the first 24 units of the collection is available from the publisher.

313. *Eighteenth Century English Provincial Newspapers.* Woodbridge, CT and Reading, England: Research Publications, 1985–.

This project was initiated by Harvester Press (since acquired by Research Publications) in association with the British Library. Plans call for publication of about 50 provincial papers. Three series have been completed so far: Bath, Derby, and Ipswich. The fourth and fifth series will cover Newcastle and Gloucester when they are completed. The *Bibliography of British Newspapers* [see 249] provides bibliographic information about these papers.

314. *Newspapers from the Depression Years, 1929–1938.* Ann Arbor, MI: UMI, n.d. 868 reels.

Beginning with the October 1929 stock market crash, this collection follows the course of the Depression through eight newspapers. The newspapers filmed are the *Wall Street Journal, Baltimore Morning Sun, San Francisco Chronicle, New Orleans Times-Picayune, Kansas City Star, Kansas City Times, Charleston News and Courier,* and *Tulsa World.*

315. *Newspapers from the Russian Revolutionary Era.* Woodbridge, CT and Reading, England: Research Publications, 1984–.

Ultimately this project will make available on microfilm the rich Russian Revolutionary Newspaper Collection at Columbia University's Herbert Lehman Library. As of 1989 some 400 reels were available. Research Publications has published a guide to the collection and plans to add further titles from the collections of the British Library. The 100 titles included in this collection cover the years 1873 to 1927.

316. *South Carolina Newspapers, 1732–1782.* Wooster, OH: Bell & Howell, 1956.

One of the earliest newspaper microfilming projects, this cumulation is enhanced by the Charleston newspaper collection of the Charleston Historical Society. Filmed newspapers include the *South Carolina Gazette, Charleston Gazette, South Carolina and American General Gazette,* and *Royal Gazette.*

317. *Underground and Alternative Press in Britain since 1961.* Woodbridge, CT and Reading, England: Research Publications, 1974–.

Another Harvester Press project acquired by Research Publications, this core collection includes varying runs of 83 papers. Since 1973 annual supplements on microfilm have been published. Through 1987 the collection had grown to include 794 microfiche and 29 reels of film. The publisher has provided an excellent guide and printed index with an alphabetical list of the papers.

318. *Underground Newspapers Microfilm Collection, 1965–1987.* Ann Arbor, MI: UMI, 1965–.

Initiated by Bell & Howell's Micro Photo division in 1965, the initial core collection was published in 1969 and consisted of 477 titles. Its scope was international and included papers from Cuba, Uruguay, Venezuela, Chile, Argentina, England (7), Belgium, Germany, Denmark, France, the Netherlands, Switzerland, Canada (6), and the United States (427). The core collection is arranged chronologically and then alphabetically by title. U.S. titles include the *Berkeley Barb,* the *Haight Ashbury Tribune* (San Francisco), *High Times* (New York), and the *New Paper* (Providence). Several supplements have been produced that add a further 73 titles and expand the coverage for the core titles still being published into the 1980s. Despite the breadth of the collection, some reviewers have complained that it was not well organized, making it difficult to use.

7.
Dissertations and Theses

Prior to 1940, bibliographical access to U.S. dissertations was largely confined to searching specialized lists published by the major doctoral-granting institutions on an irregular basis. These were generally confined to listing authors and titles. Access has improved dramatically since then, largely through the pioneering efforts of one company, University Microfilms International. It has been abstracting dissertations since 1938 and making them available for purchase as a microfilm or a paper copy. From a few institutions, this endeavor has grown to include virtually every major university in the United States and Canada, along with many others in Great Britain and Western Europe, and is available on-line and on compact disc. Retrospective listings of earlier dissertations are available through several comprehensive cumulations published since 1973. Several other recent comprehensive guides for U.S. and British dissertations were published in the 1970s.

Guides and Repositories

319. The Center for Research Libraries (CRL). 6050 South Kenwood Ave., Chicago, IL, 60637. Tel: (312) 955-4545.

This not-for-profit library was established in 1949 by ten midwestern universities in the U.S. and now has more than 100 members. It maintains the largest collection of foreign dissertations in the world. Through various exchange or deposit arrangements with major Western European universities, CRL endeavors to provide access to virtually all dissertations produced outside the U.S. and Canada. In addition to a basically complete collection of French dissertations since 1952, CRL receives dissertations from 90 universities in Denmark, Finland, West Germany, the Netherlands,

Norway, Sweden, and Switzerland. It can also obtain abstracts of doctoral dissertations from the Soviet Union. For more information on CRL's services check its annual publication, the *CRL Handbook*.

320. *Guide to the Availability of Theses*. Compiled by D. H. Borchard and J. D. Thawley. Munich and New York: K. G. Saur, 1981. 444p. ISBN 3-598-20378-0.

A helpful guide to sources of foreign dissertations, this work supplies information concerning the policies of various libraries from around the world on lending dissertations. The compilers originally surveyed 1,489 libraries in 126 countries but received replies from only 698 institutions in 85 countries. The guide is arranged alphabetically by country. At the beginning of each nation's section, various union lists and national thesis bibliographies are noted along with any programs of centralized thesis exchanges.

321. *Guide to the Availability of Theses. II. Non-University Institutions*. Compiled by G. G. Allen and K. Deubert. Munich and New York: K. G. Saur, 1984. 124p. ISBN 3-598-20394-2.

This publication serves as a supplement to the previous entry and provides information on sources of dissertations from non-university institutions such as institutes of technology (outside of the U.S.) and schools of theology, health, and art.

322. *Guide to Theses and Dissertations: An International Bibliography*. Rev. and enl. By Michael M. Reynolds. Phoenix, AZ: Oryx Press, 1985. 263p. ISBN 0-89774-149-8.

In what is by far the most complete list of dissertation and thesis bibliographies, Reynolds has arranged his material alphabetically by country and topically by subject. The most useful sections for historians are the chapters on universal sources and history sources. Of the some 3,000 titles listed, 180 deal specifically with history.

General

International

323. *Comprehensive Dissertation Index*. Ann Arbor, MI: Microfilms Inc. (UMI), 1973–. Annual. ISSN 0361-6657.

In 1973 University Microfilms International (UMI) published its landmark *Comprehensive Dissertation Index, 1861–1972* (CDI) in 37 volumes. This edition, which UMI refers to as the "main set" listed 417,000 dissertations from U.S. and Canadian institutions. Its sources of information were *Dissertation Abstracts International* [*see* 324], *American Doctoral Dissertations* [*see* 326], lists from the Library of Congress, and lists supplied by graduate schools throughout North America. This main set provides subject and keyword access in the first 32 volumes and author access in the last 5. Volume 28 is devoted to history. In 1984, UMI published a 10-year cumulative supplement for the years 1973–1982 in 38 volumes and listing an additional 351,000 dissertations. A 5-year cumulation for the years 1983–1987 was issued in 22 volumes in 1988. With the 1988 annual supplement, the CDI has begun listing British dissertations along with the North American dissertations.

324. *Dissertation Abstracts International*. Ann Arbor, MI: UMI, 1938–. Section A: *Humanities and Social Sciences*. Monthly. ISSN 0419-4209. Section C: *Worldwide*. Quarterly. ISSN 0307-6075.

In 1938 UMI published its first volume of *Microfilm Abstracts* in two parts. Volume 1, no. 1, listed two history dissertations. Its name was changed to *Dissertation Abstracts* in 1952, and bimonthly issues were inaugurated. Then in July 1966 *Dissertation Abstracts* was divided into Section A: *Humanities and Social Sciences* and Section B: *Sciences and Engineering*. International coverage was expanded in 1976 with the addition of Section C: *European Abstracts*. Beginning in July 1988, doctoral dissertations from 50 universities in Great Britain were listed in Sections A and B, and Section C was renamed *Worldwide*. History dissertations from North America and Great Britain are listed in part five of Section A. These listings include author-prepared abstracts from more than 500 participating institutions. Monthly issues provide keyword and author access. There is an annual cumulative author index. All of this forms part of UMI's dissertation data base containing bibliographic citations to one million dissertations. On-line access to *Dissertation Abstracts Online* is available through DIALOG or BRS. Access to the bibliographic citations is available back to 1861; access to the full text of the abstracts has been available since July 1980. *Dissertation Abstracts Ondisc* supplies similar access on compact disc, with 35,000 new titles added annually.

325. *Master's Abstracts International*. Ann Arbor, MI: UMI, 1962–. Quarterly. ISSN 0025-5106.

Bibliographic control for master's theses has been far less successful than that for doctoral dissertations. Currently 94 institutions provide abstracts of their theses to UMI. The arrangement is by broad general subjects with an author index. Unlike *Dissertation Abstracts International*, there is no keyword access. A 15-year cumulative index to the first 15 volumes was published in 1978 and listed 10,500 theses. In 1986 its name was changed to *Master's Abstracts International*, which reflects the increased participation of European institutions.

National

United States

326. *American Doctoral Dissertations.* Ann Arbor, MI: UMI, 1933–1934–. Annual. ISSN 0065-809X.

This annual list is compiled by the Association of Research Libraries (ARL) and is published by UMI. It began as a successor to *List of American Doctoral Dissertations* (1912–1938) issued by the Library of Congress. The new annual list includes dissertations accepted for the Ph.D. by American and Canadian institutions and is compiled from corresponding issues of the *Dissertation Abstracts International* as well as from commencement programs and information gathered directly from the institutions. Organization is by broad subject categories from "Agriculture" to "Zoology" and within these categories is arranged alphabetically by the name of the university granting the degree. There is also an author index.

Canada

327. *Canadian Theses.* Ottawa: National Library of Canada, 1947–1980. Annual, with multiyear cumulations. ISSN 0068-9874.

328. *Canadian Theses (Microfiche).* Ottawa: National Library of Canada, 1980/81–. Semiannual, with five-year cumulations. ISSN 0316-0149.

The printed volumes provide lists of theses and dissertations accepted by Canadian universities, arranged by subject based on the Dewey Decimal System and further subdivided by university. There is also an author index. They have been replaced by the microfiche bibliography, which lists all master's and doctoral theses accepted by Canadian universities, written by a Canadian outside of Canada, or written on a Canadian topic outside of Canada. The microfiche bibliography is accompanied by four cumulative indexes that include a KWOC (Key Word Out of Context) index and a Dewey Decimal Classification index for use in subject searching. All theses microfilmed by the National Library are also listed in *Canadiana* (1951–), the national bibliography issued monthly in printed and microfiche formats. The Canadian Theses Service of the National Library of Canada produces microfilm copies of doctoral and master's theses for sale or loan. Since 1965 some 80,000 theses have been microfilmed. Also listing doctoral research done on Canadian topics is *Doctoral Research on Canada and Canadians, 1884–1983* by Jesse J. Dossick (Ottawa: Minister of Supply and Services Canada, 1986). For more information on locating Canadian theses, *Theses in Canada: A Bibliographic Guide*, 2d ed. (Ottawa: Minister of Supply and Services Canada, 1986), should be consulted.

Great Britain

329. *British Reports, Translations and Theses*. London: British Library Document Supply Centre, 1981–. Monthly. ISSN 0144-7556.

Usually referred to as BRTT, this publication lists British report literature and translations produced by British government organizations, industry, universities and other learned institutions, and most doctoral theses accepted at British universities during and after 1970. It is divided into three sections: humanities and social sciences, biological and medical sciences, and engineering. Access is through monthly keyterm indexes, an annual index, and quarterly cumulative author, report number, and keyterm indexes on microfiche. All dissertations listed are available from the British Library Document Supply Centre. On-line access is offered by the SIGLE (System for Information on Grey Literature in Europe) data base, which can be accessed via Blaise-Line in the United Kingdom.

330. *The Brits Index*. Ann Arbor, MI: UMI, 1989. 3 vols. ISBN 0-576-40018-1.

This new publication was prepared by the British Library in association with UMI and lists 68,000 dissertations completed at British universities between 1971 and 1987. These were microfilmed by the British Library but never included in the UMI dissertations data base. The volumes are a large subject index divided into 8 broad categories with further subdivision into 79 disciplines. There are also accompanying author and subject indexes. Most of the titles listed in these volumes are available from the British Library Document Supply Centre. After July 1988 UMI began adding British dissertations to the UMI dissertation data base in association with the British Library, and now they appear in Sections A and B of *Dissertation Abstracts International* [*see* 324].

331. *Index to Theses with Abstracts Accepted for Higher Degrees by the Universities of Great Britain and Ireland and the Council for National Academic Awards.* London: Aslib, 1953–. Vol. 1 (for 1950–1951)–. Quarterly. ISSN 0073-6066.

Generally referred to as the *Index to Theses,* this is the British equivalent of *Dissertation Abstracts International.* It has gone through a number of changes in format and frequency of publication. In November 1986 with Volume 35, Part 1, it assumed its present structure with the addition of abstracts and an enhanced subject index. Entries for dissertations are divided into 8 broad categories, which are then further arranged under detailed subject headings. In the case of History, it is listed in section A for the Arts and Humanities and given the numerical designation of 9. There are an additional 16 subdivisions for History, ranging from Historiography (A9a) to Military Studies (A9s). Additional access is provided by author and subject indexes. Each calendar-year volume lists about 9,000 dissertations awarded by some 50 universities.

332. *Retrospective Index to Theses of Great Britain and Ireland 1716–1950.* Edited by Roger R. Bilboul and Francis L. Kent. Santa Barbara, CA: ABC-CLIO, 1975. 5 vols. ISBN 0-903450-02-X.

The purpose of this 5-volume retrospective set is to provide information to scholars on the existence of theses completed for higher degrees in Great Britain and Ireland up to 1950, when Aslib began publishing its *Index to Theses.* The first volume focuses on the social sciences and humanities, while the following 4 volumes cover the sciences. More than 13,000 doctoral dissertations and master's theses issued by 21 universities are listed in Volume 1. Coverage for most universities begins around 1900. Information supplied for the theses includes title, author, institution, degree, and date. The arrangement is alphabetical by title under specific subject headings borrowed from the *British Humanities Index* [see 227] with frequent cross-references. There is also an author index.

Historical

There are literally dozens of specialized lists of dissertations completed or in progress that are of interest to historians. Many of them are listed in *Guide to Theses and Dissertations* [*see* 322]. Numerous historical journals devoted to various countries, regions, states, or topics regularly list relevant theses and doctoral dissertations; e.g., the *Journal of American History* [*see* 188] lists completed dissertations in its "Recent Scholarship" section. The items listed below are the main guides for historical dissertations written in English.

North America

333. *Dissertations in History: An Index to Dissertations Completed in History Departments of the United States and Canadian Universities.* By Warren F. Kuehl. Vol. 1: *1873–1960.* Lexington, KY: University of Kentucky Press, 1965. 249p.; Vol. 2: *1961–1970.* Lexington, KY: University of Kentucky Press, 1972. 237p. ISBN 0-8131-1264-8; Vol. 3: *1970–June 1980.* Santa Barbara, CA: ABC-CLIO, 1985. 465p. ISBN 0-87436-356-X.

The most useful and complete guide to historical dissertations completed at U.S. and Canadian universities up to mid-1980, it lists almost 25,000 dissertations. Some 7,000 dissertations completed before 1960 appear in the first volume. The second volume has 5,891 awarded during the 1960s, and the third volume contains 10,077 dissertations finished in the 1970s. Superior subject indexing based on the headings used by the American Historical Association in its *Recently Published Articles* [*see* 085] makes it easy to locate dissertations on specific topics. Both author and subject indexes are keyed to the entry numbers assigned to each dissertation.

334. *Doctoral Dissertations in History.* Washington, DC: American Historical Association, 1976–. Annual. ISSN 0145-9929.

Published under various titles and formats, the American Historical Association has sponsored this list of completed dissertations and dissertations in progress since 1901. The primary purpose of these lists has been to register dissertation topics and so avoid duplicate research on the same topic.

335. *Register of Post-Graduate Dissertations in Progress in History and Related Subjects.* Ottawa: Canadian Historical Association, 1966–. Annual. ISSN 0068-8088.

In association with the Public Archives of Canada, the Canadian Historical Association lists master's and doctoral theses in progress at Canadian universities. The list is further enhanced by including theses in progress at non-Canadian universities dealing with topics in Canadian history. This list was published in the *Canadian Historical Review* from 1927 to 1965.

Great Britain

336. *Historical Research for Higher Degrees in the United Kingdom. Part 1: Theses Completed. Part 2: Theses in Progress.* London: University of London, Institute of Historical Research, 1931–. Annual. ISSNs 0268-6716 and 0268-6724.

Published under various titles since 1931, these lists fulfill a function similar to that of the American Historical Association's *Doctoral Dissertations in History* [*see* 334]. The British publication, however, has also recorded theses awarded the B. Litt., B. Phil., and various master's degrees as well as the Ph.D. The entries listed in Part 2 are arranged under subject headings such as Historiography or Australia. There is also an author index. Recent lists have noted about 500 theses completed annually, plus more than 3,000 in progress.

337. *History Theses, 1901–1970: Historical Research for Higher Degrees in the Universities of the United Kingdom.* By Phyllis M. Jacobs. London: University of London, Institute of Historical Research, 1976. 456p. ISBN 0-901-17934-5.

338. *History Theses, 1971–1980: Historical Research for Higher Education in the Universities of the United Kingdom.* By Joyce M. Horn. London: University of London, Institute of Historical Research, 1984. 294p. ISBN 0-901-17981-7.

The British equivalent of Kuehl's *Dissertations in History*, the first volume lists 7,633 B. Litt., master's, and doctoral theses in chronological order under broad subject categories. The second volume lists an additional 4,400 theses. Both volumes contain author and analytical subject indexes.

8.

Government Publications and Legal Sources

Historical researchers often neglect government publications even though they provide a wealth of primary information. This chapter's purpose is to introduce the major guides, indexes, and bibliographies used for locating government publications, both in the United States and in other countries. It is not meant to be totally comprehensive and tries to provide guidance to the beginning researcher. By the nature of government publications, this chapter will emphasize the twentieth century, although there are indexes covering eighteenth- and nineteenth-century documents. A distinction is made also between official government publications and archival and manuscript sources, which will be covered in a separate chapter.

It is important to understand how the United States government publishes and distributes its publications in order to understand the associated guides and indexes. Most United States documents are published by the U.S. Government Printing Office and distributed by the Superintendent of Documents to libraries participating in the Depository Library Program. These documents are divided into three main groups—congressional or legislative, judicial, and executive. They are classified by the Superintendent of Documents, or SuDoc, classification system. It is a complex system, and this chapter will discuss the introductory guides and some of the specialized indexes that support it.

Guides and bibliographies for Canadian, British, European, Soviet, Japanese, United Nations, and other international organizations' official publications will also be listed in this chapter. Another section will selectively cover guides to legal sources such as constitutions, treaties, and other international agreements, laws, and court decisions.

Government Publications

United States

Guides

339. *Government Publications and Their Use.* 2d rev. ed. By Laurence F. Schmeckebier and Roy B. Eastin. Washington, DC: Brookings Institution, 1969. 502p. ISBN 0-317-26160-6.

Although now out of date for current material, this work remains a standard as an introduction to U.S. government documents. It is an excellent guide to U.S. government publications, covering the major catalogs and indexes, bibliographies, the Superintendent of Documents classification system, congressional publications, federal and state constitutions, and federal and state legal publications. There are also topical chapters on presidential papers and foreign affairs, reports on operations, maps, and technical reports. Written in descriptive language understandable to the novice user of documents, this work is a good starting point for the beginning history researcher.

340. *Guide to U.S. Government Publications.* Edited by John L. Andriot. McLean, VA: Documents Index, 1973–. Annual.

Formerly known as *Guide to U.S. Government Serials & Periodicals,* this annual work, often referred to by documents librarians as "Andriot," is the best source for locating the SuDoc classification number, the number assigned to U.S. government documents and serial publications. It has an agency and title index, as well as a complete list of SuDoc classification numbers, including the way agency numbers have changed over the years. This historical section is valuable for locating earlier SuDoc numbers for particular agency serials that have changed classification numbers over the years. Andriot also has the advantage over the *Periodicals Supplement* to the *Monthly Catalog of United States Government Publications,* in that it lists serials that have ceased as well as current ones.

341. *Introduction to United States Public Documents.* 3d ed. By Joe Morehead. Littleton, CO: Libraries Unlimited, 1983. 309p. ISBN 0-87287-359-5.

This work, written by a recognized authority on U.S. government documents, is one of the best general introductions to the major

sources for locating U.S. government publications. Written for both
the librarian and layperson, Morehead's work contains detailed
chapters on the U.S. Government Printing Office, Superintendent of
Documents, and Depository Library System. It also covers both
depository and nondepository publications, as well as general
guides to federal publications and sources for finding legislative,
executive, judicial, and department and agency documents. Two
appendixes cover selected on-line data bases for federal government
information and list abbreviations, acronyms, citations, and personal names used in the text. A good supplement to Morehead's
work is Judith Schiek Robinson's *Subject Guide to U.S. Government
Reference Sources* (Littleton, CO: Libraries Unlimited, 1985).

Indexes

342. *Catalog of the Public Documents of the Congress and of All Departments of the Government of the United States, March 4, 1893–December
31, 1940.* Washington, DC: Government Printing Office, 1896–1945.
25 vols.

Intended to be a "comprehensive index" to both congressional and
departmental documents, the *Document Catalog* starts where Ames'
Comprehensive Index ends in 1893 (53d Congress). The work, each
volume of which generally covers a single congressional session, is
arranged in a single alphabetical sequence, with detailed entries
under author, subject, and, in some cases, title. Entries are quite
detailed, and in many cases the Serial Set volume number for individual documents is given. An essential index for locating early
twentieth-century historical documents that parallels the coverage
of the *Monthly Catalog* until 1940, this index's main drawback is that
it does not provide Superintendent of Documents classification
numbers for locating individual documents.

343. *Checklist of United States Public Documents, 1789–1909.* 3d ed.,
rev. and enl. Washington, DC: Government Printing Office, 1911.
Reprint. New York: Kraus, 1962. 1,707p.

One of the standard sources for locating historical United States
documents, this massive volume, as its title indicates, is a checklist,
containing information on congressional publications through the
close of the 60th Congress and departmental publications to the end
of the calendar year 1909. Within the *Checklist* congressional publications are arranged by congressional session, and departmental
publications are arranged by Superintendent of Documents classification number. Not very easy to use for someone unfamiliar with

the SuDoc classification system, the *Checklist* is particularly valuable because it lists the Congressional Serial Set number for many documents, which is the volume number for locating a copy of that document.

344. *CIS U.S. Congressional Committee Hearings Index, 1833–1969.* Washington, DC: Congressional Information Service, 1981–1985. 42 vols. ISBN 0-88692-050-7 (set).

This excellent index from the Congressional Information Service (CIS), a major publisher of reference aids for locating U.S. government documents, is the definitive retrospective index to congressional committee hearings. Covering from the 23d Congress (December 1833) through the 91st Congress, 1st Session (1969), the index provides detailed indexing of committee hearings for the period before the CIS annual congressional indexes began. Divided into eight parts, each covering several Congresses, the index provides access to more than 30,000 publications available for purchase on microfiche. Each index part consists of several sections, including reference bibliography volumes, listing detailed bibliographic data on individual hearings, as well as indexes by subject, organization, personal name, title, bill number, Superintendent of Documents classification number, and report or document number.

345. *CIS U.S. Serial Set Index, 1789–1969.* Washington, DC: Congressional Information Service, 1975–1979. 36 vols. ISBN 0-912380-26-8.

This is another CIS index that has greatly simplified searching for historical material in the *U.S. Serial Set,* which consists of thousands of volumes containing congressional and executive documents and reports dating back to the 1st Congress (1789). Divided into 12 parts, each covering a number of congressional sessions, the index is arranged chronologically, from the *American State Papers* (1789) through the 91st Congress, 1st session (1969), when the CIS annual indexes begin. Each part consists of a detailed alphabetical subject index, a numerical list of reports and documents arranged by Congress and session, a schedule of serial volumes, and an index of names of individuals and organizations covered by private relief and related actions. This multivolume set makes it extremely easy to locate historical material by subject in Serial Set volumes. Both the *CIS U.S. Congressional Committee Hearings Index* and the *U.S. Serial Set Index* can now be searched electronically on a CD-ROM product called *Congressional Masterfile, 1789–1969.* Researchers can search nearly 400,000 records from the four CIS retrospective indexes on a single compact disc. Also, the more recent CIS congressional index, extending from 1970 to the present, has just become available on CD-ROM as *Congressional Masterfile 2.*

346. *Comprehensive Index to the Publications of the United States Government, 1881–1893.* Compiled by John G. Ames. Washington, DC: Government Printing Office, 1905. 1,590p. 2 vols. House Document No. 754, 58th Congress, 2d session, Serial Set No. 4745-46.

Although not totally comprehensive as its title implies, Ames' work fills the gap between Poore's *Descriptive Catalogue* [see 348], which stops in 1881, and the first volumes of the *Document Catalog,* whose coverage begins in 1893. The work is basically an alphabetical keyword list of documents, with documents listed by congressional session and document number. Under a separate heading, "Congressional Documents," the Serial Set volume numbers for individual documents are listed. There is also a personal name index at the end of the volumes, referring the user to a page where an individual is mentioned. Not as detailed as the *Document Catalog,* this index is still useful for finding documents published during this period.

347. *Cumulative Title Index to United States Public Documents, 1789–1976.* Compiled by Daniel W. Lester, Sandra K. Faull, and Lorraine E. Lester. Arlington, VA: United States Historical Documents Institute, 1979–1982. 16 vols.

This multivolume work is basically an alphabetical title list to the United States documents contained in the Public Documents Library of the U.S. Government Printing Office, now known as the Printed Archives Branch of the National Archives. The entries include the following information: title, publication date, and, most important, Superintendent of Documents classification number. A key advantage of this work is that it indexes an extensive collection of documents by title, serving as a quick source for the researcher searching for the government call number for an item, without having to search several other printed sources.

348. *A Descriptive Catalogue of the Government Publications of the United States, September 5, 1774–March 4, 1881.* Compiled by Ben Perley Poore. Washington, DC: Government Printing Office, 1885. 1,392p. Senate Miscellaneous Document No. 67, 48th Congress, 2d Session, Serial Set No. 2268.

Poore's work marks the earliest attempt at publishing a complete list of all government publications, including executive, congressional, and judicial documents. Covering from 1774 to 1881, the work is divided into two parts: (1) the catalog, where the entries are arranged chronologically; and (2) the index, which refers the user to a page number where the entry is found. Poore has its drawbacks: it is not totally complete in its coverage, the index is not the most comprehensive, and the entries do not include the Serial Set volume number. However, despite these drawbacks and the fact that much of Poore's coverage has been superseded by the *U.S. Serial Set Index*, it can still be a useful guide to nineteenth-century documents.

349. *Monthly Catalog of United States Government Publications.* Washington, DC: Government Printing Office, 1895–.

This is the major index to United States government documents, serving as a bibliography of congressional, departmental, and agency publications. Published monthly since 1895, *Monthly Catalog* entries are arranged alphabetically by issuing agency, and it is indexed on a monthly and annual basis. Entries include the full bibliographic citation as well as the Superintendent of Documents classification number. Since 1941 there have been decennial cumulative indexes to the *Monthly Catalog*, covering from 1941 to 1960, and five-year indexes, from 1961 to 1980. Pierian Press has published several cumulative personal author indexes, for the period from 1941 to 1970. Carrollton Press has published a massive 15-volume *Cumulative Subject Index to the Monthly Catalog of United States Government Publications, 1900–1971*, which indexes 70 years of *Monthly Catalog* volumes in one source. The more recent years of the *Monthly Catalog*, from 1976 to the present, can now be searched electronically on CD-ROM. A number of private companies, including Marcive, Auto-Graphics, Brodart, and SilverPlatter, have CD-ROM products for searching the most recent years of this index. The *Monthly Catalog* is also available for searching on-line through vendors such as DIALOG and BRS.

350. *Monthly Checklist of State Publications.* By U.S. Library of Congress. Washington, DC: Government Printing Office, 1910–. Monthly.

Although not totally comprehensive in its coverage, this is the most complete bibliographic guide available for locating state government publications. The *Monthly Checklist* lists state publications, both monographs and periodicals, received by the Library of Congress. Monographs in each monthly issue are arranged alphabetically by state and issuing agency; periodicals are listed semiannually in June and December, with the December list the cumulative one for the year. The entries give full bibliographic information, including price and availability if known. With coverage going back to 1910, this is the best place to start for the historian looking for twentieth-century state publications.

351. *Public Documents of the First Fourteen Congresses, 1789–1817: Papers Relating to Early Congressional Documents.* Compiled by A. W. Greely. Washington, DC: Government Printing Office, 1900. 903p. Senate Document No. 428, 56th Congress, 1st Session, Serial Set No. 3879.

Covering congressional documents from 1789 to 1817, Greely's work focuses on the period before the *Tables and Index* volume [*see* 352] begins. Arranged chronologically by Congress and by type of document, this work parallels Poore's *Descriptive Catalogue* in its coverage, but the documents listed do not contain the Serial Set volume numbers. A supplement, also prepared by Greely, was published in Volume 1 of the *Annual Report of the American Historical Association, 1903.* Greely is basically a chronological catalog that has largely been superseded by the *U.S. Serial Set Index.* However, it can still be useful, because it may be necessary to check several indexes for this period to locate a specific document.

352. *Tables of and Annotated Index to the Congressional Series of United States Public Documents.* Washington, DC: Government Printing Office, 1902. 769p.

This one-volume work indexes congressional and executive documents published in the *Serial Set* from the 15th through the 52d Congresses, 1817–1893. Covering roughly the same period as Poore's *Descriptive Catalogue* and Ames' *Comprehensive Index,* the *Tables and Index* is divided into two parts: (1) tables listing the *American State Papers* and documents from the 15th through 52d Congresses by *Serial Set* volume number; and (2) a detailed subject and name index to these documents. Although the tables portion has been superseded by the *Checklist* and the *CIS Serial Set Index* provides more detailed subject searching, this work can still prove useful for finding obscure documents published during this period.

Canada

Guides

353. *Canadian Official Publications.* By Olga B. Bishop. New York: Pergamon Press, 1981. (Guides to Official Publications, Vol. 9) 291p. ISBN 0-08-024697-4.

Written by Professor Bishop, who for many years taught government documents at the University of Toronto, this work remains the best single introductory guide to Canadian publications. It focuses on Canadian federal government documents, including publications of the Canadian Parliament. Other topical chapters cover reference sources, statistics, the Public Archives of Canada, and federal-provincial relations; there is also a chapter explaining the classification and indexing schemes for Canadian documents. Bishop's work focuses only on federal publications. For an introduction to the publications of the provinces and territories consult Catherine A. Pross, *Guide to the Identification and Acquisition of Canadian Government Publications: Provinces and Territories* (Halifax, Nova Scotia: Dalhousie University School of Library Service, 1983).

Bibliographies

354. *Federal Royal Commissions in Canada, 1867–1966; A Checklist.* By George Fletcher Henderson. Toronto: University of Toronto Press, 1967. 212p. LC 68-91146.

Henderson's work is important for researchers in Canadian History because it provides a guide to the wealth of primary document material published by the federal royal commissions. Covering the period from 1867 to 1966, the *Checklist* is arranged chronologically and includes information on almost 400 of these bodies and their reports. Entries include information on the appointment of each royal commission, the names of the commissioners, whether or not its report has been printed, and where the report is located. There is a detailed index for locating commissioners, titles and authors of special studies, and the main subjects of commissions and special studies.

355. *Government of Canada Publications. Publications du Gouvernement du Canada.* Ottawa, Canada: Canadian Government Publishing Centre, Jan.–March, 1979–. Quarterly.

For the history student, this is the most comprehensive guide to twentieth-century Canadian documents. The Canadian equivalent of the United States' *Monthly Catalog*, it is the major bibliography of Canadian government publications. Now issued quarterly, this periodical, which has changed title and frequency several times over the years, began publication during the first decade of the twentieth century. Currently each issue of *Government of Canada Publications* is divided into three parts: (1) parliamentary publications; (2) departmental publications; and (3) index, which cumulates at the end of each year. The parliamentary publications are arranged by type of document, and the departmental documents are listed alphabetically by the issuing agency.

Great Britain

Guides

356. *A Guide to British Government Publications.* By Frank Rodgers. New York: H. W. Wilson, 1980. 750p. ISBN 0-8242-0617-7.

This is an excellent introductory guide to British official publications, covering Parliament as well as individual government departments. The volume is divided into three parts: (1) general; (2) parliamentary; and (3) executive agencies. Part 1 serves as a general introduction, covering the British Constitution and government and the way British government publications are organized. Part 2 covers parliamentary publications, including the Sessional Papers, Reports of Debates, and Parliamentary Committees. Part 3, the largest section, covers the government departments, arranged by subject chapters that include material on each department's origins, history, major changes in function, and publications. There is a glossary of terms and a general index at the end.

Indexes and Bibliographies

357. *Catalogue of British Official Publications Not Published by HMSO.* Cambridge: Chadwyck-Healey, 1981–. Bimonthly.

Not all British government publications are published by Her Majesty's Stationery Office (HMSO), the official publishing agency of the British government. This relatively new reference source, published by Chadwyck-Healey, fills a need by providing access to additional British government publications not published by the HMSO. The *Catalogue* appears six times a year and covers publications since 1980 of more than 500 official organizations. Publications listed include periodicals, pamphlets, technical reports, and audiovisual material. Many of the items listed in the *Catalogue* are available on microfiche from Chadwyck-Healey.

358. *General Alphabetical Index to the Bills, Reports, Estimates, Accounts and Papers Printed by Order of the House of Commons, and to the Papers Presented by Command, 1801–1948/49.* London: Her Majesty's Stationery Office, 1853–1960.

This work is the major cumulative index to all publications printed by the House of Commons or presented to the House. It presently consists of three 50-year cumulative indexes, 1801–1852, 1852–1899, and 1900–1949, which are cumulated from the earlier annual and decennial indexes. Each cumulative index is arranged alphabetically by broad subject area, and the entries give detailed locational information. These index volumes do not contain information on the papers of the House of Lords, unless they are duplicated in the House of Commons Papers. They also do not index publications of the various government bureaus and departments. The first two of these 50-year indexes are reprinted in the eight-volume *Irish University Press Series of British Parliamentary Papers* (Shannon, Ireland: Irish University Press, 1968). Until the recent Cockton compilation [*see* 361], these indexes were the best source for finding nineteenth-century British documents.

359. *Hansard's Catalogue and Breviate of Parliamentary Papers, 1696–1834.* Reprinted in facsimile with an introduction by Percy Ford and Grace Ford. Oxford: Basil Blackwell, 1953. 220p.

For the period of 1696 to 1834 an indispensable aid is this reprint of the *Catalogue of Parliamentary Reports, and a Breviate of Their Contents*. It was originally issued by the House of Commons in 1836 and indexes what is known as the "First Series" of parliamentary reports (15 volumes), the reports that appeared in the *Journals of the House of Commons*, and the reports located in the *Sessional Papers* from 1801 to 1834. These publications are classified under 26 broad subject categories, such as education and charities, trade and manufactures, agriculture, and public works. Each entry lists the location of the document and the subjects it covers. This reprint also includes a select list of House of Lords' Papers not found in the original *Catalogue*.

360. *HMSO Annual Catalogue,* 1922–. London: Her Majesty's Stationery Office, 1923–.

Although its title has varied since 1922 and earlier, these annual cumulative volumes are the British equivalent of the U.S. Government Printing Office's *Monthly Catalog*. They cumulate the monthly issues published by HMSO and serve as an index to all British government publications printed by that agency. Each annual volume is divided into sections listing parliamentary, non-parliamentary, and Northern Ireland publications, with a subject index at the end. A private publisher, Carrollton Press, has made it easier for the researcher trying to track down twentieth-century British publications by publishing a *Cumulative Index to the Annual Catalogues of Her Majesty's Stationery Office Publications, 1922–1972.* This 2-volume work covers a 50-year period and gives references to the original catalogs.

Access to British official publications is now available on CD-ROM. *UKOP: A Catalogue of United Kingdom Official Publications on CD-ROM,* a joint project of Chadwyck-Healey and HMSO Books, provides access to all British official publications, including those of both the HMSO and the departmental or "Non-HMSO" publications from 1980 to the present. It currently includes more than 160,000 records.

361. *Subject Catalogue of the House of Commons Parliamentary Papers, 1801–1900.* Compiled by Peter Cockton. Cambridge: Chadwyck-Healey, 1988. 4,800p. 5 vols. ISBN 0-85964-133-3 (set).

This massive new index set, compiled by Peter Cockton, is a companion volume to the microfiche set of nineteenth-century parliamentary papers published by Chadwyck-Healey. The *Subject Catalogue* provides detailed indexing for the Parliamentary Papers by dividing them into 19 broad subject groups, similar to those found in *Hansard,* including central government and administration, agriculture and rural society, trade and commerce, and poverty and social administration. Also within each subject group there are additional subdivisions. Entries include the citation to the volume and page number of the Sessional Papers and the Chadwyck-Healey microfiche number. At the end of the fifth volume there is a subject index to the set. This set provides more detailed indexing to nineteenth-century parliamentary papers than those published by the House of Commons and privately published sources.

European Economic Community: Guides and Indexes

362. *A Guide to the Official Publications of the European Communities.* 2d ed. By John Jeffries. London: Mansell, 1981. 318p. ISBN 0-7201-1590-6.

This is the best general guide and introduction to the publications of the European Communities. The second edition is a substantially revised, expanded, and improved version of Jeffries' original guide, published by Facts on File in 1978. Jeffries' work basically follows that of the European Communities, beginning with a brief introduction to the organization of their different agencies and their publication history. Included are chapters on the publications of the Commission, the Statistical Office of the European Communities, the Council of Ministers, the European Parliament, and the Court of Justice of the European Communities. There is also information on unofficial sources, documentation centers, depository libraries, and official catalogs.

363. *Index to the Official Journal of the European Communities*. Luxembourg: Office for Official Publications of the European Communities, 1973–. Monthly, with annual cumulations. The index has changed title and form over the years: *Index to the Official Journal of the European Communities; Alphabetical Index and Methodological Table*, 1978–1979; *Supplement to the Official Journal of the European Communities, Annual Alphabetical and Methodological Index*, 1973–1977.

This is the most detailed index to European Communities documents published in the *Official Journal*. Since 1980 the *Index* has been published in two parts—an alphabetical index and a methodological table. The alphabetical index is based on Communities terminology and is arranged by subject. Entries give references to the issue of the *Official Journal* where the document appears and the page number. The methodological table is arranged by type of document. These documents fall into two categories: (1) legislation and (2) information and notices. References are given to the number, page, and date of issues of the *Official Journal*. Documents covered include regulations, decisions, directives, orders, and removals. The index provides a good starting point for tracing recent European Communities documents on particular issues.

364. *Official Publications of Western Europe. Volume 1: Denmark, Finland, France, Ireland, Italy, Luxembourg, Netherlands, Spain, and Turkey. Volume 2: Austria, Belgium, Federal Republic of Germany, Greece, Norway, Portugal, Sweden, Switzerland, and United Kingdom.* Edited by Eve Johansson. London: Mansell, distributed in the United States by H. W. Wilson, 1984–1988. 2 vols. ISBN 0-7201-1623-6 (Vol. 1); ISBN 0-7201-1662-7 (Vol. 2).

This 2-volume set provides an excellent introduction to the official publications of 17 Western European nations, as well as Turkey. Each volume is organized into country chapters written by experts in the publications of each of these nations, which include an introduction to the political system and constitution as well as material on major publications, publication practices, bibliographic control, and library collections and availability. There is a bibliography at the end of each country chapter that includes guides to official publications. The first volume contains a good introductory chapter on the acquisition of foreign official publications, and each volume is indexed by subject, organization, and title.

United Nations and International Organizations

Guides

365. *International Information: Documents, Publications, and Information Systems of International Governmental Organizations.* Edited by Peter Hajnal. Englewood, CO: Libraries Unlimited, 1988. 339p. ISBN 0-87287-501-6.

This new study by Hajnal, who has written several other works on international organizations, is the best overall introduction to United Nations and international agency publications. The work is arranged into ten chapters, written by specialists in the area of international documentation. It begins with a chapter on the organizational setting; subsequent chapters deal with specialized topics such as inter-governmental organizations as publishers, bibliographic control, collection development, arrangement of collections, reference and information work, citation forms, documentation in microform, computerized information systems, and the user's perspective. Concentrating most heavily on the United Nations and the European Communities, this work is an excellent starting point for the researcher beginning to work with international agency documents.

Indexes

366. *Checklist of United Nations Documents, 1946–1949.* New York: United Nations, 1949–1953.

The original United Nations index, covering documents from 1946 through 1949, the *Checklist* fills the indexing gap from the earliest U.N. publications until the beginning of the next indexing source, the *United Nations Documents Index,* which began in 1950. Originally the *Checklist* was scheduled to be published in nine parts, each listing the publications of a particular U.N. agency or commission. However, only Parts 2 through 8 were published; Part 1 (General Assembly) and Part 9 (Secretariat) were never completed. Each part is cumulated for the four-year period, listing documents for each agency, and there is a detailed subject index for each part.

367. *International Bibliography: Publications of Intergovernmental Organizations.* White Plains, NY: Kraus International Publications, 1973–. Quarterly.

Until 1983 this index was known as the *International Bibliography, Information Documentation*, usually referred to by the acronym *IBID*. Since March 1976, it has served as the major index to the publications of more than 80 intergovernmental organizations, such as the International Monetary Fund and the Food and Agriculture Organization. *International Bibilography* is published quarterly, with annual cumulative title and subject indexes. Each issue is divided into two parts: a bibliographic record (documents) and a periodicals record (serials). Unlike the U.N. indexes, many of the documents listed contain abstracts, and for locating key U.N. documents this index is easier to use than the standard U.N. sources. Historians will find this the best source for finding recent publications of intergovernmental organizations.

368. *League of Nations Documents, 1919–1946: A Descriptive Guide and Key to the Microfilm Collection.* Edited by Edward A. Reno, Jr. New Haven, CT: Research Publications, 1973–1975. 3 vols. ISBN 0-89235-008-3.

This is the major guide to the publications of the League of Nations, predecessor of the United Nations. Covering the period from 1919 to 1946, this 3-volume work indexes material in the most comprehensive set of League of Nations documents, that published by Research Publications. The documents are divided into 18 broad subject categories, including administrative commissions, minorities, social questions, legal questions, and refugees. For each document, the document number is given, as well as an abstract; reel numbers are interspersed among the entries. There is a consolidated document-number index at the end of each volume. The one drawback of this index is that there is no specific subject index, beyond the broad subject categories.

369. *Ten Years of United Nations Publications, 1945 to 1955: A Complete Catalogue.* New York: United Nations, 1955. 271p.

Although certainly not the "comprehensive guide to Official Records and publications and periodicals" of the United Nations from the 1945 San Francisco Conference to the end of 1954 that it claims to be, this volume does index many of the publications of the Secretariat and General Assembly from 1946 to 1949 that were not included in the *Checklist of United Nations Documents*. The main part of the work consists of a listing of Secretariat and Official Record documents. There are author, title, and subject indexes to guide the user. For the researcher this work does provide access to early United Nations publications and fills in the gaps until the *United Nations Documents Index* begins in 1950.

370. *UNDEX: United Nations Documents Index, 1974–1978*. New York: United Nations, 1974–1980. Series C, Cumulative Edition, 1974–1978, was also published by UNIFO, Pleasantville, NY, 1979–1980.

The predecessor of the *UNDOC: Current Index*, the *UNDEX* continues the indexing to United Nations documents begun with the *United Nations Documents Index*. Different in arrangement from the earlier and later U.N. indexes, the UNDEX was issued in three series: Series A, Subject Index; Series B, Country Index; and Series C, List of Documents Issued. Series B incorporates some unique features not found in the *UNDOC*. For example, documents are arranged under each country by "type of action." Among the types of action identified are "Statements in debates" and "Voting: Abst" (Abstaining), "Voting: No," and "Voting: Yes." This unique country arrangement helps to locate a particular nation's position on various issues easily.

371. *UNDOC: Current Index; United Nations Documents*. New York: United Nations, 1979–. Quarterly, with annual cumulations. Until 1987, 10 issues a year. Since 1984, the annual cumulations are available only on microfiche.

The current and what is intended to be the most comprehensive index to United Nations publications, each quarterly issue of the *UNDOC* contains a list of documents and publications, arranged by U.N. classification number, including official records, sales publications, documents republished, new document series symbols, United Nations maps included in documents, United Nations sheet maps, and author, subject, and title indexes. There are annual author, title, subject, and checklist cumulations. A detailed user's guide at the beginning of each volume aids the researcher using this index for the first time. This is the major index for researchers looking for recent U.N. documents. It gives the United Nations classification number for locating the document in many library collections.

372. *United Nations Documents Index: United Nations and Specialized Agencies Documents and Publications, 1950–1973*. New York: United Nations, 1950–1975. Monthly, with annual cumulations beginning in 1963.

The United Nations Documents Index is the second of the four major U.N. indexes and the longest running, beginning with the end of the *Checklist* in 1950 and continuing until the end of 1973, when it was replaced by the *UNDEX*. This index was arranged into two parts: a subject index and a checklist. Prior to 1963 only the subject index was cumulated; from 1963 through 1973 both the subject index and checklist were cumulated annually. Until 1962 the index listed the publications of the specialized agencies, such as the Food and

Agriculture Organization. A four-volume cumulated index to the *United Nations Documents Index* for the period from 1950 to 1962 was published by Kraus-Thomson in 1974. This makes it considerably easier to search that period without having to look through each individual index volume.

A useful supplement to the official United Nations indexes, especially for the time period it covers, is Mary Eva Birchfield's *The Complete Reference Guide to United Nations Sales Publications, 1946–1978* (Pleasantville, NY: UNIFO, 1982). Access to United Nations documents on CD-ROM is now beginning to become available. Readex is coming out with an *Electronic Index to United Nations Documents and Publications,* which will eventually provide access to United Nations documents on CD-ROM from 1945 to the present.

Soviet Union

373. *Official Publications of the Soviet Union and Eastern Europe, 1945–1980: A Select Annotated Bibliography.* Edited by Gregory Walker. London: Mansell, 1982. 620p. ISBN 0-7201-1641-4.

Covering the period from 1945 to 1980, this work is an excellent guide to the postwar official documents of the Soviet Union and the countries of Eastern Europe. Divided alphabetically by country, each chapter begins with an introductory section giving a brief outline of political and administrative developments since the end of World War II. The main part of each chapter consists of the bibliographic entries by type of document, including general bibliographies and reference works, constitutional documents, law codes, other legislative documents, party documents, and general statistics. Brief annotations give information about many individual documents, and there is a name and title index.

Japan

374. *Japanese National Government Publications in the Library of Congress: A Bibliography.* Compiled by Thaddeus Y. Ohta. Washington, DC: Library of Congress, 1981. 402p. ISBN 0-8444-0326-1.

Compiled by the head of the Japanese Section of the Asian Division of the Library of Congress, this work serves as a guide to Japanese government publications, mainly from the post-World War II period through the end of 1977. Containing 3,376 titles, the document entries are arranged under four major sections: Legislative Branch,

Executive Branch, Judicial Branch, and Public Corporations and Research Institutes. Most of the publications listed in this bibliography are serials, but it also includes other publications such as catalogs, directories, guidebooks, handbooks, statistical surveys, census reports, and white papers. Entries include romanized Japanese titles or non-Japanese titles in the absence of Japanese titles, frequency of publication, and a holdings statement.

Legal Sources

Constitutions

375. *Constitutions of the Countries of the World.* Edited by Albert P. Blaustein and H. Franz Gisbert. Dobbs Ferry, NY: Oceana Publications, 1971–.

This is a multivolume, loose-leaf set that provides the current text in English of the constitutions of all the nations of the world. Now numbering more than 40 binder volumes, the set is divided into two parts: the current volumes and the historic constitutions volumes, which cumulate the earlier superseded constitutions, dating back to the 1970s. The volumes are arranged alphabetically by country, from Afghanistan through Zimbabwe, and contain the complete text of the constitution currently in effect, plus a summary of significant events in each country's history and a bibliography of sources. Because of its updating, this set is the best single source for current world constitutions.

376. *Sources and Documents of United States Constitutions.* Edited by William F. Swindler. Dobbs Ferry, NY: Oceana Publications, 1973–1979. 10 vols. ISBN 0-379-16175-3 (set).

The complete text of the constitutions of every U.S. state, including those in effect during the territorial period, is reprinted in this multivolume set. The constitutions are arranged alphabetically by state and contain detailed annotations by Professor Swindler, a recognized authority on constitutional law, that provide excellent analysis of the historical background. Each of the state constitutions is also indexed by subject, and in 1988 a bibliography volume was added, citing law-journal articles on each state constitution. This work is excellent for constitutional history on each state. For the text of the current state constitutions and those of the U.S. possessions and territories, the historian should consult another loose-leaf

Oceana publication, *Constitutions of the United States, National and State.*

Treaties and Other International Agreements

377. *Index-Guide to Treaties: Based on the Consolidated Treaty Series.* Dobbs Ferry, NY: Oceana Publications, 1979–1986. 12 vols. ISBN 0-379-13002-5.

This is the major index to the texts of treaties from 1648 to 1919 between countries worldwide found in the 231-volume *Consolidated Treaty Series*, edited and annotated by Clive Parry (Dobbs Ferry, NY: Oceana Publications, 1969–1981). The first five volumes of the *Index-Guide* are a general chronological list, covering from 1648 to 1919, listing treaties year by year. Volumes 6–10 are a party index, arranged alphabetically by country from Afghanistan to Zanzibar. The last two volumes list colonial, postal, and telegraph treaties chronologically from 1648 to 1920. All the volumes of the *Index-Guide* give the volume and page number of the *Consolidated Treaty Series*, where the text is actually located.

378. *Treaties and Other International Agreements of the United States of America, 1776–1949.* Compiled by Charles I. Bevans. Washington, DC: Government Printing Office, 1968–1976. 13 vols.

This multivolume work is the major retrospective index and compilation of United States treaties and other international agreements from 1776 to 1949, when the *United States Treaties and Other International Agreements* series began publication. Bevans's work is divided into three parts: (1) Multilateral treaties involving the United States; (2) Bilateral treaties, arranged alphabetically by country; and (3) General Index. It prints in English or in translation the full text of each treaty involving the United States. Historians trying to locate treaties after 1950 can check the *Cumulative Index to United States Treaties and Other International Agreements, 1950–1970* (Buffalo, NY: William S. Hein, 1973, 4 vols.) and the *Cumulative Index to United States Treaties and Other International Agreements, 1971–1975* (Buffalo, NY: William S. Hein, 1977), which index the *United States Treaties and Other International Agreements* volumes for the first 25 years.

379. *World Treaty Index.* 2d ed. By Peter H. Rohn. Santa Barbara, CA: ABC-CLIO, 1984. 5 vols. ISBN 0-87436-141-9 (set).

This is without question the most detailed index to twentieth-century national and international treaties, covering treaties from 1900 to 1980. The new edition has been extensively revised and provides access to a total of 44,000 treaties, twice the amount in the original edition. Volume 1 contains a detailed introduction to the set, including an excellent user's guide. The major part of the first volume, however, consists of "Treaty Profiles," which provide an extensive array of national, regional, and global treaty statistics. Following this introductory volume is the main part of the work, the listing of all the treaties covered, arranged in chronological order by date of signature. This is in Volumes 2 (1900–1960) and 3 (1960–1980). The detailed entries include information such as a signature date and citation, treaty number, name and title, date on which the treaty entered into force, languages of the treaty, main theme, parties to the treaty, and an annex providing postsignature treaty history. Rohn's final two volumes furnish extensive indexing to the main entry listings by party, including countries as well as international organizations (Volume 4) and keyword (Volume 5). For a good guide and collection of the key international treaties indexed by Rohn's work, the researcher should consult J. A. S. Grenville and Bernard Wasserstein's 2-volume work *The Major International Treaties, 1914–1945: A History and Guide with Texts* and *The Major Treaties Since 1945: A History and Guide with Texts* (London; New York: Methuen, 1987).

Laws and Courts

Handbooks

380. *Fundamentals of Legal Research*. 3d ed. By J. Myron Jacobstein and Roy M. Mersky. Mineola, NY: Foundation Press, 1985. 717p. Index. ISBN 0-88277-245-7.

Written by two law professors, this book stands out as a basic guide to doing legal research. It includes material on legal bibliography and legal research, making it particularly useful for the historical researcher seeking to become familiar with legal sources. This edition, which updates the second edition, published in 1981, begins with a glossary of terms used in legal research. It also includes chapters on locating and using federal and state court decisions, constitutions, legislation, administrative law, loose-leaf services, Shepards' citations, legal encyclopedias, and legal periodicals. Other chapters cover international law, English and Canadian law, federal tax research, and computer data bases and microtext sources for legal research. Particularly helpful is the last chapter, which provides a succinct general summary and chart of the research procedure for finding constitutional, statutory, case, and administrative law materials. Several appendixes contain additional material on territorial legal research, the national reporter system and its coverage, and resources listed under law-school courses. See also John Corbin's *Find the Law in the Library* (Chicago: American Library Association, 1989).

Indexes and Compilations

381. *Reports of Judgments, Advisory Opinions and Orders.* By the International Court of Justice. Leyden, Netherlands: A. W. Sijthoff's Publishing, 1947–.

This ongoing multivolume work publishes the judgments, advisory opinions, and orders of the International Court of Justice, the key decision-making body for international law. Each of the annual volumes, covering from 1947 to the present, contains the full text of the court's decisions in both English and French. There are also English and French subject indexes at the end of each volume. Prior to World War II, the current court's predecessor was the Permanent Court of International Justice. Its *Judgments, Orders, and Advisory Opinions* were also published (Leyden: A. W. Sijthoff's, 1931–1940). Earlier there were separate *Collection of Advisory Opinions, 1922–1930* and *Collection of Judgments, 1923–1930* volumes. There have also been separate collections of the decisions of the Permanent Court, including the four-volume *World Court Reports, 1922–1942* (Washington, DC: Carnegie Endowment for International Peace, 1934–1943).

382. *United States Statutes at Large.* Boston: Little, Brown, 1845–1873; Washington, DC: Government Printing Office, 1873–.

This ongoing series of volumes is the major compilation of the text of United States laws, as passed by Congress from 1789 to the present. The *Statutes at Large* volumes are arranged by session of Congress and then chronologically by the date a law was passed. Included in the volumes are the complete texts of public laws, private laws, concurrent resolutions, and presidential proclamations. The *Statutes* were where treaties were orginally published until the end of 1949, when they were published separately in the *United States Treaties and Other International Agreements* volumes. Since 1975 the *Statutes* have contained legislative histories of each public law. The more recent volumes also contain subject and individual indexes and citations to the appropriate sections of the *United States Code.* For the text of legislation since the beginning of Congress, the *Statutes* are the best source; for more recent legislation, the *United States Code and Administrative News* (St. Paul, MN: West

Publishing, 1951–) is more current and has more detailed legislative histories.

383. *United States Supreme Court Digest, 1754 to Date: Covering Every Decision of the United States from Earliest Times to Date.* St. Paul, MN: West Publishing Co., 1943–. 33 vols.

Another West publication, this digest is the major index to United States Supreme Court decisions and opinions found in the *United States Reports* volumes, extending from 1754 to the present. The first four volumes of the *Digest* serve as a descriptive word index for locating subject headings and key numbers in the main *Digest* volumes. In the main volumes the arrangement is alphabetical, with a brief summary of the case and the citations for locating the case in the *United States Reports, Lawyers' Edition of the United States Reports,* and the *Supreme Court Reporter.* Pocket parts update each of the main volumes, and two "Table of Cases" volumes help locate individual cases, if the researcher already knows the name of the case. The *Digest* has made it easy to locate individual Supreme Court cases or a series of cases on a particular legal topic.

9.

Dictionaries and Encyclopedias

Dictionaries and encyclopedias of history are useful for clarifying points of discussion, determining dates of events, and providing usually standard interpretations of historical events such as battles, wars, treaties, alliances, policies, and people. Before 1970 these types of works were generally confined to a few standard, frequently reissued general texts covering large spans of time. The past two decades, however, have seen the publication of increasing numbers of specialized topical historical dictionaries and encyclopedias. Because of this proliferation, the list that follows is of necessity selective. Emphasis has been given to recent works published since 1970.

A number of classic multivolume general histories have considerable reference value. In earlier decades they often functioned as encyclopedias, reflecting the state of historical scholarship of that time. Of particular note is the *Cambridge Ancient History*, the first edition of which was completed in 12 volumes with 5 additional volumes of plates between 1923 and 1939. This series is under revision; some volumes are in their second edition and some are in their third. As of 1990, Volumes 1–4 and 7 (part 1) have been revised.

Less up-to-date is the *Cambridge Medieval History*, published in eight volumes between 1911 and 1936. Only Volume 4 on the Eastern Roman Empire has been revised (in 2 parts, 1966–1967). More recent is the *New Cambridge Modern History*, published in 14 volumes between 1957 and 1979 and currently under revision for a second edition. This work is the successor to the earlier *Cambridge Modern History*, published in 13 volumes with an atlas between 1902 and 1926. The success of these works has inspired more specialized multivolume histories from the Cambridge University Press on various topics and regions such as Africa, China, economic history, Greek philosophy, India, Islam, Japan, and Latin America.

General

384. *Blackwell Encyclopedia of Political Institutions.* Edited by Vernon Boddanor. New York: Basil Blackwell, 1987. Index. 667p. ISBN 0-631-13841-2.

A companion volume to the *Blackwell Encyclopedia of Political Thought* [*see* 385], this work describes the key terms and concepts employed in the study of politics. It analyzes the ideas used in the study of political institutions, important forms of political organizations, and major political families. The 600 entries were written by 250 contributors from 13 countries. Individual entries are followed by short lists of additional readings and are fully cross-referenced and indexed. Both Blackwell encyclopedias appeared on several "Best Reference Books of the Year" lists in 1988.

385. *Blackwell Encyclopedia of Political Thought.* Edited by David Miller. New York: Basil Blackwell, 1987. Index. 600p. ISBN 0-631-14011-5.

From absolutism to young Hegelians, this one-volume work encompasses the whole spectrum of the history and theory of politics from Socrates to John Rawls. Some 300 entries written by 120 specialists (mostly British) include a combination of full-length survey articles with shorter definitions. Major concepts in political thought are defined and analyzed. There are brief lists of further readings accompanying the survey articles. All articles are cross-referenced and indexed.

386. *Dictionary of the History of Science.* Edited by W. F. Bynum, E. J. Browne, and Roy Porter. Princeton, NJ: Princeton University Press, 1981. 494p. Index. ISBN 0-691-08287-1.

The goal of this excellent and unique dictionary is to provide historical explanations of the fundamental concepts of science that can be understood by both laypeople and specialists. It contains no biographical entries. Instead, its 700 signed and alphabetically arranged entries deal with ideas such as evolution, quantum, and technological determinism, or related topics like the Copernican Revolution or Mayan astronomy, including obsolete ideas such as aether and phlogiston. The larger entries provide lists of additional readings. Further aid is given to readers by the provision of a general bibliography, an analytical table of contents, and a detailed biographical index. This book is available in a paperback edition.

For two works providing more extended essays *see* Ian McNeil, ed., *An Encyclopedia of the History of Technology* (New York: Routledge, 1989) and Robert Olby, Geoffrey Cantor, John Christie, and Jonathan Hodge, *Companion to the History of Modern Science* (New York: Routledge, 1989).

387. *The Discoverers: An Encyclopedia of Explorers and Exploration.* Edited by Helen Delpar. New York: McGraw-Hill, 1980. 471p. Index. ISBN 0-07-016264-6.

With signed articles from 28 historians, geographers, and librarians focusing on every aspect of discovery, this is the best one-volume guide of its type. Although emphasis is on the discoveries of Western European explorers, contributions by Chinese, Muslim, and Russians are also included. Articles are either short biographical sketches of preeminent explorers or longer articles tracing the history of exploration for a particular geographical region. There are numerous cross-references, and each article includes a short bibliography. Black-and-white photographs and maps complement the excellent text.

388. *Encyclopedia Judaica.* Jerusalem: Encyclopedia Judaica; New York: Macmillan, 1972. 16 vols. Index.

Consisting of 25,000 entries and 8,000 illustrations, this work is truly impressive. Focusing on all aspects of Jewish life and culture, the historical approach dominates the contents of these volumes. Generally the highest levels of scholarship and objectivity have been maintained by the contributors. While there are many reference books dealing with Jewish studies, this one is both authoritative and comprehensive. Also useful is the four-volume work edited by Israel Gutman, *The Encyclopedia of the Holocaust* (New York: Macmillan, 1990).

389. *The Encyclopedia of Military History: From 3500 B.C. to the Present.* 2d rev. ed. By R. Ernest Dupuy and Trevor N. Dupuy. New York: Harper & Row, 1986. 1,524p. Index. ISBN 0-06-181235-8.

This work was first published in 1970 and revised in 1977, and the second edition brings it up-to-date through 1983. It is organized in a series of 21 chronological and geographical chapters. Each chapter begins with a brief introductory essay on the principal military trends of the period, including its outstanding leaders and the general development of tactics, strategy, weaponry, and organization. There is a short bibliography and an excellent general index, as well as separate indexes of battles and sieges and wars. Some 200 maps complement this outstanding work. Also useful is George Kohn, *Dictionary of Wars* (New York: Facts on File, 1986), which is available in paperback, along with David Eggenberger's recently updated *An Encyclopedia of Battles: Accounts of over 1560 Battles from 1479 to the Present* (New York: Dover, 1989), which uses a broad definition of the term "battle."

390. *Encyclopedia of the Third World.* 3d ed. By George Thomas Kurian. New York: Facts on File, 1987. 3 vols. ISBN 0-8160-1118-4.

Now in its third edition, this set provides descriptions of the political, economic, and social systems of 124 countries. A basic fact sheet for each country supplies information on location and area, weather, population, ethnic composition, languages, religions, colonial experiences, constitution and government, freedom and human rights, civil service, foreign policy, law enforcement, health, media, and culture. Since the statistical information in sets like this one dates rapidly, more current information can be found in the *Europa Yearbook* (London: Europa, 1959–) or one of its regional volumes. Similar in format is Kurian's new *Encyclopedia of the First World* (New York: Facts on File, 1990), which provides information for the 25 major industrial nations.

391. *An Encyclopedia of World History: Ancient, Medieval, and Modern Chronologically Arranged.* 5th ed., rev. and enl. Compiled and edited by William L. Langer. Boston: Houghton Mifflin, 1972. 1,569p. Index. ISBN 0-395-13592-3.

To an earlier generation of graduate students in history, this volume was simply "Langer." The author, a Harvard history professor, published the first edition in 1940, using the German work of Karl Ploetz as a model. In putting together his magnum opus, Langer drew upon the talents of a distinguished group of historians, mostly from Harvard. Chronologically arranged, it endeavors to highlight all important events in recorded history. Of particular value are the more than 100 genealogical tables for various dynasties. Meticulously indexed, it remains one of the best one-volume historical encyclopedias for the period prior to 1970. Plans for a new American edition of the work have languished since Langer's death in 1977, although a new British edition updated to 1986 was published by Harrap/Gallery in 1987.

392. *Der Grosse Ploetz. Auszug aus der Geschichte.* 30th ed. Wurzburg: Verlag Ploetz Freiburg, 1988. 1,721p. Index. ISBN 3-87640-050-3.

The single most valuable one-volume historical dictionary in a foreign language, *Der Grosse Ploetz* has been almost continuously in print since 1863, when Karl Ploetz, a teacher of the German language, published the first edition. That original edition later served as the inspiration for William Langer's *Encyclopedia of World History* [*see* 391]. Since Ploetz's original work was translated into English, the organization of the later German editions has evolved considerably. The 30th edition of *Der Grosse Ploetz* has the advantage of currency up to 1985. It is divided into 6 sections: prehistory (60 pages), ancient history (257 pages), the Middle Ages (277 pages), Europe 1500–1945 (411 pages), the rest of the world 1500–1945 (217 pages), and recent history (607 pages). Approximately 75 German scholars authored various subsections of this work. Coverage is balanced and current. Each section has a brief introduction followed by chronological outlines. Numerous time lines, 55 dynastic charts, and hundreds of other charts complement the text, and there is a detailed 100-page index.

393. *Macmillan Concise Dictionary of World History.* By Bruce Wetterau. New York: Macmillan, 1983. 867p. ISBN 0-02-626110-3.

This single-volume dictionary of world history is arranged alphabetically rather than chronologically. Thus, unlike Langer or *Der Grosse Ploetz* [*see* 391 and 392], it is more useful for checking particular incidents, events, or personages than for reviewing the history of a region or a country. Its overall coverage is far less detailed than those two works. Besides the standard textual entries, however, Wetterau's dictionary does include chronologies. The textual entries provide essential information about a particular topic, while the chronologies cover broader topics such as individual countries or major wars. In all there are 10,000 entries and another 7,000 chronologically arranged items on world history from the beginnings of civilization to 1982.

394. *The Oxford Dictionary of the Christian Church.* 2d ed. Edited by F. L. Cross and E. A. Livingstone. London: Oxford University Press, 1974. 1,518p.

There are many reference works dealing with aspects of the history of the Christian Church, but the best general work in one volume is *The Oxford Dictionary of the Christian Church.* It consists of some 6,000 alphabetically arranged, unsigned entries written by approximately 250 specialists. All of the entries contain some additional bibliography, and many provide extensive listings. A large proportion of the entries are biographical, while others deal with events, concepts, and institutions, e.g., Synod of Dort, supralapsarianism, and World Council of Churches. *The Concise Oxford Dictionary of the Christian Church* (1989) is available in paperback. Much historical information on all religions can also be found in the massive *Encyclopedia of Religion*, edited by Mircea Eliade (New York: Macmillan, 1987, 10 vols.). Many of the individual religious denominations have their own dictionaries or encyclopedias. Classic examples of these are the 15-volume *New Catholic Encyclopedia* (New York: McGraw-Hill, 1967) and the 4-volume *Mennonite Encyclopedia* (Hillsboro, KS: Mennonite Brethren Publishing House, 1955–1959).

395. *The Simon & Schuster Encyclopedia of World War II*. Edited by Thomas Parrish. New York: Simon and Schuster, 1978. Index. 767p. ISBN 0-671-24277-6.

Although there has been a recent spate of reference books on World War II, Parrish's is still the most scholarly. With more than 47 contributors and 55 superb maps, it answers in considerable detail the most frequently asked questions about World War II. Consultant editors include a former commander of the Imperial Japanese Navy, a German general, and several U.S. brigadier generals. The work is arranged alphabetically, with minor entries averaging about a quarter of a page and major ones occupying several pages. There is a chart of the Supreme Headquarters for the Allied Expeditionary Force of June 6, 1944, a helpful glossary of terms and abbreviations, a table of equivalent ranks (U.S., British, and German), a brief chronology, and a short bibliography. Also helpful are Louis Snyder, *Historical Guide to World War II* (Westport, CT: Greenwood, 1982); Robert Goralski, *World War II Almanac 1931–1945* (New York: G. P. Putnam's Sons, 1981), which includes helpful appendixes on the costs of the war and strengths of the combatants, casualty lists, a list of comparative ranks, and lists of weapons and equipment; and Ian Hogg and Bryan Perrett, *Encyclopedia of the Second World War* (Novato, CA: Presidio, 1989), which is heavily illustrated.

United States

General

396. *Dictionary of American Diplomatic History*. Rev ed. By John E. Findling. Westport, CT: Greenwood Press, 1989. 620p. Index. ISBN 0-313-260249.

First published in 1980, this revised edition is current through July 1988 and is the best 1-volume reference work on American diplomatic history. It consists of 1,200 entries evenly divided between biographical sketches of individuals who had a significant impact on American foreign policy and nonbiographical sketches focusing on treaties, incidents, conferences, and other aspects of American foreign affairs. Sketches of most U.S. chiefs of missions are included, as are those of major congressional leaders, some foreign correspondents, and important diplomatic historians. The biographical entries are keyed to major biographical reference sources like the *Dictionary of American Biography* and *Current Biography* [*see* 482 and 474].

397. *Dictionary of American History. Bicentennial Edition.* New York: Charles Scribner's Sons, 1976–1979. 8 vols. Index (Vol. 8). ISBN 0-684-13856-5.

As originally conceived by its first editor, James Truslow Adams, this multivolume dictionary was intended to bring together in a convenient format thousands of facts about American history and to serve as a complement to the *Dictionary of American Biography* [*see* 482]. The first edition, published in 1940, included 6,425 alphabetically arranged entries written by more than 1,000 contributors. Articles ranged from 50 to 5,000 words, depending on the subject. Well received by scholars, a 1-volume supplement was published in 1961 for the period 1940–1960. Work on a revised edition began in 1970 with Louise Ketz as managing editor. As it is currently revised, the dictionary contains some 7,200 entries including 500 new ones and 300 revisions compiled by 800 scholars. All entries are signed and have a short list of additional readings. The 503-page index provides detailed access to the entire text. There is a long list of errata in the index volume. Despite the absence of any maps or charts, this is an invaluable source and the most frequently consulted for general questions about American history. An abridged version of this multivolume set was first issued by Scribner in 1962 under the title *Concise Dictionary of American History* and updated in 1983. The *Scribner Desk Dictionary of American History* is based on the bicentennial edition.

398. *Encyclopedia of American History.* Edited by Richard B. Morris. 6th ed. New York: Harper & Row, 1982. 1,285p. Index. ISBN 0-06-181605-1.

First published in 1953, this classic work is widely viewed as the best one-volume reference book on American history. The sixth edition covers events from the age of discovery to December 1981. Comprehensive in scope, the encyclopedia is divided into 4 sections. Part 1 is a basic chronology of major political and military events. Social, economic, constitutional, and cultural events are dealt with in Part 2. Part 3 is a minibiographical dictionary of 500 notable Americans, and the structure of the federal government forms the focus of Part 4. Lists of presidents and their cabinets, party strengths in Congress, the text of the Declaration of Independence, and a detailed index complete this enduring reference work.

399. *Encyclopedia of American Political History: Studies of the Principal Movements and Ideas.* Edited by Jack P. Greene. New York: Scribner, 1984. 3 vols. Index. ISBN 0-684-17003-5.

Unlike other historical encyclopedias that strive for comprehensive coverage, the intent of the editors of this set was to provide detailed coverage of a selected list of important topics in American political history. Some 90 topics are described in lengthy essays by some 90 scholars. Following a 25-page review of the historiography of American political history by Richard Jensen, the essays are arranged alphabetically, proceeding from agricultural policy to women's rights. Each essay includes a lengthy bibliography and numerous cross-references. Volume 3 contains a detailed index. Similar in arrangement and conception are Glenn Porter, ed., *Encyclopedia of American Economic History: Studies of Principal Movements and Ideas,* 3 vols. (New York: Scribner, 1980), and Alexander DeConde, ed., *Encyclopedia of American Foreign Policy: Studies of the Principal Movements and Ideas,* 3 vols. (New York: Scribner, 1978).

400. *The Encyclopedia of Southern History.* Edited by David C. Poller and Robert W. Twyman. Baton Rouge: Louisiana State University, 1979. 1,421p. Index. ISBN 0-8071-0575-9.

This volume was the first and remains the best of the regional encyclopedias of American history. It includes more than 2,900 articles from 1,100 contributors, including most of the leading scholars of southern history. The editors define the South for the purposes of this volume as encompassing the District of Columbia and all the states in which slavery was legal in 1860. There are lengthy articles on each of the southern states including notes on their geography, history, and politics. Charts list governors, and population data is provided from the decennial censuses. Several hundred biographical sketches highlight the careers of notable southerners. Alphabetically arranged, most articles are signed and include bibliographies. There are 36 maps, which are generally small and difficult to read, and 72 charts. An excellent complement is provided by Charles Regan Wilson et al., *Encyclopedia of Southern Culture* (Chapel Hill: University of North Carolina Press, 1989).

401. *Encyclopedia of the American Constitution.* Edited by Leonard Levy, Kenneth L. Karst, and Dennis Mahoney. New York: Macmillan, 1986. 4 vols. Index. ISBN 0-02-918620-X.

Winner of the Dartmouth Medal as the outstanding reference work of 1987, it is the best of a spate of new reference books published to commemorate the bicentennial of the United States Constitution. It includes 2,200 signed original articles from 262 leading constitutional scholars in an alphabetical arrangement. Each has a short bibliography, and cross-references are indicated in boldface. Topics cover constitutional history, people, Supreme Court cases, concepts and terms, and public acts. Volume 1 contains alphabetical lists of all the articles and of the contributors and their contributions. A variety of appendixes complements the text and includes the Articles of Confederation, the Constitution, a chronology of the framing of the Constitution, a list of important events in the development of American constitutional law, and a glossary of legal terms. Indexes include a case index, a personal-name index, and a subject index.

By Chronological Periods

Colonial and Revolutionary

402. *The Encyclopedia of Colonial and Revolutionary America.* Edited by John Faragher. New York: Facts on File, 1989. 448p. ISBN 0-8160-1744-1.

This is the first scholarly one-volume encyclopedia of the colonial period of American history. It includes approximately 1,500 alphabetically arranged entries, which focus on all of the people and key events that affected the area that later became the United States. Coverage ranges from early Norse explorations by Eric the Red and Leif Eriksson to the end of the American Revolution. While the coverage is most complete for the 13 English colonies, there are entries for Spanish explorers and officials in Louisiana, Texas, and New Mexico; French explorers and officials in Canada and Louisiana; and Russian trading companies in Alaska. Extensive coverage is given to women and native Americans. The majority of entries were written by the editor and contain lists of additional readings. While not a perfect reference source, it provides useful information not available elsewhere about many colonial figures.

403. *Encyclopedia of the American Revolution*. By Mark Mayo Boatner III. Bicentennial ed. New York: David McKay, 1974. 1,290p. ISBN 0-679-50440-0.

First published in 1966, this is the most detailed one-volume encyclopedia of the American Revolution. Its focus is biographical sketches, but detailed coverage of battles and issues is also included. Primary emphasis is given to events in the 13 American colonies with only a few entries on the role of Spain in Louisiana and Florida. Boatner wrote all of the entries, and the 1974 edition contains minimal changes. Many of the articles are lengthy, and a few contain short lists of additional readings. Numerous charts and maps of battles supplement the text. The bibliography is very dated, and the book lacks a good index.

Nineteenth Century

404. *Dictionary of Afro-American Slavery*. Edited by Randall M. Miller and John David Smith. Westport, CT: Greenwood, 1988. 866p. Index. ISBN 0-313-23814-6.

In preparation since 1982, this outstanding reference work is the first comprehensive reference source on Afro-American slavery. Its alphabetical arrangement contains almost 300 lengthy topical articles written and signed by 230 contributors, many of whom are distinguished historians of slavery. Each article includes a select bibliography. The United States forms the principal focus, although there are articles on African and Afro-American cultures, slave resistance, and religion that transcend national boundaries. Chronological coverage extends from the first English settlements in the seventeenth century to Reconstruction in the midnineteenth century. There is a helpful chronology of Afro-American slavery in an appendix.

405. *The Historical Times Illustrated Encyclopedia of the Civil War*. Edited by Particia L. Faust et al. New York: Harper & Row, 1986. 849p. ISBN 0-06-181261-7.

Consisting of about 2,100 entries for persons, places, events, institutions, and things connected with the American Civil War, this encyclopedia is truly impressive. The entries are arranged alphabetically and signed by the contributors, who are specialists in the period. This work is superior to the 1959 classic Mark Boatner, *The Civil War Dictionary* (New York: David McKay, rev. ed., 1988). An excellent biographical complement is the widely praised Stewart Sifakis, *Who Was Who in the Civil War* (New York: Facts on File, 1988).

Twentieth Century

406. *Dictionary of the Vietnam War.* Edited by James S. Olson. Westport, CT: Greenwood, 1988. 593p. Index. ISBN 0-313-24943-1.

This is the best of several recent reference works on the Vietnam War. Olson and 28 contributors have written a series of brief descriptive essays on the major players, legislation, military operations, and other important aspects of U.S. participation in the war. Coverage is generally balanced, and the articles are signed and include brief lists of additional readings. A series of demographic appendixes provides data on Vietnam and its ethnic groups. There is a helpful glossary of slang expressions and acronyms from the period, a chronology of the war from 1945 to 1975, and a selected bibliography. Also useful is Harry Summer's *Vietnam War Almanac* (New York: Facts on File, 1988).

407. *The Harry S Truman Encyclopedia.* Edited by Richard S. Kirkendall. Boston: G. K. Hall, 1989. 368p. Index. ISBN 0-8161-8915-3.

The second in G. K. Hall's Presidential Enyclopedia series [*see* 408], this work consists of 300 biographical and topical articles written by leading scholars that deal with virtually every aspect of Truman's life and times. Principal attention is given to the years 1945–1952. It includes numerous quick reference features such as charts and chronologies and dozens of contemporary photographs, posters, and political cartoons.

408. *Historical Dictionary of the New Deal: From Inauguration to Preparation for War.* Edited by James S. Olson. Westport, CT: Greenwood, 1985. 611p. Index. ISBN 0-313-23873-1.

The major focus of this dictionary is on domestic events in the United States from 1933 to 1940. Some 700 brief descriptive essays by 50 contributors are alphabetically arranged and describe the key people, agencies, and legislation of the New Deal. Appendixes provide a chronology of the New Deal, a list of key personnel, a bibliography of New Deal programs, and a table of common acronyms used to describe the New Deal agencies. Of related interest and with a broader scope is Otis L. Graham, Jr., ed., *Franklin D. Roosevelt, His Life and Times: An Encyclopedic View* (Boston: G. K. Hall, 1985).

409. *Historical Dictionary of the 1920s: From World War I to the New Deal, 1919–1933.* By James S. Olson. Westport, CT: Greenwood, 1988. 420p. Index. ISBN 0-313-25683-7.

Focusing on the Roaring Twenties, this work contains some 700 short, alphabetically arranged entries on prominent individuals ranging from politicians to playwrights, important legal cases, key legislation, and major social issues. There is a 12-page chronology and a lengthy bibliography at the end of the volume. The index is largely geared to proper names.

410. *Historical Dictionary of the Progressive Era, 1890–1920*. Edited by John D. Buenker and Edward Kantowicz. Westport, CT: Greenwood, 1988. 599p. Index. 0-313-24309-3.

Defining the Progressive Era as a broad-gauged response by Americans to the emergence of the U.S. as a modern industrial power during 1890–1919, this helpful dictionary includes 800 signed, alphabetically arranged entries from almost 200 contributors. The entries include important persons, events, and institutions; such subjects as the Boy Scouts of America; and notable films like *Birth of a Nation*. There is a helpful chronology and three separate indexes to names, publications, and subjects.

Ethnic

411. *Dictionary of Asian American History*. Edited by Hyung-Chan Kim. Westport, CT: Greenwood, 1986. 627p. Index. ISBN 0-313-23760-3.

This is the first comprehensive reference work to focus exclusively on Asian Americans, one of the United States' most rapidly growing ethnic minorities. It is divided into two major sections: essays and short entries. The first section consists of seven essays on the historical development of different ethnic groups from Asia and the Pacific Islands and eight essays on the place of these groups in the American social order. Contributors include historians, sociologists, and Asian-studies specialists. Eight hundred short entries written by the editor make up the second section. These focus on the historical experiences of the Chinese, Japanese, Koreans, Asian Indians, Filipinos, and various Southeast Asians. The entries highlight topics such as associations, legislation, companies, and important individuals concerned with the Asian American experience and include suggestions for additional readings. Appendixes include a select bibliography, a chronology, and 1980 census data.

412. *Dictionary of Mexican American History*. By Matt S. Meier and Feliciano Rivera. Westport, CT: Greenwood, 1981. 498p. Index. ISBN 0-313-21203-1.

Although covering the entire range of the Mexican American experience in the region of the present-day United States, the principal focus is on the period after 1835. Entries for the period 1519–1835 largely concentrate on individuals and events connected with the exploration and settlement of northern New Spain. Alphabetically arranged, the approximately 1,000 entries written by the 2 editors and 20 contributors highlight virtually every aspect of the Mexican American experience, including prominent individuals, treaties, major migrations, legislation, literature, folklore, and special terms like "braceros" and "undocumented." These are followed by a short bibliography, a chronology, a glossary of Chicano terms, census data (now somewhat dated), a list of Mexican American journals, and a series of maps. This volume is complemented by the same authors' *Mexican American Biographies: A Historical Dictionary, 1836–1987* [see 531].

413. *Harvard Encyclopedia of American Ethnic Groups.* Edited by Stephen Thernstrom. Cambridge, MA: Belknap Press of Harvard University Press, 1980. 1,076p. ISBN 0-674-37512-2.

Using a broad definition of "ethnicity," this encyclopedia includes 106 group entries and 29 thematic essays written by 120 contributors. Some of the essays are exhaustive and focus on the following topics concerning the ethnic group: origins, migration, arrival, settlements, economic life, social structure, social organization, family and kinship, behavior, culture, religion, education, politics, intergroup relations, group maintenance, and individual ethnic commitment. Each essay is signed and includes a brief bibliography of reference and secondary studies. An excellent complement is provided by *We the People: An Atlas of America's Ethnic Diversity* [see 564].

414. *The Negro Almanac: A Reference Work on the African American.* 5th ed. Compiled and edited by Harry A. Ploski and James Williams. Detroit: Gale, 1989. 1,600p. Index. ISBN 0-8103-7706-3.

Thoroughly revised and updated, the fifth edition of this acclaimed reference work focuses primarily on history, statistics, and biography. It also contains a directory of key names and addresses. The 33 chapters highlight key aspects of the Afro-American experience, including a historical chronology, significant documents, essays on the black family, data on employment and education, a compilation of black firsts, and biographical information on black Americans from every walk of life. This is the most complete one-volume source on its subject. *See also* W. Augustus Low, ed., *Encyclopedia of Black America* (New York: McGraw-Hill, 1981).

United Kingdom and Ireland

415. *Cambridge Historical Encyclopedia of Great Britain and Ireland.*
Edited by Christopher Haigh. New York: Cambridge University
Press, 1985. 392p. Index. ISBN 0-521-25559-7.

Chronologically organized, this helpful encyclopedia functions as
both a general history and a historical dictionary of the British Isles.
Some 60 contributors provided entries arranged in 7 chronological
sections from the Roman occupation to 1975. Each section consists
of an introduction followed by several articles on topics such as
government, society, and economics during that particular period of
history. Geographical coverage includes England, Scotland, Wales,
and Ireland. Numerous maps and diagrams, an alphabetical "Who's
Who," and excellent photographs complement the text of this concise general guide.

416. *A Dictionary of British History.* Edited by J. P. Kenyon. New York:
Stein and Day, 1983. 410p. ISBN 0-8128-2910-7.

This useful handbook of British history includes 3,000 alphabetically
arranged entries from prehistory up to 1970. Its geographical scope
includes Great Britain, Ireland, and the British Empire and Commonwealth. Among the various subject entries are key terms,
important places, significant events, and prominent people.
Biographical entries include not only important politicians but also
those individuals who made their contributions in the arts and
sciences. Individual entries are unsigned and generally short. Also
useful are Arthur Marwick, *The Illustrated Dictionary of British History* (New York: Thames and Hudson, 1980) and S. H. Steinberg and
I. H. Evans, eds., *Steinberg's Dictionary of British History,* 2d ed. (New
York: St. Martin's Press, 1970), a revision of *A New Dictionary of
British History.* An excellent but more specialized volume is Ben
Weinreb and Christopher Hibbert, eds. *The London Encyclopedia*
(London: Macmillan, 1984).

417. *A Dictionary of Irish History Since 1800.* By D. J. Hickey and J. E.
Doherty. Totowa, NJ: Barnes & Noble, 1981. 615p. ISBN 0-389-20160-X.

This was the first dictionary devoted solely to Irish history. Brief
quarter-page entries focus on political events, social affairs, literature, the arts, folk customs, religious developments, economics, and
population. The bulk of the entries, however, are biographical.
Cross-references are indicated by asterisks. The cabinets of the

various governments administering the Republic of Ireland between 1919 and 1977 are listed, as are the governments of Northern Ireland from 1921 to 1972 under a separate heading.

418. *A Dictionary of Scottish History.* By Gordon Donaldson and Robert S. Morpeth. Edinburgh: John Donald, 1977. 234p. ISBN 0-85976-018-9.

Containing more than 5,000 very brief entries, the book is comprehensive for events, civil and ecclesiastical institutions, titles, and offices. It is more selective for other areas. Some entries are almost too brief to be helpful, and no criteria for inclusion are mentioned. There is a brief chronology of Scottish history from 843 to 1707. A companion volume is the same authors' *Who's Who in Scottish History* (New York: Barnes & Noble, 1973).

Canada

419. *The Canadian Encyclopedia.* 2d ed. Edmonton: Hurtig, 1988. 4 vols. Index. ISBN 0-88830-326-2.

The first edition of this work was published in 1985 to widespread acclaim. The second edition is significantly expanded, with 1,700 new articles bringing the total number of entries to almost 10,000. Statistical data has been updated to include the 1986 census returns. All entries are signed and include a list of additional readings. Approximately 2,500 people, including academics, journalists, and bureaucrats, contributed to this work.

420. *The Collins Dictionary of Canadian History: 1867 to the Present.* By David J. Bercuson and J. L. Granatstein. Toronto: Collins, 1988. 270p. ISBN 0-00-217758-7.

Students of Canadian history since Confederation will be well served by this helpful one-volume dictionary. The combined talents of two of Canada's most prominent historians have produced some 1,600 entries with abundant cross-references. There are helpful time lines and many black-and-white illustrations. Various appendixes list the governors-general, prime ministers, and all provincial premiers (in chronological order by province), along with lists of principal imports and exports and other economic data.

Europe

Ancient

421. *Civilization of the Ancient Mediterranean: Greece and Rome.* Edited by Michael Grant and Rachel Kitzinger. New York: Scribner's, 1988. 3 vols. Index. ISBN 0-684-17594-0.

Like the similar sets for American history, this publication includes 97 lengthy essays arranged under 14 broad headings such as government and society, private and social life, and history. The latter is the focus of the two historical summaries on Greece and Rome. While it lacks short definitions and brief entries, the useful index makes it easy to locate information on the most frequently discussed topics of Greek and Roman history. Specialized essays describe virtually every topic of historical debate from slavery to attitudes toward birth control.

422. *Encyclopedia of Early Christianity.* Edited by Everett Ferguson et al. New York: Garland, 1990. 1,000p. ISBN 0-8240-5745-7.

This one-volume survey of the first six centuries of the Christian faith includes more than 900 signed entries from 100 scholars, ranging in length from a few paragraphs to 4,000-word essays. Articles describe doctrines, institutions, events, practices of worship, heresies, and prominent leaders and thinkers of the Church as well as pagans who had a major impact on the development of Christianity.

423. *The Oxford History of the Classical World.* Edited by John Boardman et al. New York: Oxford University Press, 1986. 882p. Index. ISBN 0-19-872112-9.

The reviewer for the *New York Times Book Review* suggested that this work should actually be titled the "Oxford Discussion of Classical History." In fact, it gives history no greater prominence than philosophy or literature. There are three general sections: Greece, Greece and Rome (covering the Hellenistic era and the Roman Republic), and Rome (dealing with the first three centuries of the Roman Empire). The 32 individually authored chapters survey antiquity from Homer to the fall of Rome. About a third of the chapters focus on history. These include essays on Archaic Greece, Classical Hellas, the Hellenistic Kingdoms, early Rome and Italy, and Roman expansion. The helpful index makes it easy to locate information on key events or themes. See also N. G. L. Hammond and H. H. Scullard's venerable *Oxford Classical Dictionary*, 2d ed. (Oxford: Clarendon Press, 1970); Michael Ari-Yonah and Israel Shatzman's *Illustrated Encyclopedia of the Classical World* (New York: Harper & Row, 1976); and the second edition of *The Oxford Companion to Classical Literature*, edited by M. C. Howatson (Oxford: Oxford University Press, 1989).

Medieval/Middle Ages

424. *Dictionary of the Middle Ages.* Edited by Joseph R. Strayer. New York: Charles Scribner's Sons, 1982–1989. 12 vols. ISBN 0-684-16760-3.

This magnificent multivolume reference work on the Middle Ages was completed in late 1988, shortly after the death of the editor in 1987. Alphabetically arranged, the 5,000 entries are divided into volumes averaging about 600 pages each. While definitions and identifications average less than 100 words in length, some of the major articles extend to 10,000 words. Each article is signed and includes a short list of recent works. The majority of the contributors were American and Canadian academics, although there were also many from European institutions. The chronological scope of this set extends from A.D. 500 to 1500. Its principal geographical focus is on the Latin West, the Slavic world, Asia Minor, the Islamic Middle East, and Muslim and Christian North Africa. Other useful but briefer sources include H. R. Lyon, *The Middle Ages: A Concise Encyclopedia* (London: Thames and Hudson, 1989); Aryen Grabois, *The Illustrated Encyclopedia of Medieval Civilization* (Mayflower, 1980); and Joseph Dalmus, *Dictionary of Medieval Civilization* (New York: Macmillan, 1984).

Renaissance/Reformation

425. *Encyclopedia of the Renaissance.* Edited by Thomas Bergin and Jennifer Speake. New York: Facts on File, 1987. 496p. ISBN 0-8160-1315-2.

The Renaissance has been less well served by historical dictionaries than the Middle Ages. Bergin and Speake's is the best of several one-volume reference works. It includes 2,500 alphabetically arranged entries describing people, events, ideas, and movements during the fourteenth through the sixteenth centuries. Generally it is quite comprehensive in its coverage, although English topics are slighted. Literature, philosophy, religion, art, science, music, architecture, and exploration are all well covered. There are also more

than 100 lavish color and black-and-white illustrations. For a more
specialized work there is J. R. Hale's *A Concise Encyclopedia of the
Italian Renaissance* (New York: Oxford University Press, 1981).

426. *The Penguin Dictionary of English and European History, 1485–
1789.* By E. N. Williams. New York: Penguin, 1980. 509p. Index.

Although this dictionary consists of only about 500 entries, it is
packed full of information on European history from 1485 to 1789.
Individual entries are limited to major subjects and provide detailed
accounts of people's careers, wars, institutions, groups, and concepts. Political, military, and diplomatic history topics predominate.
A detailed index allows more-specialized topics to be located within
larger entries. This inexpensive volume is a useful addition to any
ready-reference collection or scholar's study.

Modern

General

427. *The Penguin Dictionary of Modern History, 1789–1945.* 2d ed. By
Alan Palmer. New York: Penguin, 1983. 315p. ISBN 0-14-051-125-3.

This bargain-priced standard dictionary of recent history is a useful
addition to any historian's library. One reviewer called it a sort of
mini-encyclopedia of persons, events, and keywords. The second
edition adds 100 new entries on North America and Australia in an
attempt to balance the British and European emphasis of the first
edition. Generally the engagingly written entries deal with political
and military history. A companion volume is the same author's
Penguin Dictionary of Twentieth-Century History, 2d ed. (New York:
Penguin, 1983), which originally appeared as *The Facts on File Dictionary of 20th Century History* (New York: Facts on File, 1979). Also
useful is Chris Cook and John Stevenson's *The Longman Handbook of
Modern European History, 1763–1985* (New York: Longman, 1987).

By Region/Country

FRANCE

428. *Critical Dictionary of the French Revolution.* Edited by François
Furet and Mona Ozouf. Cambridge: Harvard University Press, 1989.
1,604p. Index. ISBN 0-674-17728-2.

Two leading members of the revisionist school on the history of the
French Revolution, both professors at the Ecole des Hautes Etudes

in Paris, have put together this very provocative new reference work. Published in France in 1988, it became something of an academic best-seller. Neither exhaustive nor encyclopedic, its entries are divided into 5 sections: Events, Actors, Institutions and Creations, Ideas, and Historians. Each lengthy entry corresponds to an important event or ideal of the French Revolution. The entries are well written, discuss controversial aspects of the subject, include sources for further reading, and provide cross-references to related topics. Of the 99 entries, the editors wrote 43, while the remaining 46 were written by 22 other historians and philosophers, many from the Ecole des Hautes Etudes. Beautiful color illustrations and name and subject indexes complement the volume. Two other recent works on the same subject are John Paxton, *Companion to the French Revolution* (New York: Facts on File, 1988) and the particularly helpful Colin Jones, *Longman Companion to the French Revolution* (New York: Longman, 1988).

429. *Historical Dictionary of the French Revolution, 1789–1799.* Edited by Samuel F. Scott and Barry Rothaus. Westport, CT: Greenwood, 1985. 2 vols. ISBN 0-313-21141-8.

430. *Historical Dictionary of Napoleonic France, 1799–1815.* Edited by Owen Connelly. Westport, CT: Greenwood, 1985. 586p. ISBN 0-313-21321-6.

431. *Historical Dictionary of France from the 1815 Restoration to the Second Empire.* Edited by Edgar L. Newman and Robert L. Simpson. Westport, CT: Greenwood, 1987. 2 vols. ISBN 0-313-22751-9.

432. *Historical Dictionary of the French Second Empire, 1852–1870.* Edited by William E. Echard. Westport, CT: Greenwood, 1985. 829p. ISBN 0-313-21136-1.

433. *Historical Dictionary of the Third French Republic, 1870–1940.* Edited by Partick H. Hutton, Amanda S. Bourque, and Amy J. Staples. Westport, CT: Greenwood, 1986. 2 vols. ISBN 0-313-22080-8.

This outstanding series contains articles on a vast number of topics concerning French history, from the outbreak of the French Revolution in 1789 to the fall of the Third Republic in 1940. Entries within each set are arranged alphabetically, signed by the contributor, and include a brief up-to-date bibliography. There are numerous cross-references, and each set contains a separate index and a chronology of events. Contributors include both well-known scholars and younger professors from North America and Europe. Unlike many other historical dictionaries, political and military affairs do not predominate, so there is broad coverage of social history, literature, education, journalism, religion, and labor.

GERMANY

434. *Dictionary of German History, 1806–1945.* By Wilfred Fest. New York: St. Martin's, 1978. 189p. ISBN 0-86043-108-8.

Historical dictionaries of German history in English are a rare commodity. This one is a short, perfunctory, alphabetically arranged guide to the important people and events of modern German history. The editor is a professor of history at the Free University of Berlin. There are occasional lists of additional readings including many German-language sources. The volume has a brief chronology, but no index.

435. *Encyclopedia of the Third Reich.* By Louis L. Snyder. New York: McGraw-Hill, 1976. 410p. ISBN 0-07-059525-9.

Still the best of several reference works on the Third Reich, this encyclopedia was reissued in paperback by Paragon in 1989. Snyder is a German emigre teaching history at the City University of New York. He wrote all of the nearly 2,000 alphabetically arranged entries. Their scope includes people, events, ideas, social life, military organization, politics, and aspects of the war. Place-names are usually entered under the German word, with the English translation in parentheses. Numerous black-and-white illustrations, including photographs, drawings, maps, cartoons, organizational charts, and stamps, add to the book's appeal. There is a bibliography of some 800 books and articles that is now somewhat dated. Regrettably there is no index. A more up-to-date but less comprehensive work is *The Third Reich Almanac* (New York: World Almanac, 1987), James Tayler and Warren Shaw, eds.

436. *The Holy Roman Empire: A Dictionary Handbook.* Edited by Jonathan W. Zophy. Westport, CT: Greenwood, 1980. 551p. Index. ISBN 0-313-21457-3.

Voltaire is said to have quipped that the Holy Roman Empire was "neither Holy, nor Roman, nor an Empire," but it did endure from 800 to 1806 and encompassed much of central and southern Europe. Zophy, a historian at Carthage College, and some 30 American contributors have compiled approximately 500 entries on the important people and events of that empire. While the emphasis is on the biographical, there are ten histories of cities, along with essays on women, Jews, witchcraft, and wars. Entries average a page or more and include lists of works about and in some cases by the biographee. Appendixes include a list of emperors and their predecessor kings, a chronology, and a list of the rulers of the Hohenzollern dynasty. There is a short bibliography.

ITALY

437. *Dictionary of Modern Italian History.* Edited by Frank J. Coppa. Westport, CT: Greenwood, 1985. 496p. Index. ISBN 0-313-22983-X.

Dictionaries of modern Italian history are not common, but this one is excellent. Coppa, a historian at St. John's University, organized a notable group of American academics as consultants and contributors to create this volume. Coverage includes eighteenth-century Italy, the Risorgimento (1796–1861), Liberal Italy (1861–1922), Fascist Italy (1922–1945), and post-World War II Italy. Following brief introductions for these periods, the signed entries are arranged alphabetically. They range from 100 to 900 words in length and occasionally include lists of further readings. There are chronologies of important events, a long list of ministries since 1848, a list of presidents of the Italian Republic, a list of kings of Piedmont and Italy, and a short list of popes since 1700. More detailed and narrower in scope is Philip V. Cannistraro's *Historical Dictionary of Fascist Italy* (Westport, CT: Greenwood, 1982).

RUSSIA/SOVIET UNION

438. *Dictionary of the Russian Revolution.* Edited by George Jackson and Robert Devlin. Westport, CT: Greenwood, 1989. 704p. Index. ISBN 0-313-21131-0.

Although narrow in focus, this alphabetically arranged dictionary provides a wealth of information about the institutions, events, and personalities that influenced the course of the Russian Revolution of 1917. More than 100 contributors from the United States, Canada, Great Britain, France, Holland, and Australia wrote some 300 in-depth articles on social forces; political parties; prominent individuals; institutions, groups, and associations; significant events; regional and ethnic studies; and other important themes. Most articles are signed and include short bibliographies of monographs in English and Russian. Appendixes include a chronology of the Russian Revolution from 1898 to the death of Lenin in 1924, a series of maps, and census statistics for 1897 and 1926. *See also* Harold Shukman, ed., *The Blackwell Encyclopedia of the Russian Revolution* (New York: Basil Blackwell, 1988).

439. *Modern Encyclopedia of Russian and Soviet History.* Edited by Joseph Wieczynski. Gulf Breeze, FL: Academic International, 1976–1987. 46 vols. Supplements, 1987–. ISBN 0-87569-064-5.

This set makes available for the first time in English articles from a variety of Russian and Soviet reference works, including the *Soviet Historical Encyclopedia*, the *Great and Small Soviet Encyclopedias*, the *Brockhaus-Efron* and *Granat Encyclopedias*, the *Siberian Soviet Encyclopedia*, and the *Russian Biographical Dictionary*. While the majority of the articles are simply translations from the Russian, others are original contributions from North American scholars. Articles vary in length and quality. Some are signed and include lengthy bibliographies. Others are short, unsigned, and without additional sources. The main set ends in the middle of Volume 46. Supplements begin in Volume 46 and reached letter P with the publication of Volume 51 in 1989. Particularly useful are the lengthy series of articles on Russian and Soviet archives in Supplement 1. Other valuable sources are the magnificent translation of the third edition of the *Great Soviet Encyclopedia* (New York: Macmillan, 1973–1983), which must be used with the index volume, and the *Cambridge Encyclopedia of Russia and the Soviet Union* (New York: Cambridge University Press, 1982).

SCANDINAVIA

440. *Dictionary of Scandinavian History*. Edited by Byron J. Nordstrom. Westport, CT: Greenwood, 1986. 703p. Index. ISBN 0-313-22887-6.

This is the only English-language historical dictionary to focus on the countries of Denmark, Norway, Iceland, Sweden, and Finland. It includes some 400 signed, alphabetically arranged entries from about 70 contributors. Articles range in length from half a page to 12 pages, depending on the topic. Each is accompanied by a short list of additional readings. Appendixes include a bibliography of works in English; lists of monarchs, presidents, and prime ministers; and a chronology. Coverage is up-to-date through 1983.

SPAIN

441. *Historical Dictionary of Modern Spain, 1700–1988*. Edited by Robert W. Kern and Meredith D. Dodge. Westport, CT: Greenwood, 1990. 688p. Index. ISBN 0-313-25971-2.

Kern and Dodge, professors at the University of New Mexico, have assembled a cast of 70 scholars from the United States, Canada, Great Britain, Spain, and Latin America to provide the first modern, comprehensive reference work on Spanish history. The focus is on seven major areas: political, governmental, institutional, cultural, social, military, and diplomatic. Maps, illustrations, tables, an index, and a selected bibliography enhance the utility of the volume. Narrower in focus is James W. Cortada's *Historical Dictionary of the Spanish Civil War,*

1936–1939 (Westport, CT: Greenwood, 1982), which describes the key persons, places, organizations, and events of the Spanish Civil War.

Asia

General

442. Asian Historical Dictionaries Series. Metuchen, NJ: Scarecrow, 1989–.

In 1989 Scarecrow Press launched another series of historical dictionaries on Asia as a successor to its earlier Historical and Cultural Dictionaries of Asia series. Like its predecessor, it will consist of one-volume general, historical dictionaries on individual countries, prepared by a specialist. The first volume in the series is William J. Duiker's *Historical Dictionary of Vietnam*.

443. *Encyclopedia of Asian History.* Edited by Ainslie T. Embree. New York: Charles Scribner's Sons, 1988. 4 vols. Index. ISBN 0-684-18619-5.

Designed as an authoritative encyclopedia for nonspecialists, this acclaimed set focuses on Iran and central Asia, China, Japan, Korea, South Asia, and Southeast Asia. It excludes the U.S.S.R. except for the central Asian republics. Entries discuss people (living and dead), places, events, geographic features, ethnic groups, the arts, historical periods, and a variety of other subjects. Articles are signed, contain lists of additional readings, and are arranged alphabetically. The text is accompanied by more than 160 black-and-white illustrations and 60 maps. The fourth volume contains a detailed subject index, various special lists, and a topical outline of subjects. Since this publication uses the Pinyin rather than the Wade-Giles system of transliterating Chinese characters, a conversion table is included. With contributions from an international cast of scholars, this is the best general encyclopedia on Asian history.

By Country/Region

China

444. *Cambridge Encyclopedia of China.* Edited by Brian Hook. New York: Cambridge University Press, 1982. 492p. Index. ISBN 0-521-23099-3.

Like similar Cambridge encyclopedias focusing on a specific country or region, this volume is intended as a general introduction to the geography, history, and culture of China. About a third of the book is devoted to history from prehistoric times to 1980. Articles are generally short, initialed by the author, and often complemented by illustrations, maps, and dynastic charts. The 70 contributors largely come from universities in Great Britain and the United States. Peculiarly, the index is placed at the beginning of the volume rather than the end. Sources for further reading are presented in a topical index at the end of the volume. A more specialized work is the three-volume *Information China: The Comprehensive and Authoritative Reference Source of New China and Its Historical Background*, compiled and translated by the Chinese Academy of Social Sciences, edited for the Pergamon Press by C. V. James (Oxford and New York: Pergamon Press, 1988).

445. *Companion to Chinese History.* By Hugh B. O'Neill. New York: Facts on File, 1987. 397p. ISBN 0-87196-841-X.

With about 1,000 entries arranged in alphabetical order, this handbook is intended as a general reference work on the most popular topics in Chinese civilization from prehistory to the mid-1980s. Since traditional Chinese names are presented surname first and the given name last, all Chinese surnames are printed in upper-case letters to avoid confusion. Most names are rendered in the Wade-Giles system of transliteration. Some articles list sources for further reading. Appendixes include a short chronology from 1506 to 1985 and 12 maps. Also useful is Michael Dillon's *Dictionary of Chinese History* (Totowa, NJ: Frank Cass, 1979), which is similar in its coverage but does include some unique terms.

India

446. *The Cambridge Encyclopedia of India, Pakistan, Bangladesh, Sri Lanka, Nepal, Bhutan, and the Maldives.* Edited by Francis Robinson. New York: Cambridge University Press, 1989. 520p. Index. ISBN 0-521-33451-9.

This regional encyclopedia is intended as a general reference work on South Asia and includes chapters on such topics as land, peoples, history, politics, economies, religions, and culture. History is well covered from prehistoric times to the present, with numerous short signed articles by specialists. Dozens of black-and-white and color maps, numerous illustrations, and lists of major states and rulers supplement the text. Longer articles include lists of books for further reading. Smaller countries or regions like Sri Lanka, Nepal, Sikkim, Bhutan, and the Maldives are separately treated. This volume is one of the best of the Cambridge encyclopedias.

447. *A Dictionary of Modern Indian History, 1707–1947*. By Parshotam Mehra. New York: Oxford University Press, 1987. 823p. Index. ISBN 0-19-561552-2.

As the first historical dictionary to focus on modern Indian history, it covers the period from the death of the Mogul ruler Aurangzeb in 1707 to Indian independence in 1947. The some 400 alphabetically arranged entries focus on people, places, battles, movements, societies, treaties, political parties, and other important topics. Numerous historical maps and a complete list of British governors, governors-general, and viceroys of India complement this useful reference work. For an older work that covers the entire span of Indian history, there is Sachchidananda Bhattacharya's *A Dictionary of Indian History* (New York: George Braziller, 1967).

Japan

448. *Concise Dictionary of Modern Japanese History*. By Janet Hunter. Berkeley: University of California Press, 1984. 347p. ISBN 0-520-04390-1.

The focus of this brief dictionary is on the period from 1853, when Commodore Matthew Perry sailed into Uraga Bay, to 1980. Entries are arranged alphabetically with short lists of additional readings. Appendixes list era names (from Tenpo to Showa), emperors since 1817, population from 1872 to 1977, a time line on Japanese political parties, and Japanese cabinets since 1885. There is a glossary of Japanese words that commonly appear in English-language texts and a Japanese-English index (not a general index) arranged according to the number of strokes in the first character of the entry.

449. *Kodansha Encyclopedia of Japan*. Tokyo: Kodansha, 1983. 9 vols. and supplement. Index. ISBN 0-87011-620-7.

Developed in response to the need for a general reference work on Japan in English, this encyclopedia was a collaborative effort between 680 Japanese scholars and 527 scholars from 27 other countries. It contains more than 9,000 articles, including 123 major pieces of more than 3,500 words, 1,429 medium-length articles of 750 to 2,500 words, and 7,865 short entries of 50 to 500 words. Approximately 40 percent of the work was written in Japanese and then translated into English. Although it is intended as a general rather than a historical encyclopedia, history and biography are exceptionally well covered. The article on the history of Japan (almost 70,000 words) is the longest in the set. There are numerous maps, genealogical and other charts, and black-and-white illustrations. All articles are signed, and the longer ones include lists of additional readings. Volume 9 is the index for the set.

Middle East

450. *Cambridge Encyclopedia of the Middle East and North Africa.* Edited by Trevor Mostyn and Albert Hourani. New York: Cambridge University Press, 1988. 504p. Index. ISBN 0-520-32190-5.

Yet another of the excellent one-volume Cambridge regional encyclopedias, this volume includes signed articles from 82 Middle East specialists, primarily British but with contributions from some American and European scholars. It is topically organized into six chapters. Chapter 2 focuses on the region's history through 1939, while Chapter 5 describes the history and politics of particular countries since 1939. Longer articles are signed and include lists of additional readings. There are the usual high-quality color and black-and-white illustrations, maps, and dynastic charts.

451. *The Encyclopedia of Islam. New Edition.* Edited by E. Van Donzel, B. Lewis, and C. Pellat. Leiden, Netherlands: E. J. Brill, 1954– (in progress). ISBN 90-04-05745-5. *Index to Volumes I–V.* By H. and J. D. Pearson, 1988. 360p. ISBN 90-04-08849-0.

Encompassing the old Arabo-Islamic empire; the Islamic states of Iran, central Asia, the Indian subcontinent, and Indonesia; the Ottoman Empire; and the various Islamic states throughout the world, this is an entirely new edition of the most important English-language reference set on Islam. Five volumes covering up to "Mahi" had been published through 1989, along with an index and several supplements in fascicles. Some ten volumes are planned. Contributors include some of the world's leading Orientalists. Articles are signed with bibliographies and describe key people, events, places, institutions, religious beliefs, manners and customs, and the industries and sciences connected with various Islamic groups. There are many black-and-white maps done to scale, including some large foldouts, various genealogical and dynastic charts, and some black-and-white illustrations. Delays have caused some of the material in this set to be dated. Still useful is the *Encyclopedia of Islam: A Dictionary of the Geography, Ethnography and Biography of the*

Muhammadan Peoples, originally published between 1913 and 1936 in four volumes with supplements. It has been reprinted as the *First Encyclopaedia of Islam* (Leiden, Netherlands: E. J. Brill, 1987) in nine volumes. *See also* Cyril Glasse, *The Concise Encyclopedia of Islam* (San Francisco: Harper & Row, 1989).

Africa

452. African Historical Dictionaries Series. Edited by Jon Woronoff. Metuchen, NJ: Scarecrow, 1974–. 43 vols. In progress.

Each of these historical dictionaries treats an individual African country and provides in dictionary form the basic information on its geography, history, economy, prominent people, significant events, and institutions. All volumes contain bibliographies. Individual volumes in this series have been widely praised. The most recent volume in the series is the *Historical Dictionary of Zaire*, edited by F. Scott Bobb, appearing in 1988. Forthcoming volumes will cover Mozambique, Malawi, Botswana, and Tunisia. Some volumes have gone through second editions.

453. *Cambridge Encyclopedia of Africa*. Edited by Rolan Oliver and Michael Crowder. New York: Cambridge University Press, 1981. 492p. Index. ISBN 0-521-23096-9.

With a largely British contingent of approximately 100 contributors, this volume provides a general introduction to the history and culture of Africa. Almost a third of the encyclopedia is devoted to history, with sections on Africa before European colonization, European occupation, European rule 1919–1939, the struggle for independence, and the postindependence period. This last section is arranged alphabetically by country. All articles are signed. Black-and-white and color illustrations are numerous. There are a number of useful historical maps. The index comes at the beginning of the volume, and there is a list of books for additional reading at the end that is up-to-date through the late 1970s. For a contemporary guide to the recent history and politics of the southern African countries of Angola, Botswana, Lesotho, Malawi, Mozambique, Namibia, South Africa, Swaziland, Tanzania, Zambia, and Zimbabwe, see Gwyneth Williams and Brian Hackland's *The Dictionary of Contemporary Politics of Southern Africa* (New York: Macmillan, 1989).

Latin America

454. *The Cambridge Encyclopedia of Latin America and the Caribbean.* Edited by Simon Collier, Harold Blake, and Thomas E. Skidmore. New York: Cambridge University Press, 1985. 456p. Index. ISBN 0-521-26263-1.

This is an authoritative standard reference work that provides a broad overview of Latin America. Approximately one-third of the volume is devoted to history, which is divided into the following chronological sections: America before Columbus, the Colonial Period, the Struggle for Independence, Latin America since Independence, and the non-Latin Caribbean since 1815. All articles are signed and include short lists of additional readings. Numerous historical maps, black-and-white illustrations, and chronologies enhance this work. Perhaps more useful, although less current, is Helen Delpar's *Encyclopedia of Latin America* (New York: McGraw-Hill, 1974). Recent history is covered by Phil Gunson, Andrew Thompson, and Greg Chamberlain in *The Dictionary of Contemporary Politics of South America* (New York: Macmillan, 1989).

455. *Enciclopedia de Mexico.* 2d ed. Mexico: Secretaria de Educacion Publica, 1987–1988. 14 vols. ISBN 968-6234-00-4.

Since Mexico is among the countries most frequently studied by North American historians, this second edition updates a useful reference work. Although it is intended as a general Spanish-language encyclopedia devoted to Mexico, its greatest concentration is biographical and geographical. More than 5,000 biographical sketches of notable Mexicans, from the colonial period to the present, are included. Several detailed indexes in Volume 14 provide easy access to the text. The first is a standard alphabetical index to persons, places, and topics. A second classified index arranges entries by subject from academies to vocabulary. Finally, a third index classifies biographical entries by occupation. Included are almost 500 sketches of prominent historians of Mexico, including some American Mexicanists.

456. Latin American Historical Dictionaries Series. Edited by A. Curtis Wilgus, Karna S. Wilgus, and Laurence Hallewell. Metuchen, NJ: Scarecrow, 1970–.

Designed as convenient source books of historical and contemporary facts and statistics for the various nations of Latin America, each book deals with a single country. The first 21 volumes in the series were edited by A. Curtis Wilgus. Volume 22 on Cuba, by Jaime Suchlicki, was published in 1988 to very favorable reviews. Other volumes vary in quality and completeness. A second edition of the *Historical Dictionary of Chile*, by Salvatore Bizzaro, was published in 1987, and other updated editions are in progress.

Australia, New Zealand, and Oceania

457. *Australians: A Historical Library*. Fairfax, Syme, & Weldon Associates. Distributed by New York: Cambridge University Press, 1988. 11 vols. Index. ISBN 0-521-34073-X.

Some 400 of Australia's leading historians, economists, archaeologists, geographers, librarians, and journalists contributed to this major historical work, published in honor of the bicentennial of European settlement in Australia. The set consists of 5 historical volumes that examine Australian history in 50-year intervals beginning with 1788, followed by 6 reference volumes. The reference volumes include "A Guide to Sources," "Events and Places," "A Historical Dictionary," "Historical Statistics," and an index volume. The most useful for general historical reference are Volume VIII, "Events and Places," and Volume IX, "A Historical Dictionary." The former is a combination chronology and gazetteer, which provides a guide to the most important and interesting happenings in Australian history, along with a summary history of more than 700 cities, towns, and geographical features. The latter has more than 1,000 entries on people, movements, ideas, and institutions that have shaped Australia's past.

458. *Bateman New Zealand Encyclopedia*. 2d ed. Edited by Gordon McLauchlan. Auckland: David Bateman, 1987. 640p. Index. ISBN 0-908610-21-1.

An updated version of the first edition published in 1984, this work was designed to be a popular yet authoritative one-volume country reference work. Its arrangement is alphabetical, and all articles are written by the editor. Many include illustrations. There are no bibliographies or lists of additional readings and no historical maps. The brief subject index lists entries by topic, but without page numbers. A selective chronology of New Zealand history is included in the appendix. There is a list of prime ministers under that name in the regular dictionary sequence.

459. *Historical Dictionary of Oceania*. Edited by Robert D. Craig and Frank P. King. Westport, CT: Greenwood, 1981. 392p. Index. ISBN 0-313-21060-8.

Despite the general title, the focus of this historical dictionary is mainly on the European penetration of the islands. Some 500 signed entries from 200 scholars are alphabetically arranged and vary in length from 250 to 4,000 words. It provides broad coverage of geographical features, personalities, politics, and education. There are the usual Greenwood appendixes, along with a bibliography and a name and subject index. This is currently the only reference work on this region.

10.

Biographical Sources

Biographical information is particularly useful and important to students of history. Not surprisingly, some of the most heavily used reference works are those supplying details about the lives of people. Collective works of biography can be current, written about living persons; retrospective, documenting the lives of deceased persons; or a combination of the two. It is also worth noting that some older editions of biographical reference works, like many of the "Who's Who" type of publication, can be quite valuable to historians even though they are out-of-date for current usage. This chapter lists those biographical reference works that are essential aids to students of history, along with a selection of more specialized works selected for their outstanding quality or their unique approach, or because they represent a common type of work.

Bibliographies

460. *ARBA Guide to Biographical Dictionaries*. Edited by Bohdan S. Wynar. Littleton, CO: Libraries Unlimited, 1986. 444p. Index. LC 86-2851. ISBN 0-87287-492-3.

American Reference Books Annual (ARBA) is well known as a source for short, authoritative reviews of current reference books of all types for nearly 20 years. This one-volume work contains entries for 718 biographical dictionaries taken largely from previous volumes of *ARBA*. The guide is divided into 23 chapters ranging from "Universal Sources" to various specialized chapters covering biographical dictionaries in the fields of "Literature," "Performing Arts," and "Sports." Each chapter begins with a short introduction that outlines some of the older biographical works as well as important current reference works. The individual entries include detailed annotations that describe and evaluate the work, along with useful comparisons to similar reference works. There is an author/title index and a detailed subject index. Although this work only deals with biographical reference works published in the past 17 years, its particular value is that it highlights the best among them. A similar work that includes the most important older works is *Biographical Sources: A Guide to Dictionaries and Reference Works*, compiled by Diane J. Cimbala, Jennifer Cargill, and Brian Alley (Phoenix, AZ: Oryx Press, 1986), which has 687 entries with detailed annotations.

461. *Biographical Books, 1876–1949*. New York: Bowker, [1983]. 1,768p.

462. *Biographical Books, 1950–1980: Vocation Index; Name/Subject Index; Author Index; Title Index; Biographical Books in Print Index*. New York: Bowker, [1980]. 1,557p. ISBN 0-8352-1315-3.

These two volumes basically can be characterized as the "Books that Were in Print" on biographical subjects in the United States, since most of the listings can no longer be purchased. Compiled out of the data base used in the publication of *American Book Publishing Record*, the two volumes list any book of a biographical or autobiographical nature. Individual entries supply the same type of biographical information found in *Books in Print*, along with additional subject classifications. The main listing is a name/subject index in which most of the entries are listed by the person's name. There are also separate vocation, author, and title indexes. The large number of works listed in these volumes makes them worth consulting for exhaustive searches.

463. *Biographical Dictionaries and Related Works: An International Bibliography of More Than 16,000 Collective Biographies, Bio-Bibliographies, Collections of Epitaphs, Selected Genealogical Works, Dictionaries of Anonyms and Pseudonyms, Historical and Specialized Dictionaries, Biographical Materials in Government Manuals, Bibliographies of Biography, Biographical Indexes, and Selected Portrait Catalogs*. 2d ed. Edited by Robert B. Slocum. Detroit: Gale, 1986. 2 vols. Index. LC 85-8163. ISBN 0-8103-0234-8.

The second edition of the eminently useful *Biographical Dictionaries* substantially cumulates and updates the first edition. It contains 4,000 new items in its total listings of 16,000. As the title indicates, it is more than an annotated bibliography of biographical dictionaries. Large numbers of related materials are also listed, making it very comprehensive in its coverage. Generally, a work has to contain 100 or more biographies to be included, and the entries must be more than a simple listing of names.

The entries are arranged in three major sections: "Universal Biography," including general works having wide range and scope of chronology, geography, or subject; "National or Area Biography," covering specific countries or regions; and "Biographies by Vocation," listing materials on specific professions and occupations. Within these broad categories many subheadings further divide the work. Entries are listed alphabetically by author or sometimes by title if that is applicable. They contain full bibliographical information, and the annotations are kept as brief as possible, while still providing an accurate and useful description. There are separate, detailed indexes for authors, titles, and subjects.

Biographical Dictionaries is well worth consulting by both beginning and advanced researchers in history. Obviously, the updated second edition is to be preferred, but the first edition and its two supplements (1972 and 1978) are still useful.

464. *Who's Whos: An International Guide to Sources of Current Biographical Information.* By Mary A. Farrell. (METRO Miscellaneous Publication No. 21) New York: New York Metropolitan Reference and Research Library Agency, 1979. 102p.

The classic *Who's Who* of Great Britain has been widely imitated, and due to its great usefulness, that imitation continues. Mary Farrell's guide lists the numerous "Who's Who" type of publications in many parts of the world that existed in 1979, excluding the familiar publications for Canada, Great Britain, and the United States. The compilation is divided into two sections: regional biographical dictionaries and individual country biographical dictionaries. The individual entries list author, title, and standard publishing information and are followed by a description and evaluation of the work, including the type of biographical information, coverage, arrangement, and special features. This useful list needs to be updated, since new current biographical works and new editions of existing works are continually being published.

Indexes

465. *Biography and Genealogy Master Index: A Consolidated Index to More Than 3,200,000 Biographical Sketches.* 2d ed. Edited by Miranda C. Herbert and Barbara McNeil. Detroit: Gale, 1980. 8 vols. ISBN 0-8103-1094-5. With annual supplements.

466. Cumulations: *Biography and Genealogy Master Index: 1981–85 Cumulation.* Edited by Barbara McNeil. Detroit: Gale, 1985. 5 vols. ISBN 0-8103-1506-8. *Biography and Genealogy Master Index: 1986–1990 Cumulation.* Detroit: Gale, 1990. 3 vols. ISBN 0-8103-4803-9.

The most useful reference work for biographical research is the *Biography and Genealogy Master Index.* It should be the first work consulted. Basically, the set is an index to the contents of hundreds of current and retrospective biographical reference works. Instead of guessing which specific works contain needed information, the *BGMI* supplies the researcher with an exact location or locations. Furthermore, if it does not contain a listing, there is a good chance that no such listing exists. Names are listed alphabetically and often include the dates of birth and death. Each entry then lists, in abbreviated form, those books of biographical reference that contain information on the individual. Unfortunately, some entries do not supply birth and death dates, making it hard to differentiate between individuals sharing a common name. In addition, some people may be listed in several locations if their name was not listed in the same form by different reference works. These problems are minor, however, when compared with the usefulness of this reference book. This work is also available for on-line searching as Biography Master Index on DIALOG files 287 and 288, which contain more than 3.5 million entries. Some libraries may hold only the much smaller *Biography Almanac,* edited by Annie Brewer (Detroit: Gale, 1981). Other, more specialized publications in the Gale Biographical Index Series simply draw their information from the larger *BGMI* data base.

467. *Biography Index; a Cumulative Index to Biographical Materials in Books and Magazines.* New York: H. W. Wilson, 1947–. Vol. 1–. ISSN 0006-3053.

Biography Index is part of the H. W. Wilson Company's series of indexes, but besides indexing some 2,600 periodicals, it also indexes monographs for biographical information along with works of collective biography. The main index is arranged alphabetically by surname with vital dates, nationality, and occupation, followed by citations to relevant periodicals and books. There is an additional detailed index to professions and occupations and separate listings of the periodicals and books covered by the index. Since it is published quarterly, it is a source of up-to-date biographical indexing. Annual and three-year cumulations help to ease the task of retrospective searching, and beginning in 1984, the index has been available on compact disc through WilsonDISC and on-line through Wilsonline. This is an excellent source to use when beginning a biographical research project.

468. *The New York Times Obituaries Index, 1858–1968.* New York: New York Times, 1970. 1,135p.

469. *The New York Times Obituaries Index II, 1968–1978.* New York: New York Times, 1980. 131p.

These two volumes list 353,000 and 36,000 obituaries respectively, including those of many non-Americans, that appeared in the *New York Times* from September 1858 to December 1978. Since obituaries are an important source of biographical information about well-known as well as lesser-known people, this is an extremely valuable source. The second volume actually reprints 50 obituaries of certain well-known individuals. Volume 1 simply lists the name and the newspaper citation for the obituary; in Volume 2 there is an additional notation as to whether the death occurred as a result of natural causes or otherwise (for instance, by violence). Another convenient source for obituaries from the late 1940s through 1978 is *Obituaries on File*, edited by Felice D. Levy (New York: Facts on File, [1979]) in two volumes. For another source of original obituaries, *see* Patricia Burgess, ed., *The Annual Obituary* (Chicago: St. James Press, 1980–).

470. *People in History: An Index to U.S. and Canadian Biographies in History Journals and Dissertations.* Edited by Susan K. Kinnell. Santa Barbara, CA: ABC-CLIO, 1988. 2 vols. ISBN 0-87436-493-0.

471. *People in World History: An Index to Biographies in History Journals and Dissertations Covering the Countries of the World Except Canada and the U.S.* Edited by Susan K. Kinnell. Santa Barbara, CA: ABC-CLIO, 1989. 2 vols. ISBN 0-87436-550-3.

These two titles are bibliographies of biographical information on 6,000 Americans and Canadians and almost 8,000 people from the rest of the world. The previous ten years of ABC-CLIO's data bases for *Historical Abstracts* [*see* 236] and *America: History and Life* [*see* 234] are the sources for this information. Entries are arranged alphabetically by the biographee's name. Individual entries supply a complete citation, an abstract, and the item's chronological coverage. Extensive indexing by subject, geography, occupation, and author, along with other useful categories, is provided.

Universal (International):
Current and Retrospective

472. *Biographie universelle: ancienne et moderne.* Edited by M. Michaud. Paris: Mme. C. Desplaces, 1845–1865. 45 vols.

473. *Nouvelle biographie generale.* Edited by De M. le Dr. Hoefer. Paris: Firmin Didot, 1853–1866. 46 vols. Reprint. Copenhagen: Rosenkilde & Bagger, 1963–1966.

These two massive French works represent classic nineteenth century projects to produce multivolume works of international biography. National biographies, pioneered by the *Dictionary of National Biography* and the *Allgemeine Deutsche Biographie,* are now the norm [*see* 489 and 493]. *Biographie universelle* is commonly cited as "Michaud" after its editor, while *Nouvelle biographie generale* is often referred to as "Hoefer." Publication of both sets was delayed because some of the earlier Hoefer volumes plagiarized from Michaud, and this resulted in a lawsuit. Articles in both sets are signed and include a bibliography. Originally Hoefer was planned to be more comprehensive than Michaud, and for the letters A–M it lists more minor figures. But from N–Z Hoefer's coverage is definitely less extensive. Generally, Michaud's articles are longer and have better bibliographies, although Hoefer's typography is superior.

474. *Current Biography.* New York: H. W. Wilson, 1940–. Vol. 1–.

This biographical periodical is published monthly, except in December, and is cumulated annually into the more familiar *Current Biography Yearbook.* It is a standard part of most reference collections. About 150 biographies are brought out each year of newsworthy people from all countries and professions. Individual entries include the person's full name, date of birth, occupation, address, a biographical sketch of approximately 2,500 words, and a list of references. The information is well presented, but the relatively small number of people covered limits the value of this source. Each annual volume contains a ten-year cumulated index, and there is also the *Current Biography Cumulated Index, 1940–1970* (New York: H. W. Wilson, 1973).

475. *New Century Cyclopedia of Names.* Edited by Clarence L. Barnhart. New York: Appleton-Century-Crofts, 1954. 3 vols.

While this fascinating and well-produced work is not solely a biographical dictionary, that is its primary utility. Containing entries for more than 100,000 proper names from all ages and areas, its scope includes "persons, places, historical events, plays and operas, works of fiction, literary characters, works of art, mythological and legendary persons and places, and any other class of proper names of interest or importance today." Still, most of the entries are biographical and provide the basic information of vital dates, nationality, and career. Generally they are somewhat more detailed than the entries in *Webster's New Biographical Dictionary* and *Chambers's Biographical Dictionary* [see 480]. Its age greatly diminishes the *New Century Cyclopedia*'s usefulness for modern topics.

476. *New York Times Biographical Service: A Compilation of Current Biographical Information of General Interest.* New York: New York Times, 1970–. Vol. 1–. Monthly.

Originally titled *New York Times Biographical Edition*, this publication reproduces major obituaries and biographical articles appearing in the *New York Times*. People, living or dead, from all nations and all forms of endeavor appear in this collection. Articles are journalistic and not academic in style. Each annual volume has a cumulative index, but there is no master index.

477. *Obituaries from The Times 1951–1960, including an index to all obituaries and tributes appearing in The Times during the years 1951–1960.* [Reading, England]: Newspaper Archive Developments; Westport, CT: Meckler Books, [1979]. 896p.

478. *Obituaries from The Times 1961–1970; including an index to all obituaries and tributes appearing in The Times during the years 1961–1970.* Reading, England: Newspaper Archive Developments, [1975]. 952p.

479. *Obituaries from The Times 1971–1975; including an index to all obituaries and tributes appearing in The Times during the years 1971–1975.* [Reading, England]: Newspaper Archive Developments; [Westport, CT]: Meckler Books, [1978]. 647p.

The obituaries appearing in *The Times* of London are well written and researched and are of great value to the historian. What these three volumes do is index all obituaries appearing in *The Times* from 1951–1975. In addition, they also print in full about 4,000 of those obituaries. Sixty percent of the entries are British. Many of these will ultimately appear in the *Dictionary of National Biography* [see 489] but many will not. Therefore, these entries and indexes form an important resource for biographical information on twentieth-century figures.

480. *Webster's New Biographical Dictionary.* Springfield, MA: Merriam-Webster, 1983. 1,130p. ISBN 0-87779-543-6.

A revision of the classic *Webster's Biographical Dictionary*, this one-volume work is the place to go for quick access to the basic biographical facts. The dictionary lists 30,000 names from all periods of time and all parts of the world. This revised edition, unlike previous editions, only lists persons who are deceased. Entries are arranged alphabetically and supply pronunciation, titles, vital dates, nationality, occupation, and other pertinent biographical information. Besides being a standard item in any library's reference collection, this work is easily affordable for the personal library. An equivalent British publication is *Chambers's Biographical Dictionary*, edited by J. O. Thorne and T. C. Collocott (Cambridge: Cambridge University Press, 1986).

National and Regional Biographical Dictionaries

United States and North America

481. *Appleton's Cyclopedia of American Biography.* Edited by James Grant Wilson and John Fiske. New York: D. Appleton and Company, 1887–1900. 7 vols. Reprint. Detroit: Gale, 1968.

Although *Appleton's* has been superseded by the *Dictionary of American Biography* [*see* 482], it remains an interesting work that is well worth consulting. Not only native and naturalized citizens of the United States appear in these volumes but also important individuals from Mexico, other Latin American countries, and Canada, along with others from abroad who are closely associated with American history. Some of the people in *Appleton's* were still living at the time of its publication. Articles are arranged in alphabetical order by surname, although articles for families are arranged chronologically. The individual entries written in a narrative fashion are fairly detailed, include little or no bibliography, and are unsigned. Scattered throughout the volumes are small black-and-white inset portraits. This work should be used with caution, as some articles contain errors and others deal with totally fictitious individuals. A further six-volume supplement titled *Cyclopedia of American Biography* was published from 1918 to 1931.

482. *Dictionary of American Biography.* Published under the Auspices of the American Council of Learned Societies. New York: Scribner,

1928–1937. 20 vols. Index. Reprint 1943. 21 vols. with 8 supplements and index, 1944–1989. ISBN 0-68416-794-8.

The *Dictionary of American Biography* (known as the *DAB*) is the most authoritative of the major biographical dictionaries of American history, although it is not the most comprehensive. It was designed to be the U.S. equivalent of the British *Dictionary of National Biography* [*see* 489]. When the original set was completed, it contained more than 13,600 entries written by professional historians. With the addition of the eight supplements, the *DAB* now consists of 18,110 entries. Each entry is signed and includes a bibliography. From the very beginning, the editors of the *DAB* sought to provide a broad coverage of significant Americans. Besides the traditional politicians, soldiers, and religious leaders, they have added scientists, businessmen, artists, musicians, and any others who have made a significant contribution to American life. The *DAB* has also been liberal in its definition of an American. Its major restrictions are that no living persons and no persons who have not resided in the present territory of the United States are included. Beginning with the fifth supplement, the individual entries have omitted some facts that had previously been included, if they were not directly relevant to the subject's career. These facts include detailed information about siblings, religious affiliations of the parents and spouses, and children's names and dates of birth. In 1989 a comprehensive index for the base set and the supplements was published. The *Concise Dictionary of American Biography*, 3d ed. (New York: Scribner, 1980), is a one-volume abridgment of the original *DAB* and the first six supplements. Salem Press's *Great Lives from History: American Series* (Englewood, NJ, 1986) contains 500 biographies that overlap heavily with the coverage of the *DAB*.

483. *Dictionary of Canadian Biography.* Toronto: University of Toronto Press, 1966–. 11 vols. in progress. Vol. I, A.D. 1000–1700; Vol. II, 1701–1740; Vol. III, 1741–1770; Vol. IV, 1771–1800; Vol. V, 1801–1820; Vol. VI, 1821–1835; Vol. VII, 1836–1850; Vol. VIII, 1851–1860; Vol. IX, 1861–1870; Vol. X, 1871–1880; Vol. XI, 1881–1890. ISBN 0-8020-3142-0.

Modeled on the *Dictionary of National Biography* [*see* 489], the excellent *Dictionary of Canadian Biography* will consist of 12 volumes when it is completed. Volume 12 will cover 1891–1900, and its publication is expected in 1990. Individual biographical entries start with the listing of the individual's occupation, vital dates, places of birth and death, and parentage. A biographical essay follows, and the entry concludes with a detailed bibliography of primary and secondary sources. Each entry is signed by the author, an expert in Canadian history. Indexes of identifications (professions and occupations), geographical places, and personal names conclude each volume. Unlike the *DNB* and the *DAB* [*see* 489 and 482], each volume of the *DCB* covers the people who died in a certain span of years (several centuries in the first volume, but only a decade in later volumes). There are between 500 and 600 entries per volume; the complete set will contain approximately 7,000 biographies. Anyone studying Canadian history will find this set to be an invaluable resource, especially U.S. historians, considering the interconnection of U.S. and Canadian history. For ready reference and twentieth-century Canadian biographies, there is the *Macmillan Dictionary of Canadian Biography* (4th ed., 1978) containing 5,000 entries.

484. *Encyclopedia of American Biography.* Edited by John A. Garraty and Jerome L. Sternstein. New York: Harper & Row, 1974. 1,241p. ISBN 0-06-01138-4.

485. *Webster's American Biographies.* Edited by Charles Van Doren and Robert McHenry. Springfield, MA: G. & C. Merriam Company, 1975. 1,233p. Indexes. ISBN 0-87779-053-1.

These two single-volume biographical dictionaries of U.S. history cover fewer people than the *Concise Dictionary of American Biography* [*see* 482], but they provide more detailed information and evaluation. "Garraty" consists of 1,000 signed entries on individuals both living and dead. The first part of each entry supplies a factual summary of the person's life, while the second part gives a historical evaluation of the individual's significance. One or two suggestions for further reading are usually provided. The 3,000 entries found in *Webster's* are unsigned and shorter, averaging 350 words with no bibliography.

486. *National Cyclopedia of American Biography.* New York: James T. White Co., 1892–1984. 62 vols. plus vols. labeled A–N63. Index.

The *National Cyclopedia of American Biography* in its permanent (numbered) volumes and current (lettered) volumes contains more than 66,500 biographical entries. Only deceased persons are listed in the permanent series, and only living persons are found in the current series. Volume N–63, which may be the last volume of the set to be published, is an exception as it contains both living and dead individuals. Each entry provides information on vital dates, parentage, education, family, outline of career, and historical significance. The information found in the entries is based on answers given to questionnaires that the publisher sent to the individual or the family of the deceased. Basically the entries read like *Who's Who* [*see* 492] entries written as a narrative. The entries are unsigned and include no bibliography. A very useful feature of the set is the inclusion of portraits. Since the individual entries do not appear in any organized fashion, it is essential to use the *Index: National Cyclopedia of American Biography* (1984), which supersedes all previous indexes and covers both the permanent and current sets. It is a detailed index that includes not only the main biographical entries but also other persons and subjects. Although it is not as scholarly and authoritative as the *Dictionary of American Biography*, the broad coverage of the *National Cyclopedia* makes it a good source for finding information on lesser figures from U.S. history.

487. *Who's Who in America.* Wilmette, IL: Marquis, 1899–. Vol. 1–. Biennial. ISSN 0083-9396.

The 45th edition (1988–1989) of *Who's Who in America* contains 77,000 biographical entries. Beginning publication in 1899, this venerable mainstay of current American biography followed the revised format of the British *Who's Who* [*see* 492]. Admission to *Who's Who in America* is limited to living persons of widespread reference interest, including government and religious officials and well-known people in private life. Not strictly limited to Americans, this work includes Canadian and Mexican government officials. Most biographical sketches are based on questionnaires filled out by the biographees, although some sketches are compiled by the Marquis staff. Individual entries provide date and place of birth, family information, an outline of the career, a list of major publications (if any), personal interests, and an address. There is an on-line version of this publication that includes *Who's Who in Science and Technology* on DIALOG File 234 with more than 100,000 entries updated quarterly. *Who was Who in America* contains selected biographies of deceased individuals, beginning with 1897, who originally appeared in the current volumes. There is also a *Who was Who in America: Historical Volume, 1607–1896* (Chicago: Marquis, 1963, rev. 1967), which consists of more than 13,000 short entries. Marquis publishes numerous other specialized "Who's Who" publications for various regions, professions, and ethnic and religious groups. There is a master index to all of these, *Marquis Who's Who Publications: An Index to All Books* (Chicago: Marquis, 1974–), published biennially. Most nations and regions are covered by some sort of "Who's Who" publication. For a listing, see Mary A. Farrell's guide [*see* 464].

British Isles

488. *A Dictionary of Irish Biography.* By Henry Boylan. New York: Barnes & Noble, 1978. 385p. ISBN 0-06-490620-5.

Approximately 1,000 biographical entries make up the contents of this work. Its scope consists of famous Irish people and others significantly associated with Ireland throughout its history until 1977. No living persons are included. Figures of dubious authenticity from the early history of Ireland have been left out. All entries are written by Boylan and provide a brief basic summary of the person's life. They include no bibliography, although there is a select bibliography for the entire volume. While this work does not rank at the forefront of collective biography, it is still useful for ready reference. It supersedes J. S. Crone's *A Concise Dictionary of Irish Biography* (1937), which, however, remains worth consulting.

489. *Dictionary of National Biography.* Edited by Sir Leslie Stephen and Sir Sidney Lee. London: Smith, Elder and Co., 1885–1901. 63 vols. Reprinted with minor revisions 1908–1909 in 22 vols. Published by the Oxford University Press since 1917. Nine supplements cover the years 1901–1980.

The *Dictionary of National Biography*, or *DNB* as it is commonly abbreviated, is the largest and oldest scholarly biographical dictionary in the English language. Including its most recent supplement, it contains 36,450 biographies of significant people in all areas of activity from the British Isles and their colonies. No living persons are listed. Each entry is signed by its author, an expert on the subject. These entries are generally concise, well written, provide a bibliography of writings by the biographee (if any exist), and list primary and secondary works for further study. Although it was largely written before World War I, there is no plan to publish a second edition of the *DNB*. In spite of its age, the information in the older volumes remains quite useful for researchers. The greatest surprise is often who can be found in the *DNB*, rather than who cannot. This work is one of the most important reference works available to students of English history and literature. It has served as the model for most other national collective biographies. Derived from it are the *Dictionary of National Biography, the Concise Dictionary: Part I, From the Beginnings to 1900* (1903. Reprint: Oxford: Oxford University Press, 1953) and the *Dictionary of National Biography, the Concise Dictionary: Part II, 1901–1950* (Oxford: Oxford University Press, 1961). *Great Lives from History: British Series* (Englewood, NJ: Salem Press, 1987) is a recent 5-volume work containing 500 biographies from all periods of British history, which overlaps heavily with the *DNB*.

490. *The Dictionary of Welsh Biography down to 1940.* By the Honourable Society of Cymmrodorion. Oxford: Blackwell, 1959. 1,157p.

Originally published in Welsh in 1953, this volume later appeared in this revised English translation. It consists of 3,500 signed biographical articles; 180 of these articles deal with families, so almost 5,000 individuals actually are discussed in the dictionary. Each article includes a bibliography. Planned as a Welsh version of the *Dictionary of National Biography*, it includes the Welsh who led significant lives as well as non-Welsh individuals who played an important part in the history of Wales. No living persons are included. Considering its age, it is not useful for recent Welsh history.

491. *The Scottish Nation: Or, the Surnames, Families, Literature, Honours, and Biographical History of the People of Scotland.* By William Anderson. Edinburgh: A. Fullerton and Company, 1878–1880. 3 vols.

No relatively modern collective biographical work for Scotland that is particularly useful exists, although there are several recent historical dictionaries of Scotland that contain biographical entries [*see* 418]. Therefore, this nineteenth-century work is the best biographical work available. It is arranged alphabetically and includes Scottish men and women from all endeavors, although political, military, and aristocratic figures predominate. Individual entries are unsigned and supply a portrait. No bibliography for further study is supplied, although works written by the biographee are listed. There is much overlap with its contemporary, the far superior *Dictionary of National Biography*.

492. *Who's Who: An Annual Biographical Dictionary.* London: Black and New York: St. Martin's, 1849–. Vol. 1–. Annual. ISSN 0083-937X.

Although this venerable patriarch of the "Who's Who" genre was founded in 1849, it did not assume its present form as a biographical dictionary until 1897. Prior to that date, *Who's Who* was a list of prominent officeholders in the British government, the Church of England, and certain prominent businesses. Afterward, it started providing biographical sketches of prominent living people from all forms of activity whose achievements have significantly affected British life. Thousands of such entries make up *Who's Who* and are based on questionnaires filled out by the biographee. The entries not only emphasize details of the individual's career but also include family information and recreations. *Who Was Who* is a publication that consists of a selection of biographies of deceased individuals up to 1980 who originally appeared in *Who's Who*. It has a separate index for 1897–1980. A complete back run of old *Who's Whos* is more comprehensive for use in historical research than the *Who Was Who*. *Who's Who in America* is almost identical in its format [*see* 487].

Western and Eastern Europe

493. *Allgemeine Deutsche Biographie*. Leipzig: Drucker, 1875–1912. Reprint 1967–1971. 56 vols.

For those who can read German, this massive set is an outstanding resource for biographical information. As the German equivalent of the *DNB* [*see* 489], it contains articles on significant Germans from earliest times to the end of the nineteenth century. Each article is signed and includes a bibliography. Their length ranges from about 200 words for less-renowned persons to more than 30 pages for Martin Luther. Later volumes contain supplementary material on people listed in earlier volumes. Therefore, it is important to consult the index in Volume 56 in order to find all the available information. Twentieth-century material can be found in *Neu Deutsche Biographie* (Berlin, 1953–1982), Volumes 1–13 in progress. This set also adds some earlier figures not included in the *ADB*, although it also omits many that can be found there. The index for each volume in the *NDB* includes references to the appropriate volumes in the *ADB* so that the two sets complement each other.

494. *A Biographical Dictionary of the Soviet Union 1917–1988*. By Jeanne Vronskaya with Vladimir Chuguev. New York: K. G. Saur, 1989. 525p. ISBN 0-86291-470-1.

Tsarist Russia and the Soviet Union are poorly served by biographical reference works in English when compared with other major countries. Therefore, this volume, containing biographies of 5,000 people in all walks of life from the post-1917 Soviet period through December 1988, is a welcome addition. The Library of Congress system of transliteration is used to list all Russian names, except where the person is far better known under a different spelling. Alternate spellings are also supplied and are followed by the individual's vital dates and occupation. Although more space is devoted to major figures— entries for Stalin and Trotsky are 1,700 and 700 words long respectively—most entries comprise about 100 words. They usually provide the place of birth, family background, education, main career events, and the place and manner of death (which is not always easy to determine if the individual was a victim of Stalin's purges). There is an index of occupations.

495. *Biographisches Lexicon zur Geschichte Sudosteuropas.* Edited by Mathias Bernath and Felix von Schroder. Munich: R. Oldenourg, 1974–1981. 4 vols.

The 1,500 entries in this German work deal with important figures from the history of Hungary, Romania, Yugoslavia, Bulgaria, Albania, Greece, Turkey, and the former Ottoman Empire for all periods up to 1945. There is also a large number of Germans and Austrians among the entries. Each entry is signed and includes a bibliography for further study. This is an excellent scholarly reference work.

496. *Dictionaire de Biographie Française.* Paris: Librairie Letouzey, 1933–1985. Vol. 16 in progress (issued in fascicles). ISBN 0-686-57087-1.

It is this set, rather than *Biographie Universelle* or *Nouvelle Biographie Generale,* that provides a collective national biography for France. Each article outlines the biographee's career and is signed by the author. Most biographies include a bibliography, although many of the minor entries do not. Volume 16 just about completes the letter G. Individual articles tend to be shorter on the average than those found in the *Dictionary of National Biography* [see 489]. The idea is that this reference work will eventually cover more people, although in less detail, than the other major national biographies.

Africa

497. *Dictionary of African Historical Biography.* 2d ed. By Martin R. Lipschutz and R. Kent Rasmussen. Berkeley: University of California Press, 1986. 328p. Indexes. ISBN 0-520-05179-3.

In spite of its title, the geographical scope of this volume is restricted to sub-Saharan or black African history. The 850 entries are largely biographical, although some supply lists of rulers or explanations of titles. While this volume attempts to be evenhanded in its coverage, the paucity of research into some aspects and time periods of African history has resulted in some areas being relatively under-represented. Native Africans and foreigners who played a significant role in African history are included, along with some living persons. 1960 was chosen as the cutoff date for the original edition, which the second edition has updated to 1980. The volume includes a useful general bibliography and a subject index. Students of African history will find this book to be a useful introductory work of reference, and it is available in paperback. Its authors recognize that this book is merely a preliminary step, but it remains all that is available, since only two volumes of the *Encyclopedia Africana: Dictionary of African Biography* (New York, 1977– in progress) have so far appeared. The Scarecrow Press series of historical dictionaries covering individual African nations, however, contains many biographical articles.

Asia and Oceania

498. *Australian Dictionary of Biography*. Melbourne: Melbourne University Press, 1966–. 9 vols. in progress. Vols. 1–2, 1788–1850; Vols. 3–6, 1851–1890; and Vols. 7–9, 1891–1939, A–Las.

Although the format of the individual entries follows that established by the *DNB* [*see* 489], the arrangement of the individual volumes is most similar to that of the *Dictionary of Canadian Biography*. The chronological scope of the set goes from 1788–1939 and is subdivided into groups of volumes covering specific periods of time. When they are completed, the set covering the years 1891–1939 will consist of six volumes. There will be about 7,000 entries in the complete work. Most will be of people who were significant to Australian history, although some will be of relatively unimportant individuals who serve as examples of types of Australians. The individual entries briefly survey the person's career and significance and include a bibliography. Most are signed, and the unsigned biographies were written by the staff of the dictionary project. There is a shorter, two-volume *Dictionary of Australian Biography* by Percival Serle (1942) that contains 1,030 biographies of people who died before 1942. More recent information on living persons can be found in the triennial *Who's Who in Australia* (1922–).

499. *Biographical Dictionary of Japanese History*. Edited by Seiichi Iwao. New York: Kodansha International, 1978. 655p. Index. ISBN 0-87011-274-0.

Translated from Japanese, the purpose of this volume is to increase Western understanding of Japanese history. Its more than 500 biographical entries have been prepared by a panel of Japanese historians. The chronological scope is from the earliest period of Japanese history to 1978. A few living persons have been included among the biographees. For the most part the people in this volume are natives of Japan who have contributed to that nation's political, military, economic, and social development, together with a few significant foreigners. Companion volumes are *Biographical Dictionary of Japanese Literature*, edited by Seachi Hisamatsu (1976), for writers, and *Biographical Dictionary of Japanese Art*, edited by Yukata Tazawa (1982), for artists.

500. *Dictionary of Ming Biography, 1368–1644*. Edited by L. Carrington Goodrich for the Association for Asian Studies' Ming Biographical History Project. New York: Columbia University Press, 1976. 2 vols. Index. LC 75-26938. ISBN 0-685-62034-4.

501. *Eminent Chinese of the Ch'ing Period (1644–1912)*. Edited by Arthur W. Hummel. Washington: Government Printing Office, 1943–1944. 2 vols. ISBN 0-8490-1761-0.

502. *Biographical Dictionary of Republican China*. Edited by Howard L. Boorman. New York: Columbia University Press, 1967–1979. 5 vols. ISBN 0-231-04558-1.

503. *Biographical Dictionary of Chinese Communism, 1921–1965*. Edited by Donald W. Klein and Anne B. Clark. Cambridge: Harvard University Press, 1971. 2 vols. ISBN 0-674-07410-6.

China is well served by specialized biographical dictionaries. These four multivolume sets together contain 2,500 biographical articles covering individuals from the period 1368–1965. The very scholarly Ming-era volumes consist of 650 signed entries from the years 1368–1644, including extensive bibliography and detailed indexing. Some 800 signed biographical articles with bibliography make up the volumes for the Ch'ing period, 1644–1912. They include considerable information on figures who lived after 1912. The period 1911–1949, however, is most authoritatively covered by the 600 essays on significant people for Republican China, both living and dead. An extensive bibliography is contained in the fourth volume, while the fifth volume is an extensive personal name index. There are 433 biographical sketches for significant people from the People's Republic of China up to 1965. These sketches were largely written by the editors. Because of the current nature of their subject, these last volumes do not contain the depth of documentation found in the earlier volumes. Current information on living persons in the People's Republic of China can be found in *Who's Who in the People's Republic of China*

(Munich: K. G. Saur, 1987). Although it is quite old, the standard single-volume biographical dictionary of Chinese history remains *A Chinese Biographical Dictionary*, by Herbert A. Giles (London: Quaritch, 1898; reprint 1968).

504. *Dictionary of National Biography* [India]. Edited by S. P. Sem. Calcutta: Institute of Historical Studies, 1972–1974. 4 vols. ISBN 0-8364-2326-7.

Consciously modeled on its namesake, the British *Dictionary of National Biography*, this Indian biographical project contains nearly 1,400 signed articles. Unlike its namesake, this work includes living persons. The chronological scope is 1800–1947, and geographically it covers present-day India, Pakistan, and Bangladesh. Each article includes a bibliography. Although people from all backgrounds and pursuits appear on its pages, the selection was heavily based on political and nationalistic considerations. For a shorter work that goes back to 1750 containing 2,500 entries and including many Britons, *see* Charles Edward Buckland's *Dictionary of Indian Biography* (London: Sonnschien, 1906. Reprint 1968). For biographical information on earlier periods of the Indian subcontinent's history, along with the Middle East, see Henry George Keene's *An Oriental Biographical Dictionary* [*see* 505].

505. *An Oriental Biographical Dictionary: Founded on Materials Collected by the Late Thomas William Beale*. Rev. ed. By Henry George Keene. London: W. H. Allen, 1894. Reprint: New York: Kraus, 1965. 431 p. ISBN 0-527-06250-7.

Written and revised in the late nineteenth century, this biographical dictionary is not a work of modern scholarship, although it is still quite useful. Its title is somewhat misleading, since it is largely concerned with Islamic Asia and excludes Chinese, Japanese, and Europeans active in Asian history. Hundreds of difficult-to-locate persons are identified. Individual entries are brief descriptions ranging from one sentence to 150 to 200 words. Each begins with an English transliteration of the name, followed by the Persian character version. Dates are given according to both the Christian and Islamic calendars. Cross-references are provided from the more familiar European version of names to the proper transliteration (e.g., Averroes, see Ibn Rashid). This volume is a good complement to the Indian *Dictionary of National Biography* [*see* 504].

Latin America

506. *Biographical Dictionary of Latin American and Caribbean Political Leaders.* Edited by Robert J. Alexander. Westport, CT: Greenwood Press, 1988. 507p. Index. ISBN 0-313-24353-0.

Latin American history has been poorly served by biographical dictionaries in the English language. This volume somewhat redresses that gap by its coverage of 450 people of political significance from the nineteenth and twentieth centuries. Living persons have been included. Each signed entry focuses on the political significance of the individual's career and includes a bibliography for further study. The contributors are experts on Latin American and Caribbean studies. It is unfortunate that this work neglects individuals who were not politicians or statesmen and persons from the colonial period of Latin America.

Chronological Periods

507. *Contemporaries of Erasmus: A Biographical Register of the Renaissance and Reformation.* Edited by Peter G. Bietenholz and Thomas B. Deutscher. Toronto: University of Toronto Press, 1985–. 3 vols. ISBN 0-8020-2507-2.

This impressive biographical collection contains 1,900 entries for those individuals mentioned in the correspondence of the famous humanist scholar Erasmus (1466?–1536). Although it was compiled primarily to supplement the *Collected Works of Erasmus,* this work also provides a valuable biographical guide to the important political, religious, and intellectual figures of the late Renaissance (particularly northern Europe) and the early Reformation. A number of obscure individuals are also included. Entries are listed in alphabetical order according to the vernacular spellings, except for those people whose Latin or Greek names are by far the most familiar. The size of the entries varies from 3,500 words to fewer than 50, depending on the fame of the individual and the availability of information. Besides providing basic biographical information, entries include a bibliography and are signed by the contributor. *Contemporaries of Erasmus* is an excellent example of recent collective biographical scholarship.

508. *Great Lives from History: Ancient and Medieval.* Edited by Frank N. Magill. Englewood Cliffs, NJ: Salem Press, 1988. 5 vols. ISBN 0-89356-545-8.

509. *Great Lives from History: Renaissance to 1900.* Edited by Frank N. Magill. Englewood Cliffs, NJ: Salem Press, 1989. 5 vols. ISBN 0-89356-551-2.

510. *Great Lives from History: Twentieth Century.* Edited by Frank N. Magill. Englewood Cliffs, NJ: Salem Press, 1990. 5 vols. ISBN 0-89356-565-2.

Each of these three biographical reference sets consists of five volumes and contains almost 500 alphabetically arranged biographical essays. Chronologically, they range from the ancient world through the twentieth century. All areas of the world are represented except for the English-speaking nations, which have their own separate *Great Lives from History* sets. Significant individuals from all aspects of human activity (politicians, rulers, religious leaders, scholars, explorers, scientists) are represented. The signed essays are written by experts on their subjects to a uniform format of 2,000 words. A ready-reference section providing vital information is followed by a biographical sketch and analysis, concluding with an annotated bibliography of readily available works for further reading. These volumes are particularly valuable since they cover many individuals not readily found in other standard reference sources, and they draw together information that has previously been scattered throughout various sources. The same judgment does not apply to the publisher's American (1986) and British (1987) sets, which basically consist of material readily found in other reference works of high quality.

511. *Makers of Nineteenth Century Culture, 1800–1914.* Edited by Justin Wintle. London: Routledge & Kegan Paul, 1982. 709p. Index. ISBN 0-7100-9295-4.

Part of the series *Makers of Culture,* this volume contains 493 signed biographical entries written by 190 contributors. Essays are interpretive in that they concentrate on the individual's contribution to modern culture and include a bibliography. Although the geographical scope of this work is worldwide, the biographees largely come from Europe and the United States. Political and military leaders are ignored for the most part. Instead, this work focuses on artists, writers, scholars, musicians, and religious figures. There is a companion volume for the twentieth century also edited by Justin Wintle, *Makers of Modern Culture* (London: Routledge & Kegan Paul, 1981).

512. *Twentieth-Century Culture: A Biographical Companion*. Edited by Alan Bullock and R. B. Woodings. New York: Harper & Row, 1983. 865p. Index. ISBN 0-06-015248-6.

In spite of its misleading title, *Twentieth-Century Culture* is a quite useful biographical dictionary of almost 2,000 individuals who, with a few exceptions, were born or active after 1900. Although it was conceived as a companion volume to the *Harper Dictionary of Modern Thought* (New York: Harper & Row, 1977), this work easily stands on its own. The idea of this work is to provide ready-reference information for the various people from all fields, e.g., arts, business, philosophy, politics, and religion, who have shaped modern Western culture. Some 300 contributors wrote the entries, which are signed with initials. Each entry provides vital dates and a summary account of the individual's career and significance. Some entries include a brief bibliography for further reading, normally no more than two items. The British title for this work is the *Fontana Biographical Companion to Modern Thought*. For a similar work, see *Thinkers of the Twentieth Century*, 2d edition, edited by Roland Turner (Chicago: St. James Press, 1987). Its approximately 450 signed essays are more detailed and include more extensive bibliographies. For an excellent ready-reference work containing 5,000 biographies with less detail and including more figures from popular culture, there is *The International Dictionary of 20th Century Biography*, by Edward Vernoff and Rima Shore (New York: New American Library, 1987). It is available in paperback.

513. *Who Was Who in the Greek World: 776 B.C.–30 B.C.* Edited by Diana Bowder. Ithaca, NY: Phaidon Book/Cornell University Press, 1982. 227p. Index. ISBN 0-8014-1538-1.

514. *Who Was Who in the Roman World, 753 B.C.–A.D. 476*. Edited by Diana Bowder. Ithaca, NY: Cornell University Press, 1980. 256p. Index. ISBN 0-8014-1358-3.

These two volumes contain respectively some 750 and 900 biographical entries for important individuals in the classical era. These biographical sketches tend to be brief and descriptive, although they also supply at least one citation for further reading. The Greek volume includes a series of essays on various periods of Greek history as its introduction. Both volumes provide helpful maps, genealogies, glossaries of terms, and bibliographies. They are also both available in inexpensive paperback editions. *Who's Who in the Ancient World*, by Betty Radice (Harmondsworth: Penguin, 1973), is a similar one-volume paperback that includes mythological as well as historical figures.

Biographical Collections for Specific Groups and Subjects

515. *American Men and Women of Science: Physical and Biological Sciences.* 17th ed. New York: R. R. Bowker, 1989. 8 vols. ISBN 0-8352-2568-2.

516. *Directory of American Scholars.* 8th ed. New York: R. R. Bowker, 1982. 4 vols. ISBN 0-8352-2568-2.

These two current biographical collections each serve basically as a "Who's Who" for scholars and scientists active in the United States, although social scientists are slighted. *American Men and Women of Science* is a triennial that began publication in 1901 and now lists 140,000 persons in one alphabetical sequence. The *Directory of American Scholars* first appeared in 1942. It is published irregularly and now contains 39,000 biographies. Its four volumes are organized by subject: Volume 1, history; Volume 2, English, speech, and drama; Volume 3, foreign languages, linguistics, and philology; and Volume 4, philosophy, religion, and law. The individual entries in both sets use a "Who's Who" format, giving name, date and place of birth, family information, education, career outline, memberships, publications, and address. Not only are these volumes an outstanding source for current biographical information, their earlier editions can also be used retrospectively. For this purpose *American Men and Women of Science Cumulative Index, Editions 1–14* (New York: R. R. Bowker, 1983) is a good research aid, while the more recent editions have been available on-line on DIALOG File 236 starting in 1979. A similar British publication that is badly in need of updating is *Academic Who's Who, 1975–1976: University Teachers in the British Isles in the Arts, Education, and Social Sciences,* 2d ed. (New York: Gale, 1975).

517. *Biographical Dictionary of American Business Leaders.* By John N. Ingham. Westport, CT: Greenwood Press, 1983. 4 vols. ISBN 0-313-21362-3.

The focus of this reference work is the "historically most significant business leaders" in American history. There are 835 biographical entries covering 1,159 people (some entries discuss families, such as the Vanderbilts and the Rockefellers). The author chose his subjects with the aid of a panel of historians of business. All entries were written solely by the author and include a bibliography. They average 750 words in length, although entries for particularly important individuals and families run much longer. Although most of the people included in this collection are deceased, it includes some living persons, e.g., Lee Iacocca and Robert McNamara. Furthermore, this work includes many individuals not found in other historical works of biography, such as Harland Sanders and Bernard H. Kroger. There is a similar work for Great Britain, *Dictionary of Business Biography: A Biographical Dictionary of Business Leaders Active in Britain in the Period 1860–1980*, edited by David J. Jeremy, 4 vols. (London: Buttersworth, 1984 in progress). For more up-to-date information, John N. Ingham has also published *Contemporary American Business Leaders: A Biographical Dictionary* (Westport, CT: Greenwood, 1990).

518. *Biographical Dictionary of American Labor*. Rev. ed. Gary M. Fink, editor in chief. Westport, CT: Greenwood, 1984. 767p. Index. ISBN 0-313-22865-5.

As an example of a single-volume biographical dictionary on a specialized group, this book is outstanding. Each of its more than 700 signed biographical entries was written by an expert in labor history. Individual entries give vital dates, an outline of the career, and a bibliography for further reading. The biographees come from all aspects and periods of American labor history and include some persons still living. A lengthy introduction provides a useful quantitative and qualitative portrait of twentieth-century labor leaders and includes numerous tables. Six appendixes organize the biographees by union affiliation, religion, place of birth, education, political preference, and public office. Anyone doing research in American labor history will want to consult this book frequently. The seven volume *Dictionary of Labour Biography*, edited by Joyce M. Bellamy and John Saville (London: Macmillan, 1972–1984), does the same thing for British labor history in much more detail.

519. *Biographical Dictionary of American Sports: Baseball*. Edited by David L. Porter. Westport, CT: Greenwood, 1987. 730p. Index. ISBN 0-313-23771-9.

520. *Biographical Dictionary of American Sports: Basketball and Other Indoor Sports*. Edited by David L. Porter. Westport, CT: Greenwood, 1989. 776p. Index. ISBN 0-313-26261-6.

521. *Biographical Dictionary of American Sports: Football*. Edited by David L. Porter. Westport, CT: Greenwood, 1987. 763p. Index. ISBN 0-313-25771-X.

522. *Biographical Dictionary of American Sports: Outdoor Sports.* Edited by David L. Porter. Westport, CT: Greenwood, 1988. 776p. Index. ISBN 0-313-26260-8.

For students of American sports history and sports buffs in general, these four volumes will form a useful and fascinating resource. The scope of the baseball and football volumes includes professionals and amateurs. Besides basketball, the figures in the indoor-sports volume come from bowling, boxing, gymnastics, wrestling, skating, and weight lifting. Outdoor sports are defined as golf, horse racing, skiing, tennis, and track and field. Each volume contains more than 500 signed biographical essays accompanied by helpful bibliographies. In all, these volumes list 2,000 individuals, both living and dead, who played a prominent role in some aspect of sports. Coverage is not limited just to athletes; sports writers, owners, and managers are also included. There are numerous appendixes found in each volume that supply information on topics such as the birthplaces of the biographees and lists of sports leagues with their duration.

523. *The Blackwell Dictionary of Historians.* Edited by John Cannon, R. H. C. Davis, William Doyle, and Jack P. Greene. New York: Blackwell Reference, 1988. 480p. Index. ISBN 0-631-14708-X.

This impressive and authoritative volume is actually more than a biographical dictionary. Besides some 450 biographical entries, the book includes 19 brief essays on the various types of history (e.g., social, legal) and 25 essays on the historiography of various nations and regions. There are also entries for specialized terms commonly used in historical writing (e.g., historicism, positivism). The historians listed in this volume come from all periods of time and parts of the world and include some individuals still living. At the same time, British and American historians have received the most attention. The editors chose individual historians for inclusion not simply because their work was first-rate but also if they helped to advance historical method and theory. This work is an excellent resource for helping students of history place a historian in his historiographical and historical context. For the most detailed information on various American historians, the *Dictionary of Literary Biography* [*see* 527] includes these three volumes: *American Historians, 1607–1865,* (1984); *American Historians, 1866–1912,* (1986); and *Twentieth-Century American Historians,* (1983), all edited by Clyde N. Wilson. For historians from other parts of the world, there is *Great Historians From Antiquity to 1800: An International Dictionary,* edited by Lucian Boia (Westport, CT: Greenwood, 1989).

524. *Contemporary Authors: A Bio-Bibliographical Guide to Current Authors and Their Works.* Detroit: Gale, 1962–. Vol. 1–. Annual. 1st Revision Series (1967–1979) 44 vols. in 11 vols. New Revision Series (1981–) Vol. 1–, irregular. Permanent Series (1975–) Vol. 1–, irregular.

As a source for biographical and bibliographical information on recent authors, both living and dead, *Contemporary Authors* is unmatched. Basically, the scope of *CA* includes anyone who has published a book in North America. The individual biographical sketches contain "Who's Who" type of information along with a bibliography of the author's works. This information is largely derived from a standard questionnaire and includes what the author's current projects are. In the case of some more famous authors, the entry will include a bibliography of secondary writings about the author. These entries also usually include biographical sketches that attempt some analysis of the author's work. The two revision series represent an updating of earlier entries in the annual series for authors who are still active. The permanent series contains the final updated entries concerning authors who have died or definitely retired. Each annual volume has a cumulative index for all the current-, revision-, and permanent-series volumes.

525. *Dictionary of American Negro Biography.* Edited by Rayford W. Logan and Michael R. Winston. New York: W. W. Norton, 1982. 680p. ISBN 0-393-01513-0.

Although numerous works of collective biography for black Americans had been published before the *Dictionary of American Negro Biography*, it is the first work whose primary purpose was scholarly and not apologetic. Its 800 signed entries were elegantly and concisely written by 280 scholars. No living person was included, and the cutoff date was 1 January 1970. The chief criterion for inclusion was historical significance, rather than fame or merely being the "first" black to do something. Many of the people included in this volume had little impact on the mainstream of American history, but they were very influential in the development of the largely segregated black community. This work is an indispensable supplement to the *Dictionary of American Biography* [*see* 482] and *Notable American Women* [*see* 532 and 533]. For more recent biographies, there is *The Negro Almanac* [*see* 414].

526. *Dictionary of American Religious Biography.* Edited by Henry Warner Bowden. Westport, CT: Greenwood, 1977. 572p. Index. ISBN 08371-8906-3.

The primary purpose of this volume is to illustrate the religious diversity of the United States. It consists of 425 biographical entries, all written by Henry Warner Bowden. Each entry supplies vital dates, a narrative survey of the life, a selected bibliography of the subject's writings, and a selected bibliography of primary and secondary sources. Persons from all denominations and faiths are represented. A special effort was made to include individuals outside of the mainstream of institutional religion. Two appendixes organize the biographees by denomination and birthplace. This work both complements and supplements the *Dictionary of American Biography*. It is also important to keep in mind that many Christian denominations have their own biographical dictionaries.

527. *Dictionary of Literary Biography.* Detroit: Gale Research, 1978–. Vols. 1–.

Originally, the *DLB* was limited to American literary figures, but in 1982 the scope was broadened to include British, Commonwealth, and modern European writers. The definition of writers and literary figures is not limited to authors of fiction; the *DLB* includes historians, journalists, and other authors of nonfiction. By 1988, the main *DLB* reached 79 volumes. There are also separate documentary and yearbook volumes. Individual volumes are devoted to specific topics, e.g., *American Newspaper Journalists, 1873–1900* or *Jacobean and Caroline Dramatists.* The biographical essays are signed and focus on the individual's literary career. They include pictures, a bibliography of the biographee's works, and a list of references. Each new volume provides a cumulative index to all the previous volumes. Although primarily a tool of literary reference, the *DLB* deals with many topics of potential interest to students of history.

528. *Dictionary of Saints.* By John J. Delaney. Garden City, NY: Doubleday, 1980. 647p. ISBN 0-385-13594-7.

529. *The Oxford Dictionary of Saints.* 2d ed. By David Hugh Farmer. New York: Oxford University Press, 1987. 478p. Index. ISBN 0-19-869149-1.

Hagiography, the study of the lives of saints, is a complex subject. Truly exhaustive works on saints of Latin Christianity, Greek Christianity, or even Ireland require many volumes. But for most students of history, these brief but comprehensive one-volume works will be sufficient. The 5,000 entries in John J. Delaney's dictionary make it the most comprehensive. In comparison, the *Oxford Dictionary of Saints* contains only 1,000 biographies and leans strongly toward British saints, although its entries are more detailed and include bibliography. It is available in paperback, as is Donald

Attwater's similar *Penguin Dictionary of Saints*, 2d ed. (New York: Penguin, 1983). Delaney is also available in an abridged paperback edition containing 1,500 entries (New York: Doubleday, 1983).

530. *Dictionary of Scientific Biography.* Charles Coulston Gillespie, editor in chief. New York: Scribner, 1970–1989. 16 vols. with Supplement II. ISBN 0-08-030399-4.

The *DSB* was envisioned as the scientific counterpart of the *Dictionary of National Biography* and the *Dictionary of American Biography* [*see* 489 and 482]. This very scholarly work consists of 5,300 entries written by more than 1,200 expert contributors. Each entry is signed, surveys the individual's career, and supplies a bibliography for further study. The scope of the set is international and includes all periods of history. No living persons were included, nor were individuals in technology, medicine, behavioral sciences, and philosophy whose work was not closely connected with scientific research. Two areas where coverage is weak are twentieth-century scientists and scientists from India, China, and Japan. This situation reflects gaps in the available Western scholarship. Volume XVI is a detailed index to the dictionary. *Supplement II* adds entries for 600 scientists who died in the late twentieth century and were not included in the original set. For anyone doing research in the history of science, the *DSB* is a fundamental reference work. It is supplemented by the excellent *Women in Science, Antiquity through the Nineteenth Century: A Biographical Dictionary with Annotated Bibliography*, by Marilyn Bailey Ogilvie (Cambridge, MA: MIT Press, 1986).

531. *Mexican American Biographies: A Historical Dictionary, 1836–1987.* By Matt S. Meier. Westport, CT: Greenwood, 1988. 270p. Index. ISBN 0-313-24521-5.

Allthough this work is titled "historical," almost 200 of its 270 alphabetically arranged biographical entries are for contemporary Mexican Americans. The basic criterion used for including individuals was the recognized significance of their career. Each individual's entry was written to highlight their impact on Mexican-American history and includes a bibliography to guide further study. Unfortunately, the author either had to eliminate some people because they failed to respond to his requests for information or else he used alternative sources of information that were not always particularly up-to-date. Therefore, this is not a biographical reference work of the highest standard, but it is the only one-volume work available on the subject. Its deficiencies reflect the embryonic state of Hispanic American studies.

532. *Notable American Women 1607–1950: A Biographical Dictionary.* Edited by Edward T. James. Cambridge: Harvard University Press, 1971. 3 vols. ISBN 0-674-62731-8.

533. *Notable American Women, the Modern Period: A Biographical Dictionary.* Edited by Barbara Sicherman and Carol Hurd Green. Cambridge: Harvard University Press, 1980. 773p. ISBN 0-674-62732-6.

The four volumes of *Notable American Women* are the most comprehensive and authoritative biographical reference works available for the history of women in America. Entries are well written with bibliographies to guide further study. They are generally about two pages long and follow the approach and format used in the *Dictionary of American Biography.* Their authors are all experts in the field of American history. The original three volumes contained 1,400 biographies and ended with the year 1950. Another 442 biographies for women who died between 1951 and 1975 are supplied by the fourth volume. Women from all fields, such as politics, religion, business, and entertainment, can be found. Historical significance, as judged by the editors, an advisory board, and a large pool of consultants, forms the main criterion for inclusion. Although the 2,000 entries in this collection overlap somewhat with the *Dictionary of American Biography,* there are many unique entries that make this work the premier resource for its subject. It is also available in paperback. For a one-volume work containing 1,000 biographies, see Robert McHenry's *Famous American Women: A Biographical Dictionary from Colonial Times to the Present* (New York: Dover, 1983), which is a reprint of a work originally titled *Liberty's Women* (1980). Information on famous women from outside the United States can be found in Jennifer S. Uglow's *International Dictionary of Women's Biography* (New York: Continuum, 1982). British women are covered in 1,000 entries by Anne Crawford, editor of *The Europa Biographical Dictionary of British Women* (Detroit: Gale, 1983).

534. *The Oxford Dictionary of the Popes.* By J. N. D. Kelly. Oxford: Oxford University Press, 1986. 346p. Index. ISBN 0-19-213964-9.

Prior to the publication of this volume, no convenient and scholarly one-volume biographical work on the papacy existed. The purpose of this dictionary is to provide summary biographies of all the popes and antipopes (those persons who claimed to be popes but were not officially recognized by the Roman Catholic church), which also include introductory bibliographies to the relevant primary and secondary sources. Entries are arranged in chronological order, and the datings generally follow those found in the *Annuario Pontifico* of

1984. John Paul II is obviously the last pope listed. A separate alphabetical list of popes and antipopes, along with their dates and page locations, allows the reader to find entries for individual popes. The detailed index allows important topics to be followed throughout the volume. In addition, certain unfamiliar terms and concepts are marked by asterisks that refer the reader to the index. There the page reference printed in italics indicates where a definition of the term or concept can be found. This dictionary is well written and researched and is available in paperback. It supersedes *The Popes: A Concise Biographical History,* by Eric John (New York: Hawthorn Books, 1964).

11.

Geographical Sources and Atlases

In his book *Cosmographie* (1652), the ecclesiastical historian Peter Heylyn observed that "if joined together, [history and geography] crown our reading with delight and profit; if parted, [they] threaten both with a certain shipwreck." And it is true. Geography has had a big impact on the unfolding of historical events. Maps are, therefore, an essential component of many history books. To further aid historical research, many excellent historical atlases have been published, and more are being added all the time. This chapter lists some of the main geographical reference works and atlases of interest to historians, along with a representative selection of specialized historical atlases.

Dictionaries, Directories, and Guides

535. *Guide to U.S. Map Resources.* Compiled by David A. Cobb. Chicago: American Library Association, 1986. 196p. Index. ISBN 0-8389-0439-4.

Basically this publication is a directory of 919 map collections in the United States, arranged alphabetically by state and then by city. Each entry provides the name of the institution, address, telephone number, hours, and a detailed description of the collection, including special strengths (if any), size of the collection, classification system used, the state of its cataloging, staff, and copying facilities. It is important to keep in mind that the map collections listed in this guide are basically those of large public libraries, state libraries, historical society libraries, and various colleges and universities. A map collection does not have to be of research quality to be included in this list, which makes it useful for the local researcher who is looking for the nearest basic map collection. Following the main directory are several lists of useful addresses: U.S. Geological Survey Depositories, Defense Mapping Agency Depositories, National Cartographic Information Centers, State Information Resources, State Mapping Advisory Committees, and Map Societies. *Guide to U.S. Map Resources* overlaps heavily with the 804 entries of David Carrington and Richard Stephenson's *Map Collections in the United States and Canada: A Directory*, 4th ed. (New York, Special Libraries Association, 1985), going beyond it in the breadth and depth of its coverage, although omitting Canadian map collections. For map collections in the rest of the world, consult John A. Wolter's *World Directory of Map Collections*, 2d ed. (Munich/New York: K. G. Saur, 1986). The work and products of the U.S. Geological Survey are described by Morris M. Thompson in *Maps for America: Cartographic Products of the U.S. Geological Survey and Others*, 2d ed. (Washington, DC: Government Printing Office, 1981).

536. *Historical Geography of the United States: A Guide to Information Sources*. By Ronald E. Grimm. Detroit: Gale, 1982. 291p. Index. ISBN 0-8103-1471-1.

Historians interested in geographical approaches to their subject will find Grimm's guide invaluable when studying the United States. It consists of 686 annotated entries divided into 20 chapters. Subjects of the individual chapters include "Historical Atlases," "Land Records," and "Historical Cultural Geography." These chapters are arranged under three broad headings: "Cartographic Sources," "Archival and Other Historical Sources," and "Selected Literature in Historical Geography." The third section on secondary literature covers the years 1965–1980, which is where Douglas R. Manis's *Historical Geography of the United States: A Bibliography* (Eastern Michigan University, Division of Field Services, 1965) stops. It is unfortunate that similar volumes are not available in English for other parts of the world. The entire discipline of geography is covered by Stephen Goddard, ed., in *A Guide to Information Sources in the Geographical Sciences* (Totowa, NJ: Barnes & Noble, 1983).

537. *Longman Dictionary of Geography: Human and Physical*. By Audrey N. Clark. White Plains, NY: Longman, 1985. 724p. ISBN 0-582-35261-4.

Containing more than 10,500 entries, this dictionary is a convenient, accurate, and concise reference work for both the specialist and the nonspecialist. The terms defined include plants, animals, topographical features, and geographical techniques and concepts.

Many of the entries are relevant to historians investigating the geographical aspects of their subject. Unlike Sir Dudley Stamp's *Longman's Dictionary of Geography* (London: Longman, 1966), Clark's dictionary does not have entries for specific people or places. For more detailed dictionaries of human geography, see R. J. Johnson, ed., *Dictionary of Human Geography* (New York: Free Press, 1981) and Robert P. Larkin and Gary L. Peters, *Dictionary of Concepts in Human Geography* (Westport, CT: Greenwood Press, 1983).

Gazetteers and Place-name Dictionaries

538. *Columbia Lippincott Gazetteer of the World.* Edited by Leon E. Seltzer. New York: Columbia University Press, [1962]. 2,148p., 22p., 1961 supplement.

Although some aspects of this massive work are starting to show their age, it remains the most comprehensive one-volume gazetteer available with more than 130,000 entries and 30,000 cross-references. The places listed in the entries can be natural geographic features or man-made places, such as cities, countries, or provinces. Each entry provides alternative spellings and pronunciation, along with the place's population (if appropriate) and its geographic and political location. A brief description supplies information on the economy and history of the place. Since the information in this gazetteer is 25–35 years old, it should be used with caution, even though the vast bulk of it remains accurate. A similar work useful for identifying an obscure place or geographical feature is an irregular serial publication of the U.S. Board on Geographic Names', *Gazetteer* (Washington, DC: Government Printing Office, 1955–1984), which has so far published 129 volumes.

539. *Concise Oxford Dictionary of English Place-names.* 4th ed. By Eilert Ekwall. Oxford: Clarendon Press, 1960. 546p.

A place-name dictionary, such as this one, serves a different function than a gazetteer. Besides listing 15,000 names and locations, the *Concise Oxford Dictionary of English Place-names* also provides their etymology and the older forms of that place-name with the dates of usages, along with some references to sources. Occasionally an entry will give the pronunciation of the place-name. A reference work of this nature is valuable because it helps the researcher to identify unfamiliar places that are mentioned in primary sources. For more detailed information on English place-names, the work to consult is the English Place-Name Society's multivolume *Survey of English Place-names* (Cambridge: Cambridge University Press, 1924–, in progress). Because of the importance of place-names in the study of history, geography, folklore, and linguistics, similar works also exist for many other countries.

540. *The Encyclopedia of Historic Places.* By Courtlandt Canby. New York: Facts on File, 1984. 2 vols. ISBN 0-87196-126-1.

Although the contents of this encyclopedia heavily duplicate other standard geographical dictionaries and gazetteers, its historical focus gives it a special appeal for students and researchers in history. Each of the 100,000 entries provides information on alternative spellings, location, and a brief description of the place's historical significance. Quite often Canby's entries provide little more historical detail than can be found in *Webster's New Geographical Dictionary* or the *Columbia Lippincott Gazetteer* [*see* 542 and 538]. However, his entries, written in a narrative form with complete sentences rather than as clipped and abbreviated dictionary entries, are always easier to read. *See* and *see also* references are generously provided. Although the *Encyclopedia of Historic Places* has a wide appeal for students of history at many levels, it is unaffordable for most individuals and many school and college libraries. Joseph Nathan Kane's *The American Counties: Origins of County Names, Dates of Creation and Organization, Area, Population including 1980 Census Figures, Historical Data, and Published Sources*, 4th ed. (Metuchen, NJ: Scarecrow, 1983), is a far more specialized and detailed work.

541. *A Guide to the Ancient World: A Dictionary of Classical Place Names.* By Michael Grant. New York: H. W. Wilson, 1986. 708p. ISBN 0-8242-0742-4.

Michael Grant is well known as a historian whose prolific writings have made the latest scholarship on ancient history accessible to educated laymen. In *A Guide to the Ancient World,* Grant has provided descriptions of cities and towns along with some physical features, such as mountains and rivers. Each of the 900 entries (which are generally 300–800 words in length) discusses the historical, geographical, and archaeological aspects of each place, along with any artistic or mythological aspects when applicable. The places included in this dictionary range chronologically from the Bronze Age to the late fifth century A.D. *See* references lead the user to alternative entries, and 15 black-and-white maps help locate the places described by the entries. Information in the individual entries is not documented, although a substantial bibliography of primary and secondary sources has been included. For most undergraduate and ready-reference type questions, this dictionary is satisfactory and more than sufficient. When there is a need for a more specialized and scholarly reference work, the book to consult is *The Princeton Encyclopedia of Classical Sites,* edited by Richard Stillwell (Princeton, NJ: Princeton University Press, 1976), containing 3,000 documented entries.

542. *Webster's New Geographical Dictionary.* Springfield, MA: Merriam-Webster, 1984. 1376p. ISBN 0-87779-446-4.

As a classic of the general reference collection, this frequently revised work continues to retain its value. Its compact size, reasonable price, and comprehensive character (47,000 entries with 15,000 cross-references) make it a natural choice for ready-reference collections, the classroom, and the personal library. Each entry briefly provides (when applicable) information about pronunciation, location, population (based on the latest censuses), economy, and history. While not as comprehensive, this work is handier to use and more readily available than the *Columbia Lippincott Gazetteer of the World* [*see* 538] and is more up-to-date. *Webster's New Geographical Dictionary* also contains 218 black-and-white maps to aid the user. Similar in scope is David Munro's *Chambers's World Gazetteer: An A–Z of Geographical Information* (New York: Chambers/Cambridge, 1988).

Indexes to Maps

543. *Index to Maps in Books and Periodicals.* Map Department, American Geographical Society. 10 vols. Boston: G. K. Hall, 1968, with supplements for 1971 and 1976.

Many useful and interesting maps are found in books and articles other than atlases. This index locates many of these maps found in various books and approximately 80 international periodicals (mostly geographical) and lists them alphabetically by subject and geographical-political divisions. Originally this index was compiled as a card file maintained by the Map Department of the American Geographical Society. It has been made more accessible by the publisher G. K. Hall, who has made a photo-reproduction of that card file. The index is well worth consulting for the location of maps on subjects not routinely included in most atlases, although the latest supplement (1976) is unfortunately not current.

General Atlases

544. *National Geographic Atlas of the World.* Washington, D.C.: National Geographic Society, 1981. 383p. Index. ISBN 087044-347-X.

National Geographic is rightfully a familiar and trusted name in atlas publishing. The latest *National Geographic Atlas of the World* is the fifth edition of that title, and a sixth edition is expected soon. This work is one of the best comprehensive, general world atlases available in one reasonably priced volume. Its 126 maps are well chosen, readable, and attractive, and the 155,000-entry gazetteer is quite useful. Only the *New International Atlas* and the *Times Atlas of the World (Comprehensive Edition)* equal or surpass it as one-volume atlases [*see* 545 and 548].

545. *The New International Atlas.* Chicago: Rand McNally, 1988. 1 vol. various pagings. Index. ISBN 0-528-8311-46.

Many people consider this atlas to be the best one-volume reference atlas published in the United States. It is truly comprehensive in its coverage of the world, and its extensive index/gazetteer has 160,000 entries. Like the *Times Atlas of the World (Comprehensive Edition)*, its maps indicate topography in greater detail than the *National Geographic Atlas of the World*. However, for most geographical questions, any of these three atlases would be an excellent reference source. It should also be kept in mind that the *New International Atlas* is virtually identical to the *Brittanica Atlas*, which is included with the *New Encyclopedia Brittanica*.

546. *Oxford Economic Atlas of the World.* 4th ed. Oxford: Oxford University Press, 1972. 239p. Index. ISBN 0-19-894107-2.

The Cartographic Department of the Clarendon Press excels in the production of readable topical maps. Their *Oxford Economic Atlas of the World* is an example of and a tribute to their great mapmaking abilities. Geographical coverage by this atlas is worldwide, with the map subjects ranging from soil types to the distribution of computer usage. Furthermore, since the economic specialization of this atlas is broadly defined, it is definitely a valuable work for general reference. A gazetteer lists the map(s) where various place-names appear, and a country-by-country statistical supplement provides further useful economic information. Unfortunately, the information in the supplement is dated, and it is time for a new edition of this fine atlas to be produced. From a historical point of view, however, dated editions of works like this one can be a source of much hard-to-find and detailed information. There are also smaller regional versions of the *Oxford Economic Atlas* available.

547. *Rand McNally Commerical Atlas & Marketing Guide.* 118th ed. Chicago: Rand McNally. Index. Annual. ISBN 0361-9923.

As a source for up-to-date geographical information on population, economic activity, and transportation facilities in the United States and Canada, the *Rand McNally Commercial Atlas & Marketing Guide* is both convenient and reliable. It is arranged into six sections: "United States and Metropolitan Area Maps," "Transportation and Communications Data," "Economic Data for the United States," "Population Data," "State Maps and United States Index of Statistics and Places by States," which is the largest section of the atlas, and "Canada: Population Data." The maps, tables, and charts contained in this atlas are all well designed and readable. Unfortunately, as each new edition of the atlas appears, the Rand McNally Company requires the return of the previous edition, precluding the collection by libraries of back files of this atlas for historical-research purposes.

548. *Times Atlas of the World: Mid-Century Edition.* London: Times Publishing Co., 1955–1959. 5 vols. 524p.

What the *Oxford English Dictionary* is to dictionaries, the *Times Atlas of the World: Mid-Century Edition* is to atlases—the biggest and the best general reference book in its field. The *Times Atlas* has been rightly praised for its balanced coverage of the world's geography. For the most difficult geographical questions, this is the work to consult. Furthermore, this work has spawned two other important geographical reference works. One is the *Times Atlas of the World (Comprehensive Edition)* (New York: Times Books, 1980), possibly the best one-volume general atlas available. The other is the *Times Index-Gazetteer of the World* containing 345,000 locations. These entries are listed with latitude and longitude so that each entry can be located on any map with sufficient precision.

Historical Atlases: World

549. *Atlas Historique Larousse.* Edited by Georges Duby. Paris: Librairie Larousse, 1978. 324p. Index. ISBN 2-03-053305-X.

The *Atlas Historique Larousse* is a somewhat less ambitious French equivalent to the *Times Atlas of World History* [see 557]. Its chronological coverage ranges from prehistory to 1977 and begins with a large section of general maps on ancient and medieval history. This section is followed by general European-history maps and an alphabetical country-by-country section of maps. After that comes individual sections for Asia, Africa, and the Americas. European history receives the most attention in this atlas. Although it is not specifically a historical atlas of France, it is a good source for French maps. The cartography is very good, and the index is detailed.

550. *Atlas of Western Civilization.* 2d rev. ed. By Frederic van der Meer, English version by T. A. Birrell. Princeton, NJ: Van Nostrand, 1960. 240p.

The focus of this excellent atlas is the culture of Western civilization from ancient Greece to 1918. There are 52 maps in this collection arranged in chronological order, which are accompanied by an explanatory text and a large number of well-chosen black-and-white illustrations. Except for brief views of the Byzantine Empire, early Islamic civilization, and the western hemisphere, the maps are largely confined to Western Europe, which follows a description of the classical era. Artistic, intellectual, and religious themes figure as prominently in these maps as political developments. Historians of art and ideas will find this atlas to be of special interest to them, and browsers will find it a delight.

551. *Grosser Historischer Weltatlas.* Munich: Bayerischer Schulbuch-Verlag, 1978–1981. Erster Teil: *Vorgeschichte und Alterum.* 56p. 19p. index. Zweiter Teil: *Mittelalter.* 134p. 57p. index. Dritter Teil: *Neuzeit.* 110p. 36p. index. ISBN 3-7627-6021-7.

The *Grosser Historischer Weltatlas* is one of the more impressive achievements of German cartography. Arranged in three chronological volumes, it is one of the most comprehensive collections of maps available. Although the emphasis is European, with particular attention paid to Germany, many interesting and detailed maps are provided for other areas (e.g., a map of Nestorian Christianity in Asia during late antiquity and the early Middle Ages [Volume II, p. 72]). Another outstanding feature of this atlas is its many fine overlay maps (e.g., an overlay map of ancient Rome that fits over a map of the city in 1950 [Volume I, p. 35]). The indexing of each volume is extensive. Whenever it is available, this atlas is definitely worth consulting as a reference or even simply for browsing.

552. *Harper Atlas of World History.* Edited by Pierre Vidal-Naquet. New York: Harper & Row, 1987. 340p. Index. ISBN 0-06-181884-4.

More than an atlas, the *Harper Atlas of World History* also supplies a succinct narrative, attractive and abundant illustrations, and a running chronology. This reflects its origin in France, where it was published as *Le Grand Livre de l'histoire du monde* (Paris: Hachette, 1986). The information presented is arranged in chronological order and is most detailed for Europe and the United States, although Asia and Africa are given more attention than they usually receive in works of similar scope. This atlas is a helpful introductory work for the layman or the student and would be a good addition for the home library. For scholarly reference it is less useful, but that was not the primary purpose for which it was published.

553. *Muir's Historical Atlas: Ancient, Medieval, and Modern.* 10th ed. By Ramsey Muir and edited by R. F. Treharne and Harold Fullard. New York: Barnes & Noble, 1964. Various pagings. Index.

The many editions of this atlas testify to its status as a classic, while the coverage of its maps further reveals it as the product of an earlier age. *Muir's* is definitely what is called a "Eurocentric" work. Asia, Africa, Latin America are only portrayed in their relation to Western Europe. The United States is adequately covered, although even Eastern Europe and Russia are left on the periphery of this volume's vision. Religion, culture, population, and economics are also given scant attention. Still, if a traditional approach to political history is desired, Muir's maps are amply detailed and attractively done. Whether you refer to the complete edition or one of its subdivisions, this atlas remains well worth consulting.

554. *The New Cambridge Modern History Atlas.* Edited by H. C. Darby and Harold Fullard. Cambridge: Cambridge University Press, 1970. 319p. Index. LC 57-14935.

Although this atlas was made to accompany the *New Cambridge Modern History* as Volume XIV, it can stand on its own as a reference work. Its geographical coverage is worldwide, and its chronological coverage is from the midfifteenth century to the late 1960s. About 300 color maps fill the pages of this atlas, and although the volume's page size is smaller than normal for an atlas, most of the maps are quite readable, thanks to the excellent cartography. The arrangement of the maps is geographic, beginning with world maps showing various changes from the fifteenth to the twentieth century. That section is followed by a large group of maps illustrating wars and treaties of the modern era. From that point onward, the maps are grouped by region and country, beginning with Europe and followed by the individual European countries. Numerous maps for the other continents follow. It should be kept in mind that the index for this atlas is for subjects and not place-names. Another important consideration for individuals is that this atlas can be purchased separately from the *New Cambridge Modern History* and is available in paperback for the personal library.

555. *Rand McNally Historical Atlas of the World*. R. I. Moore, general editor. Chicago: Rand McNally, 1981. 192p. Index. ISBN 0-528-83124-0.

The approximately 100 maps in this atlas range from prehistory through the late 1970s in their chronological coverage. They are arranged into five sections: "The Ancient World," prehistory to A.D. 500; "Heirs to the Ancient World," A.D. 500 to 1500; "The Age of European Supremacy," 1500–1900; "The Emergence of the Modern World," 1900–1970s; and "United States Historical Maps." Europe is the focus of this atlas and receives the most attention. Political and military developments are also more commonly portrayed in the maps than religion, economics, and population. The maps that do appear for these topics, however, are done very well. In fact, the overall cartography of the atlas is attractive and easy to understand, and the accompanying text enhances the usefulness of the maps. This atlas definitely supersedes R. R. Palmer's *Rand McNally Atlas of World History* (Chicago: Rand McNally, 1957). Furthermore, although *Shepherd's Historical Atlas* [see 556] has more maps, the *Rand McNally Historical Atlas of the World* is more up-to-date and the cartography is clearly superior to the older and minimally revised *Shepherd's*. The *Rand McNally Historical Atlas of the World* is also available in a reasonably priced paperback for addition to the personal library.

556. *Shepherd's Historical Atlas*. 9th ed., rev. and updated. By William R. Shepherd. New York: Barnes & Noble, 1980. 115p. Index. ISBN 0-389-20155-3.

For generations of historians and students, the words "Shepherd" and "historical atlas" seem to go together as part of the natural order of things. Unfortunately, this older standard of historical atlases is beginning to show its age and has not been substantially revised since 1964. A few new maps have been added, but otherwise, the basic contents remain the same. Chronological coverage ranges from ancient Egypt to the present (ca.1970). Shepherd's emphasis is very much oriented toward Western Europe, and its many full-color, highly detailed and tipped in maps are accompanied by a large index. There is no accompanying text to explain and supplement the maps. In terms of sheer numbers of maps, Shepherd's remains superior to most of the world-history atlases available.

557. *The Times Atlas of World History*. 3d ed. Edited by Geoffrey Barraclough. Maplewood, NJ: Hammond, 1989. 358p. Index. ISBN 0-7230-0304-1.

This volume represents a significant revision and updating of the original 1978 and the 1984 editions of the much-acclaimed *Times Atlas of World History*. If possible, the newer edition should be consulted, although all three editions are masterpieces of the mapmaker's art. More than 100 plates depict the broad sweep of global history from prehistoric times to the present (ca.1980s) as arranged in seven chronological sections. As a result of such a wide geographical and chronological scope, some detail is lost, especially at the level of national history. Maps for military events are also overly generalized (e.g., the American Civil War is depicted by one map with an inset). Of course, more specialized atlases exist to supply such details, and it is the goal of the *Times Atlas of World History* to present a broad interpretive overview. Toward that end, it has been quite successful; it is the best and most comprehensive atlas of world history available in English. There is also a *Times Concise Atlas of World History* based on the second edition, which is available in paperback. Another excellent recent addition to the Times atlases is *The Times Atlas of the Second World War* (New York: Harper & Row, 1989).

558. *Westerman Grosser Atlas zur Weltgeschichte*. Braunschweig: Georg Westerman, 1981–1982. 170p. of maps, 78p. of summary and index. ISBN 3-14-100919-8.

German cartography is deservedly famous for its high quality and eye-pleasing appearance. The simple act of browsing through Westerman's historical atlas will be a distinct pleasure for any map lover. Its more than 400 maps are well designed and magnificently produced in full color. They begin with prehistory and proceed through to the world in the year 1981. Although political maps form the bulk of this atlas, there are also many maps dealing with culture, economics, population, and religion, along with numerous maps of cities. There is no explanatory text in the 1981/1982 edition, although the 1968 edition included a narrative introduction to the list of maps at the beginning of the volume. Europe is the main focus of this atlas, although Asia and Africa receive a fair amount of attention. The United States and the rest of the western hemisphere, however, are definitely slighted. Except for the last four pages of color maps dealing with 1981, there is no difference between the 1968 edition of this atlas and the 1981/1982 edition.

Historical Atlases: United States

559. *The American Heritage Pictorial Atlas of United States History.* Edited by Hilde Heun Kagan. New York: American Heritage, 1966. 424p. Index.

Beginning with prehistory, this atlas covers United States history up to 1965. Clear and attractive cartography, accompanied by an informative text and illustrations, characterize this impressive production. Although all aspects of history are dealt with, military subjects dominate, including a selection of interesting pictorial maps for the American Revolution and the Civil War. Like all American Heritage books, this volume is a pleasure to browse and to study. A generous index further enhances its value. Unlike the *Atlas of American History* [see 560], this atlas excels in depicting the motion and dynamics of history. It is unfortunate that it has been allowed to go out of print.

560. *Atlas of American History.* 2d rev. ed. New York: Scribner's, 1984. 306p. Index. ISBN 0-684-18411-7.

Originally produced in 1943 as a companion volume to the *Dictionary of American History*, this newly revised and expanded atlas can also stand on its own as an outstanding reference tool. Unlike many atlases, the Scribner's atlas does not have any accompanying text with its 200 maps. The maps are composed solely in black and white with a lucid presentation free of the clutter of unnecessary detail. Chronological coverage ranges from the Age of Discovery through 1982, with the population figures based on the 1980 census. Many topics are dealt with, such as politics, religion, the economy, and military affairs. The military maps generally only show places and do not depict movements of troops. There are also no individual battlefield maps. For the reader seeking historical place-name maps, the *Atlas of American History* is the best source. If dynamics, change, and battlefields are wanted, however, then *The American Heritage Pictorial Atlas of United States History* [see 559] is a better and more attractive atlas. Another classic work is Charles O. Paullin's *Atlas of the Historical Geography of the United States* (Washington, DC:

Carnegie Institution, 1932). A recent addition is Robert H. Ferrell and Richard Natkiel's *Atlas of American History* (New York: Facts on File, 1987). Many states have historical atlases, and the University of Oklahoma Press is publishing a serviceable series of historical atlases for individual states. Another valuable reference, edited by John H. Long, is the *Historical Atlas and Chronology of County Boundaries, 1788–1980* (Boston, MA: G. K. Hall, 1984).

561. *Atlas of Early American History: The Revolutionary Era, 1760–1790.* Edited by Lester J. Cappon et al. Princeton: published for The Newberry Library and The Institute of Early American History and Culture by Princeton University Press, 1976. 157p. Index. ISBN 0-911028-00-5.

As an example of the heights that historical cartography can reach, the *Atlas of Early American History* is unsurpassed. All aspects of American life from 1760–1790 form the subject of its 286 well-conceived and beautifully produced maps. Population, religion, cultural activity, political and legislative distributions, and economic activity all provide topics for the many detailed maps found in this atlas. Where did the various members of the American Philosophical Society live in 1790? What did Detroit look like in 1760? How did the news of Lexington and Concord spread? All of these questions and more are answered by the maps and text of this atlas. It is the final word for the time period it covers, and it is to be hoped that further volumes of similar quality will someday be published.

562. *Historical Atlas of Religion in America.* Rev. ed. By Edwin Scott Gaustad. New York: Harper & Row, 1976. 189p. Index. ISBN 0-06-063089-2.

Gaustad's volume is a convenient and useful reference work for the geographical and statistical history of Christianity and Judaism in the United States from 1650 to 1975. A rich text and many detailed figures and tables supplement and explain the approximately 70 black-and-white maps. The material is arranged into four parts, beginning with the colonial religious situation from 1650 to 1800. The major religious denominations in the United States from 1800 to 1975 are dealt with in the second and largest part of the book. In the third section, minor denominations (at least with regard to the United States) are discussed, and the fourth section looks at American Indian religion, Judaism, blacks in American religion, and the special religious situations of Hawaii and Alaska.

563. *The Historical Atlas of United States Congressional Districts, 1789–1983*. By Kenneth C. Martis. New York: Free Press, 1982. 302p. Index. ISBN 0-02-920150-0.

This important work of reference accomplishes several things: it supplies maps of all congressional districts for the United States House of Representatives, it has descriptions of these districts based on the legal documents, and it identifies all the representatives elected to Congress with their proper district. The atlas is divided into three parts: (1) an introduction that explains how the maps were compiled and how they might be used; (2) a section consisting of 97 national congressional district maps and a list of members for each congress; and (3) a section tracing the congressional redistricting of each state. A companion atlas is *The Historical Atlas of Political Parties in the United States Congress: 1789–1988*. (New York: Macmillan, 1989) Furthermore, Martis' atlas supersedes Stanley B. Parsons, William W. Beach, and Dan Hermann's *United States Congressional Districts 1788–1841* (Westport, CT: Greenwood Press, 1978). The latter work is much less comprehensive, but it does provide some information on population for each district that is not included in the Martis volume.

564. *We the People: An Atlas of America's Ethnic Diversity*. Edited by James P. Allen and Eugene J. Turner. New York: Macmillan, 1988. 315p. Index. ISBN 0-02-901420-4.

Students of immigration and ethnic studies will find a useful tool in this impressive atlas. It consists of 111 color maps with another 4 in black and white showing the distribution of 67 ethnic groups in the United States. The county is used as the geographical unit of study. There are also numerous appendixes of county-by-county ethnic census information. A useful complement is *This Remarkable Continent: An Atlas of United States and Canadian Society and Culture* (College Station, TX: Texas A&M University Press, 1982), edited by John F. Rooney, Jr., Wilbur Zelinsky, and Dean R. Louder, which looks at such diverse topics as music, food, house types, and sports.

565. *The West Point Atlas of American Wars*. Edited by Vincent J. Esposito. New York: Praeger, 1959. 2 vols. No pagination.

Published in two handsome volumes, this atlas is one of the finest reference works on military history available. Volume 1 covers the years 1689–1900, and Volume 2 contains the years 1900–1953. Unfortunately, the Vietnam War is not included in this atlas, which necessitates that it be updated. Otherwise, it is a fine atlas consisting of simple black-and-white topographical maps with troop positions superimposed on them in red and blue and a detailed text that accompanies and explains the maps. Where it is needed, great detail is provided (e.g., 11 maps illustrate the troop movements of the Chickamauga campaign of 26 June–20 September 1863). That is not to imply that this atlas is exhaustive in the information that it presents. Actions against the Indians are entirely left out, and three maps are all that are provided to illustrate the action of the four French and Indian Wars from 1689 to 1763. Only the most famous Civil War campaigns are included in the atlas, which means that minor actions in the Red River Valley, Arkansas, Missouri, and other places are ignored. It should also be mentioned that the Civil War maps have been extracted and published separately as the *West Point Atlas of the Civil War* (New York, Praeger, 1962).

Historical Atlases: Other Nations and Regions

566. *An Atlas of Russian and East European History.* By Arthur E. Adams, Ian M. Matley, and William O. McCagg. New York: Praeger, 1967. 204p. Index.

This atlas would be better titled *An Atlas of East European and Russian History,* since it contains so many maps dealing with Eastern Europe, and several other atlases for Russian history already exist [see 574]. There are 101 black-and-white maps in this atlas with an accompanying text. After starting with the usual maps of physical features and climate, the organization is chronological beginning with the fourth century A.D. and ending with the Communist world in 1965. This atlas is particularly useful because most general atlases of world history tend to neglect Eastern Europe. For those who read French, there is also Pierre Kovalevsky's *Atlas Historique et Culturel de la Russie et de Monde Slave* (Paris: Elsevier, 1961).

567. *Historical Atlas of Africa.* Edited by J. F. Ade Ajayi and Michael Crowder. New York: Cambridge University Press, 1985. 1 vol. various pagings. ISBN 0-521-25353-5.

Africa's history and geography have been beautifully served by Cambridge University Press's publication of the *Historical Atlas of Africa.* It contains some 300 maps that are arranged into 72 sections. An excellent brief introduction tells how to use this atlas and also explains the basic purposes and limitations of any historical atlas. The first few sections of maps deal with questions of physical features, climate, geology, and distribution of flora, fauna, and language groups. After that the maps are arranged in a chronological sequence, starting with prehistory and ending with 1980. The maps are classified into three types by their makers: "event" maps, depicting wars and political changes; "process" maps, illustrating the spread or movement of things over time, such as cattle, religions, or ethnic groups; and "quantitative" maps that supply numerical information and allow for comparisons between different areas or the same area over a period of time. An index allows people, places, and geographical features to be located easily on the various maps. Prior to the appearance of this atlas, the best atlas of African history was J. D. Fage's still useful *An Atlas of African History*, 2d ed. (New York: Africana Publishing, 1978).

568. *Historical Atlas of Britain*. Malcolm Falkus and John Gillingham, eds. New York: Continuum; distr., New York: Crossroad Publishing, 1981. 223p. Index. ISBN 0-8264-0179-1.

Falkus and Gillingham have produced the best and most attractive atlas of Britain to date. It consists of eight chapters, of which the first six are a chronological presentation of British political history from prehistoric times to 1981. The seventh and eighth chapters deal with economic and social history topics, such as population, wealth distribution, transportation, and agriculture. Color maps are integrated with a survey text and supplemented by well-chosen color or black-and-white illustrations and genealogical charts. England receives the lion's share of attention in this atlas, although useful maps are provided for aspects of Scotland, Wales, and Ireland's history. There is also a falling off in the coverage of this volume for the years following 1945. Still it is superior to Martin Gilbert's *British History Atlas* (New York: Macmillan, 1968) and G. S. P. Freeman-Grenville's *Atlas of British History* (London: Rex Collings, 1979).

569. *Historical Atlas of Canada*. Vol. I, *From the Beginning to 1800*. Edited by R. Cole Harris. Toronto: University of Toronto Press, 1987. 198p. Index. ISBN 0-8020-2495-5.

This handsome volume is the first of a three-volume set. It consists of 69 color plates dealing with Canadian prehistory, exploration, French and British settlement, and the situation of Canada in 1800. The cartography is excellent, and the topics illustrated by the maps are all based on extensive research. When this set is finished, it will be in the forefront of historical atlases concerned with an individual nation.

570. *An Historical Atlas of China*. By Albert Herrmann with new edition by Norton Ginsburg. Chicago: Aldine, 1966. 88p. Index.

China, like many countries and areas, needs a new up-to-date historical atlas based on the latest scholarship and cartographic techniques. In the meantime, what is currently available for China is better than what exists for most countries. Albert Herrmann's atlas first appeared in English in 1935 and was based on the highest standards of scholarship for that time. It was reprinted in 1966, and as a resource for both Chinese and general Asian history from prehistory to just prior to the nineteenth century it remains quite useful. The cartography is excellent and combines great detail with clear presentation. For the modern period, it is best to consult Caroline Blunden and Mark Elvin's *Cultural Atlas of China* (New York: Facts on File, 1983).

571. *An Historical Atlas of Islam*. Edited by William C. Brice. Leiden, Netherlands: E. J. Brill, 1981. 71p. Index. ISBN 90-04-06116-9.

The history of Islam is inextricably tied to the history of large parts of Asia and Africa. This atlas reflects that fact and was compiled as a companion volume to the massive and erudite *Encyclopedia of Islam*, also published by E. J. Brill. Its 60 color maps are well designed and excellently reproduced and cover many topics not found in other historical atlases of the world. The index is quite detailed, but there is no explanatory text to go with the maps and to aid beginners in the subject. Furthermore, the coverage of the twentieth century is quite weak. For maps dealing with that time period, it is best to use Francis Robinson's *Atlas of the Islamic World since 1500* (New York: Facts on File, 1982), which is as much an encyclopedia as an atlas.

572. *A Historical Atlas of South Asia*. Joseph E. Schwartzberg et al., eds. Chicago: University of Chicago Press, 1978. 352p. Index. ISBN 0-226-74221-0.

The history of South Asia, which is defined in this case as the area of the present nations of India, Pakistan, Bangladesh, Afghanistan, Nepal, Bhutan, Sri Lanka, and the Maldives, is impressively depicted in this excellent atlas. A dedicated team of scholars labored for more than a decade to produce its 650 well-researched, four-color maps, which deal with cultural, social, demographic, and economic topics as well as political ones. Chronologically the maps range from the Stone Age to 1977, although more than half of the atlas is concerned with the post-1857 period. Furthermore, the emphasis of the maps in this atlas is to portray periods of time rather than specific points in time (e.g., "1526–1707" rather than simply "1526"). A text of more than 100 pages helps to explain the maps, and an index with 15,000 entries will aid the reader in the location of places and subjects. There is also a bibliography of more than 4,000 entries on South Asian history and related topics. Inserts at the back of the volume consist of two transparent overlay maps and three chronological charts. This work is one of the most scholarly atlases available in English and is definitely the best source for the historical geography of South Asia.

573. *Latin American History: A Teaching Atlas.* By Cathryn L. Lombardi and John V. Lombardi. Madison: University of Wisconsin Press, 1983. 104p and 40p. Index. ISBN 0-299-09710-2.

The Lombardi atlas was published by the Conference on Latin American History and consists of 104 black-and-white maps. The organization is basically chronological, beginning with the pre-conquest Indians and proceeding to the late 1970s. Many maps deal with their subjects in a detail found in few or no other atlases (e.g., the voyages of the Dutch privateer Piet Heyn during the 1620s). The cartography is simple and clear. Although this is a quite serviceable atlas, it is surprising that as important a field as Latin American studies is not served by an atlas of the stature of the *Historical Atlas of Africa* [*see* 567]. Still, this atlas is the best one available and is a major improvement over its predecessor A. Curtis Wilgus's *Historical Atlas of Latin America: Political, Geographic, Economic, Cultural* (New York: Cooper Square, 1967).

574. *Russian History Atlas.* By Martin Gilbert. New York: Macmillan Company, 1972. 146p. 15p. index.

Atlases in English of non-English-speaking countries are rare. Hence Martin Gilbert's atlas of Russian history, which ranges from prehistory to 1970, is particularly welcome. Its more than 140 maps are done in black and white with no accompanying narrative or explanatory text. The cartography is clear and serviceable, although by no means a work of art. Although the maps are primarily political and military in their subject matter, religion, economics, and culture also appear on some maps. This atlas is particularly useful for its detailed treatment of medieval and early modern Russia, the Russian Civil War, and the non-Muscovite ethnic groups. Another useful atlas is Allen F. Chew's *An Atlas of Russian History: Eleven Centuries of Changing Borders* (New Haven, CT: Yale University Press, 1967). It consists of 34 maps in black and white, accompanied by an explanatory text.

Historical Atlases: Specific Periods and Topics

575. *Atlas of Classical History.* Edited by Richard J. A. Talbert. New York: Macmillan, 1985. 217p. Index. ISBN 0-02-933110-2.

Richard Talbert and his 25 contributors have performed a great service by providing an up-to-date atlas of classical history that will be of use to readers from high school through graduate school. Its 132 maps may be only in black and white, but they are generally clear and attractive in their design and are always accompanied by a lucid explanatory text. The chronological coverage of this atlas is from Bronze Age Greece to A.D. 314. A 28-page gazetteer is a further aid to the reader, along with an introductory bibliography. The emphasis of these maps is the location of places and boundaries of significance to political, religious, military, cultural, and economic history. Particularly interesting are the many city maps and the maps of Roman provinces showing the extensive system of roads. This atlas is a tribute to what can be accomplished without using the most expensive cartographic techniques. Also of interest is Nicholas G. L. Hammond's very competent *Atlas of the Greek and Roman World in Antiquity* (Park Ridge, NJ: Noyes Press, 1981).

576. *Atlas of Maritime History.* By Richard Natkiel and Antony Preston. New York: Facts on File, 1986. 256p. Index. ISBN 0-8160-1132-X.

From the ancient Phoenicians to oceanic trade in the 1980s is the chronological scope of this excellent atlas. All maritime topics are covered in this work, although military subjects predominate. There is some bias toward English and European history, which is much more heavily represented than naval episodes from American history. Text, illustrations, and the many detailed maps are nicely integrated. The maps are produced in black, white, and blue with fine attention to detail, yet remaining clear and uncluttered in their presentation. A small but useful glossary and a simple index conclude this volume. This atlas is far superior to Christopher Lloyd's *Atlas of Maritime History* (New York: Arco, 1975).

577. *Atlas of the Jewish World.* By Nicholas de Lange. New York: Facts on File, 1984. 240p. Index. ISBN 0-87196-043-5.

Facts on File atlases tend to be more encyclopedias than atlases. *The Atlas of the Jewish World* certainly follows this format in its coverage of Jewish history and culture from antiquity to the present. Besides approximately 50 color maps, there is an ample narrative text and an excellent selection of illustrations. The material is divided into three sections: "The Historical Background," "The Cultural Background," and "The Jewish Way of Life." For a more straightforward atlas, with a larger number of maps but of inferior cartographic quality, there is Martin Gilbert's *Jewish History Atlas*, 2d ed. (New York: Macmillan, 1977).

578. *Historical Atlas of the Religions of the World*. By Ismail Ragi al Faruqi. New York: Macmillan, 1974. 346p. Indexes. ISBN 0-02-336400-9.

As much an encyclopedia as an atlas, the *Historical Atlas of the Religions of the World* is divided into three parts: "Religions of the Past," e.g., ancient Egyptian and Greco-Roman paganism; "Ethnic Religions of the Present," e.g., Sikhism and Shinto; and "Universal Religions of the Present," e.g., Christianity and Islam. There are 65 maps distributed through 20 illustrated chapters that are each written by an expert on the subject. The text is followed by an appendix of chronologies for the various religions. Another more specialized atlas is Henry Chadwick and Gillian Evans's recent *Atlas of the Christian Church* (New York: Facts on File, 1987).

579. *The Macmillan Bible Atlas*. By Yohanan Aharoni and Michael Avi-Yonah. New York: Macmillan, 1968. 184p. Index. ISBN 0-02-500590-1.

The 264 three-color maps of this atlas range from the prehistoric Near East to the extent of Christianity in the second century A.D. Although biblical events form the primary focus of its maps, this atlas also deals extensively with large segments of the history of the ancient Near East. It is the product of two well-respected Israeli archaeologists who have produced clear and uncluttered cartography and a readable accompanying text. There is also a detailed biblical chronology and an index. When it is relevant, each map is related to the appropriate section of the Bible. A more recent atlas on the same subject is James B. Pritchard's *The Harper Atlas of the Bible* (New York: Harper & Row, 1987).

580. *The World Atlas of Archaeology*. Boston: G. K. Hall, 1985. 423p. Index. ISBN 0-8161-8747-9.

"Beautiful" and "impressive" are the two adjectives that justly describe this atlas. Its coverage is truly worldwide, with the ancient Near East, Meso-America, China, and other regions of the world all getting their fair share of attention. The 19 sections are organized on a partly chronological and partly geographical basis, with further subdivisions within each section. Ninety experts have produced a text that is well integrated with a multitude of maps and illustrations, most of which are in color. Cartographically, the maps are a pleasure to look at and are easy to read. This work, as well as the excellent *Past Worlds: The Times Atlas of Archaeology,* edited by Chris Scarre (New York: Hammond, 1989), are intended for the layman and the novice in archaeology.

12.

Historical Statistical Sources

Statistical sources are of value to the historian, particularly those publications compiling a wide range of statistics over a period of time. Most of the data in these statistical compilations comes from the nineteenth and twentieth centuries; data on earlier periods is difficult or impossible to obtain in any convenient form. Historical statistics are diverse and include data ranging from population and climate to religion and agriculture. The terminology used in these statistical sources may be unfamiliar to the novice in historical research. *Time-series* data, for example, refers to any series of data collected or recorded at regular intervals of time, and the term *national accounts* is defined as the totaling of various economic accounts to provide an estimate of national income.

This chapter is designed to make the student of history aware of basic historical statistical sources. These include general bibliographies and indexes, periodicals and time series, as well as international, regional, and country sources of statistical information. Many of these sources are available on computer tapes or diskettes and CD-ROM. The chapter does not attempt to be exhaustive, but seeks to provide a good introduction to the topic.

General

Bibliographies and Indexes

581. *Bibliography of Official Statistical Yearbooks and Bulletins.* By Gloria Westfall. Alexandria, VA: Chadwyck-Healey, 1986. 247p. ISBN 0-85964-124-4.

This recent volume provides detailed information on 374 statistical yearbooks and bulletins, covering data published by the national statistical offices of more than 180 countries. The main part of the work is divided into five broad geographical headings: Africa, the Americas, Asia, Europe, and Oceania. Within these headings the material is arranged alphabetically by country. Entries include the title of the yearbook or bulletin, publisher, length and frequency of publication, and detailed information about the subjects covered (e.g., demography, economic affairs). Information on sources of historical statistics for each country is also provided, when available. Data from many of the statistical yearbooks listed in Westfall's work can also be found in a convenient microfiche set: *Current National Statistical Compendiums* (Bethesda, MD: Congressional Information Service, 1974–).

582. *Index to International Statistics (IIS): A Guide to the Statistical Publications of International Intergovernmental Organizations.* Bethesda, MD: Congressional Information Service, 1983–. ISSN 0737-4461. Monthly, with annual cumulations.

The *Index to International Statistics* (IIS) serves as a comprehensive guide to the English-language statistical publications of 95 international organizations, including the publications of the United Nations, the Organization for Economic Cooperation and Development, the European Community, and the Organization of American States. Covering the years from 1983 to the present and indexing more than 1,700 titles, IIS is arranged similarly to another Congressional Information Service index, the *American Statistics Index* (ASI). IIS is divided into two parts—indexes and abstracts. In the index volume, sources are indexed by subject, name, geographic area, category, issuing source, title, and publication number. There are detailed abstracts for each publication, many of which are available on microfiche from IIS. It is an excellent index for finding international statistics on a wide variety of subjects. Two other publications that also provide subject access to a large number of U.S. and international statistical publications are *Data Map* (Phoenix, AZ: Oryx Press, 1983–) and *SISCIS: Subject Index to Sources of Comparative International Statistics* (Beckenham, U.K.: CBD Research, 1978).

583. *Statistics Sources, 1990.* 13th ed. Edited by Jacqueline Wasserman O'Brien and Steven R. Wasserman. Detroit: Gale Research, 1989. 2 vols. ISBN 0-8103-4699-0.

This massive two-volume work is extremely useful as a subject-finding guide to sources of statistics, including sources of data on industry, business, society, education, finance, and other subjects both for the United States and the rest of the world. It contains nearly 60,000 citations. *Statistics Sources* covers U.S. government statistical publications as well as statistical publications from the United Nations, other international organizations, and various national statistical offices. The volumes are arranged alphabetically by subject, and the subject entries contain information about publications where statistics on that topic can be found. Within each country, citations refer to that country's national statistical office, the major printed sources, and the basic printed compilation that provides economic, financial, and monetary data on that country. *Statistics Sources* is a good starting place for finding statistical publications on a number of topics.

Periodicals and Time Series

584. *Cross-Polity Time-Series Data.* By Arthur S. Banks and the Staff of the Center for Comparative Political Research, State University of New York at Binghamton. Cambridge: MIT Press, 1971. 300p. ISBN 0-262-02071-8.

Although a single volume, this unique work presents a wide range of statistical time-series country data drawn from the data archive at the Center for Comparative Political Research at the State University of New York at Binghamton. The data is drawn from a number of sources, including the *Statesman's Year-Book, Europa Yearbook,* and the United Nation's *Statistical Yearbook,* and covers the period from 1815 to 1966. Banks' work is divided into ten sections, each containing statistical data on particular subjects, such as population, area, national government revenue, transportation, economic data, and domestic conflict. Within each section the data is arranged alphabetically by country and chronologically. For the historian, this work brings together information on more than 100 topics for many different countries, covering, in some cases, a time period of more than 100 years.

The historian should also be aware that there is an enormous amount of statistical time-series data on the United States and other countries available in machine-readable form through the Inter-University Consortium for Political and Social Research (ICPSR), located in Ann Arbor, Michigan. Many research libraries belong to this organization and can obtain the data tapes for researchers. For a complete list of ICPSR's holdings check their latest *Guide to Resources and Services.*

585. *The Statesman's Year-Book.* London: Macmillan; New York: St. Martin's Press, 1864–. ISSN 0081-4601. Annual.

Since its first publication in 1864, this annual volume has contained a wealth of statistical information about different countries of the world. The most recent volumes are divided into two parts: (1) "International Organizations" and (2) "Countries of the World," listed alphabetically. Concise information is supplied for each country, including its history, area and population, climate, constitution and government, defense, economy, energy and natural resources, communications, judicial system, religion, education, and diplomatic representatives. Much of the information is statistical, and at the end of each country's profile there is a bibliography of references. Since it was first published, this extremely useful reference source has more than doubled in size. Material in the early volumes is less comprehensive, but for the historian, it is a good source of statistical information on various countries dating back to the midnineteenth century.

United Nations

586. *Demographic Yearbook; Annuaire Demographique.* New York: United Nations, 1948–. Index. ISSN 0082-8041. Annual.

The United Nations is the major publisher of recent international statistical information, including a number of serial statistical publications. One major statistical reference source published by the U.N. is the *Demographic Yearbook,* prepared by its Statistical Office. Published annually since 1948, this yearbook supplies detailed world and country data on population and vital statistics, such as birthrates, infant and maternal mortality, general mortality, marriage, and divorce. Each volume is divided into two parts: (1) statistical tables and (2) special topics tables, for example, mortality statistics updating earlier tables. In 1979 a special *Historical Supplement* of the *Demographic Yearbook* was published, containing time-series data on population, natality, mortality, and nuptiality from 1948 to 1978. The 1948 volume, the first one in the series, also contains annual data for the years 1932–1947. Since the *Yearbook* is not totally current, more up-to-date information can be found in the U.N.'s quarterly *Population and Vital Statistics Report,* which updates many of the statistical tables found in the main *Yearbook* volumes.

587. *Statistical Yearbook; Annuaire Statistique.* New York: United Nations, 1948–. ISSN 0082-8459. Annual.

This is the major statistical compendium of social and economic data published by the Statistical Office of the United Nations. It draws on a number of other more specialized U.N. and international agency publications. Beginning in 1948, the *Yearbook* has been published annually and contains statistics on more than 200 countries. Much of the data covers ten-year periods and includes world and country statistics on population and manpower, national accounts, wages, prices, consumption, balance of payments, finance, health, education, agriculture, manufacturing, energy, trade, transportation, and communications. Although the annual volumes of the *Yearbook* are not quite current, they can be updated by the U.N.'s *Monthly Bulletin of Statistics,* which contains more recent data. Since the United Nations publishes a wide range of other statistical publications, the *Directory of International Statistics* (New York: United Nations, 1982) should be consulted for a listing of these sources, which are also indexed in the *Index to International Statistics* [*see* 582].

United States

588. *American Statistics Index: A Comprehensive Guide to the Statistical Publications of the U.S. Government.* Bethesda, MD: Congressional Information Service, 1973–. ISSN 0091-1658. Annual, with monthly supplements.

This Congressional Information Service (CIS) index has greatly simplified locating statistical information published by the federal government. Similar in arrangement to the *Index to International Statistics* [*see* 582], the *American Statistics Index* (ASI) is the most comprehensive index to recent U.S. government statistical publications, covering 5,000 titles, including 600 periodicals. There is a *Retrospective Edition,* which indexes publications from 1960 to 1973, and the annual cumulative volumes, beginning in 1974. The ASI is divided into two parts—index and abstracts. Items are indexed by subject and name, category, title, agency report numbers, and Superintendent of Documents (SuDoc) numbers. Abstracts are extremely detailed, providing the SuDoc number and an extensive description of the statistical material contained in a particular publication. The ASI can also be searched on-line through major services such as DIALOG. Since 1980 another CIS publication, the *Statistical Reference Index* (SRI), has indexed statistics published by private organizations and state agencies. This index, along with ASI and IIS, is now available from CIS on CD-ROM under the title *Statistical Masterfile*. Almost all the documents indexed on ASI, SRI, and IIS are available on microfiche from CIS.

589. *Bureau of the Census Catalog of Publications, 1790–1972.* Washington, DC: Government Printing Office, 1974. 591p. Index.

The publications of the United States Bureau of the Census are a valuable source of historical and current statistics about all aspects of American life. For the historian interested in using census publications, this one-volume *Catalog of Publications* is an excellent bibliographic guide. It is in reality a compilation of two catalogs: *The Catalog of United States Census Publications, 1790–1945* (Washington, DC: Government Printing Office, 1950) and the more recent *Bureau of the Census Catalog of Publications, 1946–1972*. Within the volume, publications are arranged by broad census subject areas, such as population, housing, and agriculture. There are detailed descriptions of individual publications and subject indexes to each of the two catalogs. For more recent information on current census publications, the researcher should check the annual *Census Catalog & Guide* (Washington, DC: Government Printing Office, 1947–). Recent census information is searchable through the data base CENDATA, and more of it is produced in various machine-readable forms, as well as CD-ROM, by both the federal government and private publishers. Also helpful as a guide to census material are three recent volumes by Suzanne Schulze: *Population Information in Nineteenth Century Census Volumes*, *Population Information in Twentieth Century Census Volumes, 1900–1940*, and *Population Information in Twentieth Century Census Volumes, 1950–1980*, all published by Oryx Press in 1983, 1985, and 1988.

590. *Historical Statistics of the United States, Colonial Times to 1970.* Bicentennial ed. Washington, DC: Government Printing Office, 1975. 1,200p. 2 vols. Index. Reprint. White Plains, NY: Kraus International, 1989. ISBN 0-525-91756-7 (set).

This volume is the third and most recent in the *Historical Statistics* series published by the Bureau of the Census, which is a supplement to the *Statistical Abstract of the United States* [see 591]. The current two-volume work conveniently compiles federal statistics from the colonial period to 1970, including more than 12,500 time series, representing a 50 percent increase over the previous edition. Statistics compiled in these volumes cover every social and economic area, including population, vital statistics, labor, consumer income and expenditures, agriculture, manufactures, transportation, energy, business enterprise, and government. There are entensive notes before each chapter that list statistical sources and explain the type and reliability of the data. Data in the tables is mainly annual, and there is a chapter at the end on colonial and pre-federal statistics. The volumes are indexed by time period and by subject. Most of the current time-series tables found in *Historical Statistics* are updated in the annual volumes of the *Statistical Abstract of the United States*, beginning with the 1973 issue. Also, a *Supplement to Historical Statistics of the United States* will be published by Kraus International Publications, updating the current volume.

591. *Statistical Abstract of the United States.* Washington, DC: Government Printing Office, 1879–. Index. Annual.

Published annually since 1879, this single volume is the standard ready-reference source of U.S. government political, social, and economic statistics. It contains a wide-ranging selection of statistics drawn from many federal and private statistical publications. Within the volume, the data is arranged into chapters by subject (e.g., population, elections). Usually the tables cover the past several years, although some tables cover 15 to 20 years. There is a detailed index, and several appendixes include material on guides to sources of statistics, metropolitan statistical areas and their components, and statistical methodology and reliability. In recent years there have been two supplements to the *Statistical Abstract*: the *County and City Data Book* (Washington, DC: Government Printing Office, 1952–) and the *State and Metropolitan Area Data Book* (Washington, DC: Government Printing Office, 1980–). The tabular data published in the *Statistical Abstract* and its supplements is now also available on diskette and CD-ROM.

Canada

592. *Historical Statistics of Canada.* 2d ed. Edited by F. H. Leacy. Ottawa: Statistics Canada, 1983. ca. 900p. Index. ISBN 0-660-11259-0.

The Canadian equivalent to the *Historical Statistics of the United States*, this volume publishes in one location Canadian statistics from 1867 through the mid-1970s. This second edition updates the earlier *Historical Statistics of Canada* (Toronto: Macmillan, 1965). Arranged by broad subjects, as in the U.S. volume, chapters include time-series data on population and migration, vital statistics and health, price indexes, agriculture, and energy and electric power. At the beginning of each chapter there is a detailed explanation and list of the sources. A subject index ends the volume. For more current Canadian statistics, the researcher should check the annual volumes of the *Canada Year Book* (Ottawa: Statistics Canada, 1906–), which updates the historical volume and is the Canadian version of the *Statistical Abstract of the United States* [see 591]. Also useful as an index to available Canadian statistics is the recent *Canadian Statistics Index* (Toronto: Micromedia, 1985–).

Europe

General

593. *The East European and Soviet Data Handbook: Political, Social, and Developmental Indicators, 1945–1975.* By Paul S. Shoup. New York: Columbia University Press, 1981. 482p. ISBN 0-231-04252-3.

Shoup's work makes available to researchers a great deal of historical data on the Soviet Union and the countries of Eastern Europe. Covering the period from 1945 to 1975, it also contains data from the period before World War II. This volume is structured to provide cross-national and historical comparisons. After a lengthy general introduction describing the types of data collected and the reliability of that data, the *Handbook* is arranged by sections. These include chapters on population, party membership, national and religious affiliation, level of education, classes, background of party leaders, occupations, and developmental indicators and standard of living. Some of this material is not available in other sources. There are a number of appendixes as well as a bibliography, a summary of sources, and a listing of sources for individual tables. This work is an excellent source of political and social statistics of the region during the post-World War II period.

594. *European Historical Statistics, 1750–1975.* 2d rev. ed. By B. R. Mitchell. New York: Facts on File, 1980. 868p. ISBN 0-87196-329-9.

This work is valuable because it brings together in one volume a compendium of statistics for individual European countries covering the period from 1750 to 1975. The second edition is an update of an earlier volume, published in 1975, and corrects some of the errors and revises some of the tables in the original work. Mitchell's work draws heavily on the official statistical publications of the European governments. It supplies statistical data on 26 European countries in 75 tables arranged under 11 broad subject areas. These include climate, population and vital statistics, labor force, agriculture, industry, external trade, transport and communications, finance, prices, education, and national accounts. The comprehensiveness of the data varies from country to country. Each chapter includes a brief introduction to its statistical tables. One drawback of this work is the lack of a detailed subject index for quickly locating material. For recent statistics on Western Europe, there are the statistical yearbooks of individual countries and the many statistical publications of the Organization for Economic Cooperation and Development (OECD) and the European Communities.

Great Britain

595. *British Historical Statistics.* By B. R. Mitchell. Cambridge: Cambridge University Press, 1988. 886p. Index. ISBN 0-521-33008-4.

This volume, which is an updating of two earlier volumes—*Abstract of British Historical Statistics* and the *Second Abstract of British Historical Statistics*, is the best single source for social and economic statistics for the history of Great Britain. The emphasis is on economic statistics, but the new volume includes a greater amount of social statistics than the earlier volumes. Mitchell's work is arranged into 16 chapters, including the broad topics of population and vital statistics, labor force, agriculture, external trade, public finance, and prices. There is a detailed explanatory introduction before each chapter, followed by the tables. These present data from a wide range of years, in some cases dating back to the fourteenth century. Most of the annual data covers the nineteenth and twentieth centuries, and there is a subject index at the end of the volume. For more recent statistics on Great Britain, see the *Annual Abstract of Statistics* (London: Her Majesty's Stationery Office, 1840/1853–).

France

596. *Annuaire Statistique de la France.* Paris: Institut National de la Statistique et des Etudes Economiques, 1878–. Index. Annual, with occasional historical volumes.

Written in French, this yearbook is the best statistical source for all aspects of French political, economic, and social life. Published since

1878, these annual volumes are arranged by broad subject categories, including climate, environment, population, vital statistics, agriculture and food, commerce and business, education, housing, and labor. Most of the statistical tables give five to ten years of data. There is a subject index at the end of each volume, along with a list of French and international statistical agencies and publications. Certain volumes in the series provide historical statistical data (e.g., the volumes for 1946, 1951, 1961, and 1966), and the volumes from 1881 to 1939 include data from earlier periods.

Germany

597. *Statistisches Jahrbuch fur die Bundesrepublik Deutschland.* Wiesbaden, West Germany: Statistisches Bundesamt, 1952–. Index. Annual.

Published since 1952, this is the major statistical yearbook for West Germany. Written in German, it includes statistics on climate and environment, population, vital statistics, agriculture, industry, education, housing, and religion. Most of the data covers the previous four years. In addition to the national data, the yearbook includes material on individual states, districts, counties, and municipalities. There is a section on East Germany and a subject index to each volume. For earlier German statistics, there is the *Statistisches Jahrbuch fur das Deutsche Reich*, published by Statistisches Reichsamt, which covers the years from 1880 to 1942. There is a separate statistical source for East Germany: *Statistisches Jahrbuch der Deutschen Demokratischen Republik* (Berlin: Staatliche Zentralverwaltung fur Statistik, 1955–).

Soviet Union

598. *USSR Facts & Figures Annual.* Gulf Breeze, FL: Academic International Press, 1977–. Annual. ISSN 0148-7760.

The best and most reliable English-language annual for statistics on the Soviet Union, it has been published since 1977. Each volume contains a wide variety of statistics. After a brief introductory overview of current developments in the Soviet Union, the most recent volume is divided into chapters covering such topics as the Communist Party, armed forces, population, economy, foreign aid, science, education, welfare, and nationalities. Most of the information is in the form of tables, some containing data going back as far as 1940. A special-topics chapter concludes the volume and contains a list of recent obituaries of prominent individuals, a chronology of events, and a list of recent books on the Soviet Union. It is important to note that the latest volume in the series does not cumulate the earlier ones. Each volume in this series contains a great deal of material that is not found in the other volumes.

Latin America

599. *International Historical Statistics: The Americas and Australasia.* By B. R. Mitchell. Detroit: Gale Research, 1983. 949p. ISBN 0-8103-0520-8.

This is the third in a series of historical statistics volumes including *European Historical Statistics* and *International Historical Statistics: Africa and Asia* [see 594 and 602]. This volume contains statistical information drawn mainly from the statistical yearbooks of the countries of North and South America, as well as Australia, Fiji, and New Zealand. Individual chapters supply data on climate, population and vital statistics, agriculture, trade, finance, prices, education, and various other topics. While most of the tabular data is for the twentieth century, there is also statistical information for much of the nineteenth century. The amount of information supplied by the tables varies according to the topic and the country.

600. *Statistical Abstract of Latin America.* Los Angeles: UCLA Latin American Center Publications, 1955–. Index. Annual. ISSN 0081-4687.

This is the best and most detailed annual compilation of social and economic statistical data on the countries of Latin America. Published since 1955, the most recent of these volumes contains data from more than 200 sources on 20 South and Central American countries, including Cuba, Haiti, and the Dominican Republic. This latest volume consists of ten sections with tables on the topics of geography and land tenure; transportation and communications; population, health, and education; politics, religion, and the military; working conditions, migration, and housing; industry, mining, and energy; sea and land harvests; foreign trade; financial transactions; and national accounts, government policy and finance, and prices. Tables contain both recent and time-series data. Since 1970 the Latin American Center has published supplements to the *Abstract* containing data on more specialized topics. Two other sources, the *Statistical Bulletin of the OAS* and the *Statistical Yearbook for Latin America and the Caribbean,* also contain recent statistical information on Latin America.

Africa and Asia

General

601. *African Statistical Yearbook.* Addis Ababa: United Nations Economic Commission for Africa, 1974–. Annual. ISSN 0252-5488.

Beginning publication in 1974, this work provides detailed statistical information for 52 African countries. The *Yearbook* is divided geographically into four parts: "North Africa," "West Africa," "East and Southern Africa," and "Central Africa and Others in Africa." Each volume is arranged alphabetically by country and contains country statistics on such topics as population and employment, national accounts, agriculture, industry, prices, education, and health. The volumes cover data from the most recent ten-year period available. The *Yearbook* is not completely current, and more recent statistical data on African countries can be found in a number of United Nations publications. The most current U.N. source is the *Monthly Bulletin of Statistics.*

602. *International Historical Statistics: Africa and Asia.* By B. R. Mitchell. New York: New York University Press, 1982. 761p. ISBN 0-8147-5385-X.

A companion volume to the earlier *European Historical Statistics* [see 594], this volume draws heavily upon the official statistical publications of the countries of Africa and Asia (data on the People's Republic of China is not included). Its statistical data is organized into tables by broad subject categories, such as climate, population, agriculture, external trade, prices, education, and national accounts. Although there is coverage in some tables going back well into the nineteenth century, much of the annual data is for the twentieth century. Basically, this volume provides the same types of historical statistical data for the countries of Africa and Asia as the earlier volume covered for Europe. Also included in this volume are historical statistics on the countries of the Middle East, such as Egypt and Israel. More recent data can be found in the various statistical yearbooks of these countries.

603. *Statistical Yearbook for Asia and the Pacific.* Bangkok, Thailand: United Nations Economic and Social Commission for Asia and the Pacific, 1973–. ISBN 92-1-119447-4. Annual. ISSN 0252-3655.

Continuing an earlier United Nations' publication, *Statistical Yearbook for Asia and the Far East,* this annual volume contains detailed statistics on 44 Asian and Pacific countries, including China, Vietnam, Japan, and Korea. Each statistical volume covers a broad range of topics, including population, national accounts, agriculture, forestry and fishing, industry, transportation and communications, external trade, wages, prices and consumption, and finance and social statistics. The statistics are taken from international and national statistical agencies and generally contain data covering the past ten years. Since the most recent volume of the *Statistical Yearbook* is not totally current, it can be updated by consulting the *Quarterly Bulletin for Asia and the Pacific,* which contains more recent data for many of its tables. For historical statistics on many Asian countries, there is the *International Historical Statistics: Africa and Asia* [*see* 602].

China

604. *Statistical Yearbook of China.* Hong Kong: Economic Information Agency, 1982–. Annual. ISSN 0255-6766.

This is the official and most detailed volume of social and economic statistics for the People's Republic of China. The most recent volume is arranged into 16 chapters that provide detailed statistical tables on population, labor, agriculture, industry, transport, telecommunications, construction, domestic trade, public finance, prices, education, science, culture, and sports. In some tables, data goes back to 1949. Two useful appendixes provide statistics on the "Principal Economic Indicators of Taiwan Province" and "Major Economic and Social Indicators of China in Comparison with Foreign Countries." A detailed explanatory note is included at the end of the volume. Also useful for statistics on China and more current than the *Yearbook* is the annual *China Facts and Figures Annual* (Gulf Breeze, FL: Academic International Press, 1978–). For the most recent economic data on China, there is the new publication *China Statistics Monthly* (Chicago and Beijing: University of Illinois at Chicago and China Statistical Information and Consultancy Service Center, 1988–).

Japan

605. *Japan Statistical Yearbook*. Tokyo: Statistics Bureau, 1949–. Index. Annual. ISSN 0389-9004.

Continuing the *Statistical Yearbook of the Empire of Japan*, which was published from 1882 to 1941, the *Japan Statistical Yearbook* is the most comprehensive source for social and economic statistics about Japan. Published in both Japanese and English, the *Yearbook* contains extensive statistics on a wide variety of subjects, including climate, population, labor, agriculture, manufacturing, energy, prices, national accounts, health, education, and disasters and accidents. There are two appendixes in the most recent volume, listing key statistics and a guide to sources, although these are listed only in Japanese. Another drawback is that the index is also solely in Japanese. The volume also contains a section with international statistics from other countries. Although the section on key statistics contains data in time series going back as far as 1945, much of the data in the most recent volume is from the past several years. An explanation of the materials covered in the tables precedes each chapter.

13.

Guides to Archives, Manuscripts, and Special Collections

Serious research in history requires the use of primary documents, which include archival, manuscript, and special collection material. The term *archives* often refers to the official records of a nation, an institution, or an organization. It can also refer to the repository that contains these types of records. *Manuscripts* usually refers to a collection of primary documents housed in an archive, library, or research institution. *Special collection material* can include manuscripts, but can also contain other types of primary source documents.

This chapter covers guides to archives, manuscripts, and special collections. It is not designed to be totally comprehensive; its purpose is to provide an introduction to the specialized reference works that aid researchers using these primary materials. The main part of the chapter deals with guides to archives and manuscript collections, arranged by country. This is followed by sections on guides to specific archives and special topic or subject guides, as well as a closing section on guides for locating special collection sources. It is hoped that this chapter will provide the researcher with a sound grounding in the major reference works available for finding material in these specialized collections.

Archives and Manuscript Collections

General

606. *International Directory of Archives*. Edited by Andre Vanrie. Munich: K. G. Saur, 1988. 351p. Index. ISBN 3-598-21233-X.

Issued by the International Council on Archives, this is a revision of the *Internationale Jahrbuch der Archive* and is the only directory for locating archives throughout the world. It includes information about all archives of historical significance that are open to the public, including archives that are not members of the International Archives Committee. This work is arranged alphabetically by country and contains the following information about each archive: name of the director, address, telephone and telex number, opening hours, statistical data on collections, and facilities available for the researcher. The *Directory* is useful as a starting point for the historian interested in archival research in a particular country, but it should be supplemented by the more specialized country and regional guides mentioned in this chapter.

United States

607. *The Archives: A Guide to the National Archives Field Branches.* By Loretto Dennis Szucs and Sandra Hargreaves Luebking. Salt Lake City: Ancestry Publishing, 1988. 340p. Index. ISBN 0-916489-23-X.

While much has been written about the records in the National Archives, this volume serves as a guide to the holdings of the 11 field branches of the National Archives system, which, when combined, contain more than 300,000 cubic feet of archival material. The *Guide* covers records spanning 200 years of American history, including agency records from the General Accounting Office, the Bureau of Indian Affairs, and the Office of the Army Surgeon General. Szucs and Luebking's work mainly focuses on the National Archives' field branches, providing information on these locations and their holdings, noting those records common to all the branches and those available only at particular locations. The *Guide* includes detailed descriptions of specific record groups as well as a subject and name index. It is an essential source for researchers seeking information about sources scattered around the country in the field branches of the National Archives.

608. *Directory of Archives and Manuscript Repositories in the United States.* 2d ed. By National Historical Publications and Records Commission. Phoenix: Oryx Press, 1988. 853p. Index. ISBN 0-89774-475-6.

This second edition, published by Oryx Press, updates and expands the earlier volume published by the National Archives and Records Service in 1978. The new edition includes information on historical document collections in 4,560 corporate, academic, city, and state archives in all 50 states, and includes the District of Columbia, Puerto Rico, and the U.S. Virgin Islands. Comprised of material largely gathered from questionnaires, the second edition of the *Directory* contains information on 1,400 repositories not included in the earlier edition, as well as updated material on entries already listed in the earlier volume.

The *Directory* is arranged alphabetically by state and, within each state, by city and institution. Individual entries contain the following information: institution name, street address, mailing address, telephone number, days and hours of operation, user fees, access restrictions, copy facilities, acquisitions policies, volume of total holdings, a brief description and inclusive date of the holdings, and references to other guides and finding lists. There are repository and subject indexes at the end of the volume. The new edition of this standard work will be very useful to researchers seeking current information on special collection materials located in all areas of the United States. For a more general introduction to U.S. archival sources, see John C. Larsen's *Researcher's Guide to Archives and Regional History Sources* (Hamden, CT: Library Professional Publications, 1988).

609. *A Guide to Archives and Manuscripts in the United States.* Compiled for the National Historical Publications Commission by Philip M. Hamer. New Haven: Yale University Press, 1961. 775p. Index.

Although dated and largely superseded by the *Directory of Archives and Manuscript Repositories in the United States*, the *National Union Catalog of Manuscript Collections*, and Chadwyck-Healey's *National Inventory of Documentary Sources in the United States*, Hamer's work deserves mention as the standard for guides to archival and manuscript material. This single-volume work directs the researcher to the most important archival and manuscript collections located throughout the United States. Unlike the *National Union Catalog*, this *Guide* does not claim to be comprehensive, although it does cover archival and manuscript holdings in roughly 1,300 locations in all 50 states and includes the papers of more than 7,600 individuals. The work is arranged alphabetically by state, then by city and repository. Each repository's entry includes names and addresses as well as a brief description of the contents of the collection; entries also include some material on holdings and mention guides to the material. There is a detailed name and subject index. Hamer's *Guide* is a useful starting point for researchers, but definitely needs to be supplemented by the sources mentioned above.

610. *A Guide to Manuscripts in the Presidential Libraries.* Compiled and edited by Dennis A. Burton, James B. Rhoads, and Raymond W. Smock. College Park, MD: Research Materials Corporation, 1985. 451p. Index. ISBN 0-934631-00-X.

This work will prove useful to researchers of the recent presidency; it is the first attempt to compile in one volume a guide to manuscript collections located in the seven presidential libraries administered by the National Archives and Records Administration, chronologically covering the libraries of Herbert Hoover to Gerald Ford. The *Guide* is arranged alphabetically and includes descriptions of manuscript collections, microfilm, and oral-history material located in the presidential libraries. Each entry includes collection reference numbers, name of the collection, size, the presidential library where the material is located, a detailed description of the collection, and the *National Union Catalog of Manuscript Collections* number. Much of the material in the book comes from information found in the printed guides of the individual libraries, recent announcements in *Prologue: Journal of the National Archives,* and recent accessions by the seven presidential libraries. The work has a detailed subject and name index for easy access to the main listings. It also gives a good general description of and the current research hours of each of the presidential libraries.

611. *A Guide to Manuscripts Relating to America in Great Britain and Ireland.* A revision of the 1961 *Guide* edited by B. R. Crick and Miriam Alman. Edited by John W. Raimo. Westport, CT: Published for the British Association for American Studies by Meckler Books, 1979. 467p. Index. ISBN 0-930466-06-3.

This work is an expanded and updated version of the original *Guide,* edited by B. R. Crick and Miriam Alman; 95 percent of the original material has been traced, and locations have been updated. The *Guide* has also been expanded to include more than 100 new entries and is 65 percent larger than the original. Raimo's work includes not only manuscripts related to political history but also material in the areas of economic, social, and immigration history.

The *Guide* attempts to provide a location and brief description of all the manuscripts in Great Britain and Ireland dealing with the American colonies and the United States that are not covered in earlier guides. This work covers archives in England, Wales, Scotland, Northern Ireland, Isle of Man, Channel Islands, and Ireland. It is arranged by country, then county, city, and alphabetically, by archive holding the records. There are detailed descriptions of the

American holdings of many different archives and a detailed subject and name index to specifically locate individual items in the main part of the *Guide*. Although this work is now a bit dated, it still contains a great deal of information for researchers seeking primary material on American history located in British archives.

612. *A Guide to Research Collections of Former Members of the United States House of Representatives, 1789–1987*. Bicentennial ed. Prepared under the direction of the Office for the Bicentennial of the United States House of Representatives, Raymond W. Smock, historian and director; Cynthia Pease Miller, editor in chief. Washington, DC: U.S. House of Representatives, 1988. 504p. House Document No. 100-171.

This *Guide*, a product of the staff of the Office for the Bicentennial of the House of Representatives, contains information on research collections containing historical material on 3,300 former members of the House of Representatives, which are located in 592 archives throughout the United States. The House members covered include all former representatives and territorial delegates from all 50 states who served in the House before 31 December 1987. Based on a survey conducted by the Office for the Bicentennial, the work is arranged alphabetically by representative. Each entry gives the name of the individual, birth and death dates, abbreviation for state or territory represented, and an alphabetical listing of repositories that hold historical material on that person's career. Information on individual collections includes such things as dates of the collection, its size, and a brief description of the type of material available. If the former members' papers are part of a larger collection, that is noted. After the main part of the volume covering research collections, there is information on members whose papers' location is unknown, a listing of repositories by state, a listing of current documentary-editing projects related to the history of the federal government, a listing of the dates of each congressional session, and a copy of the survey reporting form. This *Guide*, along with the recent *Guide to Research Collections of Former United States Senators, 1789–1982* [see 613] provides researchers with ready access to the amount and locations of historical material on former members of Congress at archives all over the United States.

613. *Guide to Research Collections of Former United States Senators, 1789–1982*. Prepared under the direction of William F. Hildenbrand, secretary of the Senate; Kathryn Allamong Jacob, editor in chief. Washington, DC: Historical Office, United States Senate, 1983. 362p. U.S. Senate Bicentennial Publication #1; Senate Document No. 97-41.

This *Guide*, published by the United States Senate Historical Office, is the predecessor and companion to *A Guide to Research Collections of Former Members of the United States House of Representatives, 1789–1987* [*see* 612]. It provides access to research materials on 1,800 former Senate members in 350 archives throughout the United States, including personal papers, portraits, photographs, oral-history transcripts, and memorabilia. The main part of the work is arranged alphabetically. Each entry gives the name and location of the archive where the papers and, more recently, oral-history transcripts of individual senators are to be found, as well as a brief description of the scope of the collection. Several appendixes list state and party abbreviations; senators by state, with information about party, dates of service, offices held, and birth and death dates; and a listing of archives by state, as well as the senatorial collections each archive contains. A brief supplement to the *Guide,* published in April 1985, updates the original entries, providing changes of locations and new information.

614. *Guide to the National Archives of the United States.* Washington, DC: National Archives and Records Administration, 1987. 896p. Index. ISBN 0-911333-23-1.

The National Archives is the major repository of the government's historical records, and this volume is the key guide to this wealth of information, totaling more than one million cubic feet of material. This massive volume is basically a reissue by the National Archives of its earlier 1974 *Guide,* with a new introduction and new descriptions of major record groups added to the archives between 1970 and 1977. The *Guide* contains detailed administrative histories and descriptions of the records of a large number of federal agencies. It is divided into six parts: (1) U.S. government—general; (2) records of the legislative branch; (3) records of the judicial branch; (4) records of the executive branch; (5) records of or relating to other governments; and (6) other holdings.

The main part of the work is taken up with detailed descriptions of the contents of individual record groups available in the National Archives, including the volume and type of records. There are several appendixes, including a list of record groups arranged by record group number. At the end of the volume there is a subject index to organizational units, names, functions, and broad subjects mentioned in the *Guide,* but it is not a detailed index to individual records in the National Archives. This work is a good general introduction to the holdings of the National Archives, but it does not substitute for more detailed finding aids to the records themselves. Historians doing research at the archives should contact them directly for more information and also check Chadwyck-Healey's

National Inventory of Documentary Sources in the United States [*see* 682] for more detailed descriptions of finding aids.

615. *Guide to the Records of the United States House of Representatives at the National Archives, 1789–1989.* Bicentennial ed. By National Archives and Records Administration. Washington, DC: U.S. House of Representatives, 1989. 466p. Index. House Document No. 100-245.

616. *Guide to the Records of the United States Senate at the National Archives, 1789–1989.* Bicentennial ed. By National Archives and Records Administration. Washington, DC: U.S. Senate, 1989. 356p. Index. U.S. Senate Bicentennial Publication #7; Senate Document No. 100-42.

Both of these *Guides,* compiled by the staff of the National Archives and Records Administration, were published to commemorate the bicentennial of the Congress. They provide detailed descriptions of nearly 46,000 cubic feet of House and Senate records located in the National Archives. Both *Guides* follow a similar arrangement; after a brief introductory chapter on research in the records of Congress, the bulk of each volume is arranged alphabetically, with chapters on individual committees. Within each chapter, there is information on the history and jurisdiction of each committee and detailed descriptions of the types of records produced. Following these chapters, there are additional chapters on other records and recent records of both branches. There are a number of useful appendixes at the end of each volume, such as listings of congressional leaders, select bibliography, glossary of legislative and archival terms, session dates, National Archives finding aids, and microfilm publications of congressional records. Both volumes are indexed. These two *Guides* are very useful for congressional researchers, making it easy to locate detailed information about Senate and House records stored in the National Archives.

617. *Members of Congress: A Checklist of Their Papers in the Manuscript Division, Library of Congress.* Compiled by John J. McDonough, with the assistance of Marilyn K. Parr. Washington, DC: Library of Congress, 1980. 217p. ISBN 0-8444-0272-9.

This checklist provides information on locating the papers of members of Congress from 1774 to 1979 (First Continental Congress to the end of the 95th Congress) that are located in the Manuscript Division of the Library of Congress. The volume lists material on the papers of 894 senators, members of the House of Representatives, and delegates to the Continental Congress. Based on the members listed in the *Biographical Directory of the American Congress, 1774–1971*

(Washington, DC: Government Printing Office, 1971) and other biographical sources, the work is arranged alphabetically by name. Each entry lists the member, dates of their service in Congress, state they represented, type of material and number of items in the collection, and *National Union Catalog of Manuscript Collections* number, if they are listed in that source. There are two appendixes listing members by state and Congress. Although selective, this volume does provide researchers with a convenient source of information about congressional research collections located in the Manuscript Division of the Library of Congress.

618. *National Inventory of Documentary Sources in the United States.* (For full information, see listing in "Reference Works on Microforms, Microform Publishers, and Individual Microform Collections")

619. *National Union Catalog of Manuscript Collections.* Washington, DC: Library of Congress, 1962–. Began with volume for 1959–1961; recent volumes have been published annually. ISSN: 0090-0044.

This ongoing work, now in its 23d issue, is the most comprehensive guide to locating manuscript collections in the United States. The most recent issues consist of a volume containing the current entries and a separate index volume that is eventually replaced by cumulative index volumes. The *Catalog*, often referred to as *NUCMC*, is a continuing series; each new volume contains additional entries and is not a cumulation of previous volumes. Since its inception, *NUCMC* has included descriptions of "approximately 56,435 collections located in 1,321 different repositories." Entries are arranged by the last two digits of the year of the volume and then numerically. They include such information as the name of the collection, its location, years covered, numbers of items, brief description of its contents, donor, and finding aids. The contents of many of the collections listed consist of personal papers, but beginning in 1970, *NUCMC* began including oral-history interview transcripts, and it now includes sound recordings. *NUCMC* is indexed by names, places, and subjects, as well as by genre or form of the material, such as diaries or oral history. Recently an additional two-volume index to *NUCMC* has been published, *Index to Personal Names in the National Union Catalog of Manuscript Collections, 1959–1984* (Alexandria, VA: Chadwyck-Healey, 1988). This has greatly aided researchers by providing quick guidance to the locations of particular names in all the previous *NUCMC* volumes through 1984.

620. *Presidents' Papers Index Series.* Washington, DC: Manuscript Division, Library of Congress, 1960–1976.

This series of indexes is worth mentioning because it provides access to the microfilm editions of the collections, located in the Manuscript Division of the Library of Congress, of 23 presidents. The presidents included in this series are Washington, Jefferson, Madison, Monroe, Jackson, Van Buren, William Henry Harrison, Tyler, Polk, Taylor, Pierce, Lincoln, Andrew Johnson, Grant, Garfield, Arthur, Cleveland, Benjamin Harrison, McKinley, Theodore Roosevelt, Taft, Wilson, and Coolidge. There is an individual, computer-generated index to the papers of each of these presidents, arranged by correspondent and date. One drawback of using these indexes is that they do not provide access by subject. However, they do provide researchers access to a wealth of primary documents in the history of these presidents and their presidencies. These indexes can be supplemented by the *Public Papers of the Presidents of the United States* series (Washington, DC: Federal Register Division, National Archives and Records Service, General Services Administration, 1930–1932/1933, 1945–), which index and include many of the papers of recent presidents from Hoover to Reagan.

621. *Records of the Presidency: Presidential Papers and Libraries from Washington to Reagan.* By Frank L. Schick, with Renee Schick and Mark Carroll. Phoenix, AZ: Oryx Press, 1989. 309p. Index. ISBN 0-89774-277-X.

This work contains a wealth of useful factual and historical information about presidential papers from Washington to Reagan. It is divided into four parts. Part 1 deals with the agencies responsible for the maintenance of presidential records, legislation relating to presidential libraries, guides to presidential records, and presidential book collections at historic sites. The last three parts of the work cover in detail presidential papers in the Manuscript Division of the Library of Congress, presidential papers in historical societies and special libraries, and presidential libraries operated by the National Archives. There are short biographical sketches of each president as well as detailed descriptions of the records drawn from visits to the actual locations and material provided by the Manuscript Division of the Library of Congress, National Archives, historical societies and special libraries, and the historical literature in general. This work also contains detailed descriptions and historical material on each of the current presidential libraries, from Franklin Roosevelt to Ronald Reagan. Four appendixes include statistical material on the resources, staff, funding, and use of presidential libraries; a directory of major presidential record collections; a directory of presidential historic sites; and an overview of the White House filing system. There is also a bibliography of major works on each president. This guide is a good general starting point for researchers seeking information on the location and availability of presidential papers.

Canada

622. *Union List of Manuscripts in Canadian Repositories.* Rev. ed. Robert S. Gordon, director, and E. Grace Maurice, editor. Joint Project of the Public Archives of Canada and the Humanities Research Council of Canada. Ottawa, Canada: Public Archives, Canada, 1975. 2 vols., with supplements.

This two-volume work, with its series of supplements that update the main volumes, is the definitive list of major manuscript collections located in Canada. The two main volumes include material from 171 archival institutions, totaling 27,000 entries. Entries, which represent units or collections of papers, are arranged alphabetically and include names of individuals, corporate bodies, and government agencies. The material also includes birth and death dates of individuals, their principal occupation and place of residence, type of papers, dates and size of collection, location, ownership of originals, and finding aids. Locations are given by a numerical symbol referring to a specific archive, and there is a list of locations at the end of each volume. At the end of the second volume, entries are arranged by repository, and there is a general index. Several supplements, although not completely current, bring the original list up-to-date by adding new entries. This work is an essential source for researchers using Canadian archives.

Latin America

623. *Guide to Materials on Latin America in the National Archives of the United States.* By George S. Ulibarri and John P. Harrison. Washington, DC: National Archives and Records Service, 1974. Reprint 1988. 489p. Index. ISBN 0-911333-22-3.

This guide, one of a series of subject guides to records in the National Archives, supersedes and updates an earlier archives publication, *Guide to Materials on Latin America in the National Archives,* published in 1961. The work is arranged first by general U.S. government records and then by records of the individual branches—legislative, judicial, and executive. Most of the work describes the Latin American holdings by the different executive departments, with the rest of the book focusing on the holdings of independent executive and other government agencies. Within each agency or department the coverage is arranged by record group, with detailed descriptions about the type, purpose, content, chronological span, and quantity of Latin American material in the records. The *Guide* does not attempt to describe all the major documents on Latin America in the National Archives, but gives detailed information on enough representative documents to aid the researcher. Several appendixes contain useful information on National Archives microfilm publications relating to Latin America and the diplomatic and consular records from Latin America located in the National Archives. This guide contains a wealth of information on archival sources for researchers in Latin American history, particularly on the relationship between Latin America and the United States.

624. *A Handbook of Latin American & Caribbean National Archives.* By Ann K. Nauman. Detroit: Blaine Ethridge Books, 1983. 127p. ISBN 0-87917-088-3.

The *Handbook,* written in English and Spanish, contains information on a total of 27 Latin American and Caribbean national archives. Derived from questionnaires sent out to these repositories, the information listed for each archive includes name and address, administrator, hours, history, description of the collection, cataloging, services provided, and requirements for use. The work also provides a list of sources containing more in-depth information on the contents of the archives mentioned in the main body of the handbook. This is a good starting place for researchers planning a trip to work in Latin American archives.

625. *Research in Mexican History: Topics, Methodology, Sources, and a Practical Guide to Field Research.* Compiled and edited by Richard L. Greenleaf and Michael C. Meyer for the Committee on Mexican Studies, Conference on Latin American History. Lincoln: University of Nebraska Press, 1973. 226p. ISBN 0-8032-5773-2.

626. *Research Guide to Central America and the Caribbean.* Edited by Kenneth J. Grieb. Madison: University of Wisconsin Press, 1985. 431p. Index. ISBN 0-299-10050-2.

627. *Research Guide to Andean History: Bolivia, Chile, Ecuador, and Peru.* John J. TePaske, coordinating editor. Durham, NC: Duke University Press, 1981. 346p. Index. ISBN 0-8223-0450-3.

These three guides contain detailed information for researchers interested in Latin American history. Each of the guides includes in-depth articles by specialists in the field covering the historiography of individual countries as well as archival resources and specific archives. Information provided on specific archives includes material on their organization and holdings along with names, addresses, telephone numbers, hours, and photocopying policies. Some of the articles are quite extensive in their descriptions of doing research in Latin American archives. While the guides generally discuss archives in the area, the volume on Central America and the Caribbean contains material on archives outside the region. The research guides to Central America and the Caribbean and Andean history are indexed, but the Mexican history volume is not. Each of the guides contains a great deal of valuable information on Latin American archival sources, particularly for the young scholar planning historical research in any of these countries.

Great Britain

628. *British Archives: A Guide to Archive Resources in the United Kingdom.* 2d ed. By Janet Foster and Julia Sheppard. New York: Stockton Press, 1989. 750p. Index. ISBN 0-935859-74-8.

This is a new, expanded edition of the main printed guide to British archival materials. Containing more than 1,000 entries, the *Guide* is arranged alphabetically by town; entries include name and address of the archive, telephone number, where to send inquiries, hours, and a brief description of their major collections, finding aids, and publications. There is a good name and subject index at the end of the work, as well as a select bibliography on archival materials. This *Guide* is a good starting point as a source for finding archival collections in many local repositories in Great Britain. For more detailed information on particular finding aids the researcher should also check Chadwyck-Healey's *National Inventory of Documentary Sources in the United Kingdom and Ireland* [*see* 681], which reprints many of these sources.

629. *Guide to the Contents of the Public Record Office.* London: Her Majesty's Stationery Office, 1963–1968. 3 vols.

This three-volume work, a revision of the 1923–1924 *Guide* by M. S. Guiseppi, is the principal printed guide to the holdings of the Public Record Office in Great Britain, one of the major archival collections in the world. The first two volumes give detailed descriptions of all the British government records acquired by the Public Record Office through 31 August 1960. Each volume covers a different set of records. The first volume deals with legal records, arranged by different areas of the British government, and the second volume includes the State Papers since the accession of Henry VIII and the records of different government departments, arranged largely by administrative agency. In both volumes there are detailed descriptions of the Public Record Office's holdings of these records, as well as a key to regnal years with a chronological index to statutes cited in the text. There are also lists of abbreviations; indexes by person, place, and subject; and in the first volume, a glossary of some of the technical terms used in the *Guide,* and a general introduction to the British records system. The third volume is a supplement to the first two, listing new classes and changes in existing classes of records through the end of 1966. These three volumes provide the researcher with an excellent introductory guide to the collections of the Public Record Office.

630. *Index of Manuscripts in the British Library.* Cambridge, U.K.: Chadwyck-Healey, 1984–1986. 10 vols. ISBN 0-85964-140-6.

The British Library has one of the leading historical manuscript collections in the world, and this massive ten-volume set serves as an index to many of the individual collections located there. Published by Chadwyck-Healey, this index provides access to person and place entries for collections in the British Library. Entries are derived from their *Catalogues of Additions* and ten other catalogs specific to their collections. The index covers person and place entries only for collections acquired up to 1950 and does not provide indexing by subject. Entries are arranged alphabetically, with place names preceding personal names; thus, rulers of particular countries are listed alphabetically under the country, for example, entries for Napoleon are under France. An effort is made to group all entries relating to the same person or place together in one location. Most of the entries are taken from the *Catalogue of Additions,* but for entries taken from other specific manuscript collections the abbreviated name of the collection to which a specific item belongs is listed immediately above each entry or group of entries. This index provides access to a wealth of manuscript material in the British Library, but is limited by not having direct subject access to these collections.

France

631. *Libraries and Archives in France: A Handbook.* Rev. ed. By Erwin K. Welsch. New York: Council for European Studies, 1979. 147p.

This work, which was considerably expanded and updated from the earlier 1973 edition, remains the best general guide to information about French libraries and archives. It is divided into three main sections: (1) libraries in the Paris region, (2) archives in the Paris region, and (3) libraries and archives elsewhere in France. There are detailed descriptions of the Bibliotheque Nationale and the Archives Nationales at the beginning of the first two sections, followed by material on other libraries and archives in the Paris region. After coverage of the Bibliotheque Nationale, other Paris libraries are arranged by broad subject area. Information on each library and archive includes material on their major areas of collection, hours, holdings, access, collection use, catalogs, photocopying, and publications. The third section contains much briefer descriptions of departmental archives and libraries outside Paris. At the end of the volume there are brief bibliographies on the holdings and specializations of French libraries, sources on archival holdings related to French history since 1789, and departmental archives and libraries. Three appendixes describe the classification systems at the Archives Nationales and the departmental archives, as well as information on locating manuscripts in French libraries. This slim volume contains a great deal of useful information for researchers planning trips to French archives. See also *Les Inventaires des Archives Nationales de Paris*, published on microfiche by Chadwyck-Healey, which reproduces more than 700 finding aids for important collections in this major French archive.

Germany

632. *Libraries and Archives in Germany*. By Erwin K. Welsch. Pittsburgh: Council for European Studies, 1975. 275p.

This guide, like the earlier volume on France, was written by Welsch, Bibliographer for Western Europe at the University of Wisconsin Library, and is meant to be a handbook for first-time researchers using German archival sources. Welsch's work is divided into two main sections—libraries and archives. The library section contains descriptions of libraries in both the Federal Republic of Germany (West Germany) and the German Democratic Republic (East Germany), beginning with the major national libraries and then other libraries arranged by city. Library descriptions include information on national, state, regional, and special libraries, as well as general information on manuscript collections, research collections, and regional catalogs and union lists.

The archives section also begins with some general comments and then gives descriptions of the major archives in both West and East

Germany. Information on both libraries and archives includes material similar to that found in the volume on France, including collection areas, holdings, access, hours, catalogs, and publications. Material on East Germany is much more limited because of the limitations on access for research. Welsch's work, like his earlier volume on France, may be a bit dated, but it still remains a good general introduction for researchers using German archives and manuscript collections.

Eastern Europe and Soviet Union

633. *Archives and Manuscript Repositories in the USSR: Moscow and Leningrad* (Studies of the Russian Institute, Columbia University). By Patricia Kennedy Grimstead. Princeton, NJ: Princeton University Press, 1972. 436p. Index. ISBN 0-691-05149-6.

634. *Archives and Manuscript Repositories in the USSR: Estonia, Latvia, Lithuania, and Belorussia* (Studies of the Russian Institute, Columbia University). By Patricia Kennedy Grimstead. Princeton, NJ: Princeton University Press, 1981. 929p. Index. ISBN 0-691-05279-4.

These two volumes were designed to provide information to researchers about the development, holdings, and published reference aids to archives and manuscript collections in the Soviet Union. They serve as a starting point for foreign researchers planning to do research in the Soviet Union and also give foreigners an awareness of the development and overall organization of archives and manuscript repositories in that country. Grimstead's first volume focuses on giving a brief historical survey of the Soviet archival system and procedural information about working in Soviet archives. Otherwise, the organization of the two volumes is the same; the first part of each work contains detailed information on Soviet archival bibliography and research aids, and the other parts focus on the different archives and manuscript collections in the areas covered by each volume. The author attempts to give detailed information for each individual institution, including a brief historical survey and general characterization of the nature and extent of their holdings as well as a bibliography of finding aids. Appendixes at the end of both volumes give additional information, and there are author-title and subject indexes at the end of each volume. These volumes provide an excellent starting place for researchers seeking detailed guidance about Soviet archival and manuscript repositories.

635. *Eastern Europe and Russia/Soviet Union: A Handbook of Western European Archival and Library Resources* (Joint Committee on Eastern Europe Publication Series; no. 9). By Richard C. Lewanski. New York: K. G. Saur; Detroit: distributed by Gale Research, 1980. 317p. Index. ISBN 0-89664-092-2.

This handbook, a publication of the Joint Committee on Eastern Europe of the American Council of Learned Societies and the Social Science Research Council, is both an inventory and directory of the major research resources, facilities, and services available for the study of Slavic, Eastern European, and Russian/Soviet archival and library materials located in Western Europe. Written by the noted Slavic scholar and bibliographer Richard Lewanski, the *Handbook* covers sources available in 1,000 repositories, including institutions of higher learning, libraries, archives, and museums in 22 European countries. The subjects covered in the guide are mainly in the humanities and social sciences, with some coverage of the natural sciences. Lewanski's handbook is arranged alphabetically by country, then within each country by locality, and within each locality by name of institution. Each entry attempts to provide such information as the name of the director or librarian, subject profile of the collection, holdings, size, special collection material, photocopying facilities, hours, and restrictions. There is a broad subject index at the end of the work. This handbook is essential for researchers seeking archival information on Eastern Europe and the Soviet Union in Western European sources. *See also* Paul G. Horecky's *East Central and Southeast Europe: A Handbook of Library and Archival Resources* (Santa Barbara, CA: Clio Press, 1976).

Africa

636. *African Studies Information Resources Directory.* Compiled and edited by Jean E. Meeh Gosebrink. Oxford, England: Published for the African Studies Association by Hans Zell Publishers, K. G. Saur, 1986. 572p. Index. ISBN 3-598-10657-2.

Produced by the African Studies Association, this work is the most detailed guide to all areas of African Studies research in the United States. The *Directory* focuses on the countries of Subsaharan Africa and lists 437 sources of information and documentation on this area, including special collections, archives, documentation centers in government agencies, religious and missionary organizations, museums, learned societies, historical societies, professional and academic associations, and major publishers, book dealers, and distributors of African Studies materials. Included in this directory is information on library holdings, archival and manuscript sources, collections of computerized data, and information and documentation services. Derived from questionnaire information, this work is divided into four chapters: (1) an alphabetical list of collections and information services in libraries and other repositories; (2) an alphabetical list of entries by religious denomination of church and mission organizations that have done work in Africa; (3) a list of bookstores, book dealers, and distributors of Africa-related materials; and (4) a list of major American publishers of Africa-related materials. At the end of the volume there is a bibliography, as well as a subject, name, place, and institution index. This directory only lists holdings for larger African Studies archival and manuscript collections. For more detailed coverage of archival sources on Africa in the United States the researcher should consult two publications compiled by Aloha South, *Guide to Federal Archives Relating to Africa* (Waltham, MA: Crossroads Press, 1977) and *Guide to Non-Federal Archives and Manuscripts in the United States Relating to Africa* (London; New York: Hans Zell Publishers, 1989).

637. *International Guide to African Studies Research/Etudes Africaines. Guide International de Recherches.* 2d ed. Edited by the International African Institute, compiled by Philip Baker. Munich; New York: Hans Zell, K. G. Saur, 1987. 264p. Index. ISBN 0-905450-25-6.

This work is an expansion and updating of the first edition of this guide, published in 1975, and it includes material on more than 1,100 academic institutions, research centers, and public and governmental agencies that carry out African Studies research. The entries in the *Guide* usually include information about the interests of research staff at particular institutions or agencies, as well as material on library collections and publications. Several different indexes make it easier for the user to find specific information. There is a country index, which arranges institutions by country according to research areas, and an index of ethnonyms and language names, which lists the research centers working on certain ethnic or linguistic groups. Also there is a serial publications index, which lists current titles published at African Studies institutions, and a personnel index, which provides a current list of African Studies subject specialists. This work is the best guide to worldwide research in African Studies, and it will be of definite interest to researchers working in that area.

Asia

638. *Asia and Oceania: A Guide to Archival & Manuscript Sources in the United States.* Edited by G. Raymond Nunn, with contributions from Alberta Freidus, Walter Pierson, and the Center for Asian and Pacific Studies, University of Hawaii. London; New York: Mansell Publishing, 1985. 5 vols. ISBN 0-7201-1713-5 (set).

This massive set is the definitive guide to research collections on Asia and the Pacific area in the United States. The *Guide* provides information on the holdings of 450 archives in the United States; the first four volumes are arranged alphabetically by state, then by city and institution. Entries contain information such as address of the repository, telephone number, hours, collection restrictions, photocopying, holdings, and detailed descriptions of the collections. Most of the materials covered are Western-language sources, although there are also Japanese and Sino-Vietnamese archival documents. Individual collections are broken down by folder and by reels of microfilm when that information is available. The fifth volume of the set serves as an index to the main volumes, providing detailed access by personal, corporate, geographic, and political names, as well as by subject. This source is essential for any researchers in Asian and Pacific subject areas or United States-Asian relations seeking the location of primary documents in the United States.

Guides to Specific Archives

639. *Catalogue of Manuscripts in the Houghton Library, Harvard University.* Alexandria, VA: Chadwyck-Healey, 1986. 8 vols. ISBN 0-89887-040-2.

After the Library of Congress, Harvard's Houghton Library has one of the greatest manuscript collections in the United States, and this multivolume set serves as a guide to this material. The *Catalogue,* which describes the library's holdings up to April 1985, is arranged in a single alphabetical sequence by author. It attempts to give a detailed description of the library's manuscript holdings, even giving shelf marks and accession numbers. The *Catalogue* provides researchers with a source for finding out detailed information about manuscripts in one of the world's largest research libraries.

640. *Directory of Business Archives in the United States and Canada.* Chicago: Business Archives Committee, Society of American Archivists, 1975. 38p.

This brief pamphlet updates the previous edition of this work, published in 1968. It does not cover all business archives in the United States and Canada, but it does provide information particularly on those archives held by private business firms. The entries list name, address, and telephone number of the firm, the name of an individual in charge, a description of the types and quantity of material, and any restrictions on access. This is a very brief guide, and the information in it is dated. However, it remains the only directory specifically focusing on business archives. For more current information, the researcher can check under subject and name in the *Directory of Archives and Manuscript Respositories in the United States* [see 608].

641. *Guide to Ethnic Museums, Libraries, and Archives in the United States.* By Lubomyr R. Wynar and Lois Buttlar. Kent, OH: Program for the Study of Ethnic Publications, School of Library Science, Kent State University, 1978. 378p. Index.

This work is the major source for locating information on ethnic research collections in the United States. The *Guide* contains material on museums, libraries, and archives covering more than 70 ethnic groups and a total of 828 cultural institutions. Based on information collected from questionnaires, the guide is arranged alphabetically by ethnic group (e.g., Afro-American, Swiss-American, etc.). Entries contain information about name and type of institution, address, phone number, sponsoring organization, personnel, date founded, scope, staff, access, admission, visitors, publications, collection size, and comments about the organization. The guide does not claim to be complete for larger ethnic groups, such as American Indians, but does provide a list of additional sources for those groups. There are name and geographic indexes at the end of the work. This is a good example of a guide to archival sources on particular cultural groups.

642. *Guide to Jewish Archives.* Edited by Aryeh Segall. New York: World Council on Jewish Archives, 1981. 90p.

Published by the World Council on Jewish Archives, this work serves as the latest guide to the archives, libraries, research institutions, and other repositories that contain archival sources on the Jewish people. The *Guide* is based on information generated from questionnaires and includes Jewish archival sources around the world, with country coverage on the United States, Israel, Canada, and Australia; the European countries are listed individually under the chapter heading "Europe." Within the country or continent chapters, the repositories are arranged alphabetically and individual entries include material on their location, director, history and scope of the collection, and size of the holdings. There is no separate index, but the table of contents serves as the main index to finding material in the *Guide*. This would be the best guide to check for Jewish archival sources, particularly for researchers planning trips to institutions outside the United States.

643. *Guide to the Hoover Institution Archives* (Hoover Bibliographical Series, 59). By Charles G. Palm and Dale Reed. Stanford, CA: Hoover Institution Press, 1980. 418p. Index. ISBN 0-8179-2591-0.

This work serves as a descriptive guide to the archival and manuscript holdings of the Hoover Institution on War, Revolution and Peace, located at Stanford University. The *Guide* describes a total of 3,569 items covering a total of 18,000 linear feet; subject areas covered include political, social, economic, and military history from the late nineteenth century to the present. Geographically, the *Guide* describes primary research materials from North America, Eastern Europe and the Soviet Union, Western Europe, East and Southeast Asia, Latin America, Africa, and the Middle East. It includes information on organizational records, individual papers, special collections, and audiovisual and microfilm materials. The *Guide* describes material acquired by the Hoover Institution through 1978; items are arranged alphabetically into two sections: (1) archival and manuscript material and (2) microfilms of archival and manuscript materials held privately or in other libraries. Entries include information on the main entry, title, volume of material, form of material, scope and content of the collection or item, finding aids, restrictions, and donor or source of the item. There is an appendix listing bibliographic works based on the Hoover collections and a name and subject index, referring the user to an entry number. This work is a good example of a specialized source for researchers seeking information on a particular archive and its holdings.

Special Topic or Subject Guides

644. *Black History: A Guide to Civilian Records in the National Archives.* Compiled by Debra L. Newman. Washington, DC: National Archives Trust Fund Board, General Services Administration, 1984. 379p. Index. ISBN 0-911333-21-5.

This guide is another of the supplements to the *Guide to the National Archives of the United States,* focusing on the records of the civilian agencies located in the National Archives dealing with blacks and black history. The work is arranged into chapters by record group number, which usually means the records of a particular federal agency. Within each chapter the material is further broken down and numbered sequentially, paragraph by paragraph. There are a total of 453 record groups listed in the *Guide,* with detailed descriptions of their holdings on blacks, including specific information on the arrangement and the volume of this material within the collection. Certain types of material are highlighted by showing them in boldface type, and there is an index at the end of the work. This guide is essential for researchers planning to work with black history topics using federal government records. For a good general guide to material on blacks during the earlier slave trade, African colonization, and back-to-Africa movements, the historian should also check the *Guide to Federal Archives Relating to Africa* (Waltham, MA: Crossroads Press, 1977).

645. *The Confederacy: A Guide to the Archives of the Government of the Confederate States of America.* By Henry Putney Beers. Washington, DC: National Archives and Records Administration, 1986. (First published as the *Guide to the Archives of the Government of the Confederate States of America,* Washington, DC: Government Printing Office, 1968) 536p. Index. ISBN 0-911333-18-5.

646. *The Union: A Guide to Federal Archives Relating to the Civil War.* By Kenneth W. Munden and Henry Putney Beers. Washington, DC: National Archives and Records Administration, 1986. (First published as *Guide to Federal Archives Relating to the Civil War,* Washington, DC: Government Printing Office, 1962) 721p. Index. ISBN 0-911333-46-0.

These two volumes are reprints of the guides produced in the 1960s, largely through the efforts of Beers, a former National Archivist. They have not been revised or updated, but are published in new bindings to make them more attractive for purchase for library reference collections. The *Union* volume describes in detail records relating to the federal side in the Civil War held in the National Archives, Federal Records Centers, and other federal agencies. The *Confederacy* volume describes Confederate records in the National Archives, but also includes those in a number of separate collections, such as the Alabama Department of Archives and History and the Georgia Historical Society. Each of the volumes has a similar organizational arrangement, beginning with general records, followed by the records of Congress, the judiciary, the presidency, and those of the executive departments and agencies. Within each chapter, there is a historical statement regarding the functions and responsibilities of the department or agency listed, followed by detailed descriptions of general records, records of particular bureaus or offices, as well as material on bibliographic references, finding aids, and other sources. There are detailed indexes at the end of each volume. These two volumes provide an abundance of detailed information for Civil War researchers; their only limitation is the lack of updated information on records acquired in the past 20–25 years. Researchers on the Confederacy may also want to check James C. Neagles' *Confederate Research Sources: A Guide to Archive Collections* (Salt Lake City: Ancestry Publishing, 1986) for more current location information.

647. *Guide to Genealogical Research in the National Archives.* Washington, DC: National Archives and Records Service, 1982. 304p. Index. ISBN 0-911333-00-2.

This work is a revision and enlargement of the 1964 *Guide to Genealogical Records in the National Archives.* It includes records not described in the earlier edition, as well as numerous illustrations, photographs, citations to microfilm publications, and more detailed descriptions of previous records. This volume covers records in the National Archives and those located in the 11 Federal Archives and Records Centers all over the country. The *Guide* is arranged into four sections—population and immigration, military records, records relating to particular groups, and other useful records. Among the materials covered are census records, passenger arrival lists, naturalization records, pension records, records of American Indians, records of black Americans, land records, and court records. Each of these is dealt with in individual chapters, which give detailed information on researching and locating these documents. Two appendixes list record groups and microfilm publications cited in the text; there is also a subject index at the end of the work. This is a very useful guide for genealogy researchers seeking information about the wealth of material in the holdings of the National Archives.

648. *A Reference Guide to United States Department of State Special Files.* By Gerald K. Haines. Westport, CT: Greenwood Press, 1985. 393p. Index. ISBN 0-313-22750-0.

This work is an example of a specialized guide to twentieth-century U.S. diplomatic history. It provides detailed information on

Department of State "Special Files," mainly covering the period from 1940 to 1959, which contain a great deal of primary source material on a wide variety of foreign policy subjects. Drawing on State Department and National Archives material, the work is organized in much the same way as the department itself; for example, files are arranged by geographic areas and subjects, with a detailed list of contents at the front of the volume guiding the user to the appropriate location in the text where information on a particular agency is found. There is detailed material on each of the files, including the special file number, short title of the file, inclusive dates, description of the file, finding aids, restrictions, volume of material, and location of the records. At the end of the volume, there are organization charts showing the State Department from World War II to 1959, a numeric list of all files cited in the volume, a list of key abbreviations, and a name and subject index. This *Guide* would be very useful for historians of American foreign policy in the post-World War II period.

649. *Women's History Sources: A Guide to Archives and Manuscript Collections in the United States.* Edited by Andrea Hinding. Vol. 2 edited by Suzanna Moody. New York: R. R. Bowker, 1979. 2 vols. Index. ISBN 0-8352-1103-7 (set).

This is the major guide to archival and manuscript collections in women's history in the United States. Based on a nationwide survey conducted by the Social Welfare History Archives at the University of Minnesota, this work contains descriptions of 18,026 collections in 1,586 repositories throughout America. It covers collections that include material in all fields of women's history from the colonial period to the present, containing diaries, journals, and other first-person accounts, as well as public records in the National Archives. The first volume contains the main body of the work; information about collections is arranged alphabetically by state and city, and then within each city by institution or repository and collection title. Entries include material such as the collection title, type of documents, date and size of the collection, access, bibliographic control, repository name, and description of contents. There is a directory of contributing repositories at the end of the first volume, and the second volume serves as a detailed index by name, subject, and geographic access to the collections listed in the main volume. This two-volume set is the definitive guide for researchers trying to find out about women's history materials in both large and small repositories in the United States. Researchers interested in women's history sources should also check Anne R. Kenney's *Archival Sources*

*for Women's History: An Annotated Bibliography of Guides, Inventories,
and Catalogs to Archives and Manuscript Collections in the United States*
(New York: Garland Publishing, 1986).

Guides to Special Collections

650. *Directory of Libraries and Special Collections on Asia and North Africa.*
Compiled by Robert Collison, with the assistance of Brenda E. Moon.
Hamden, CT: Archon Books, 1970. 123p. Index. ISBN 0-258-96789-7.

651. *Directory of Libraries and Special Collections on Eastern Europe and the
U.S.S.R.* Edited by Gregory Walker, in collaboration with J. H. Bowyer,
P. A. Crowther, and J. E. Wall. London: Crosby, Lockwood & Son;
Hamden, CT: Archon Books, 1971. 159p. Index. ISBN 0-258-96837-0.

These two guides, products of the British Standing Conference of
National and University Libraries (SCONUL), serve as directories
for locating library and special collection material in Great Britain
on Asia, North Africa, Eastern Europe, and the Soviet Union. Each
directory is arranged alphabetically by city, with each library listed
alphabetically within the city. The *Directory* on Eastern Europe and
the Soviet Union contains an additional section listing names,
addresses, and telephone numbers of other sources on Eastern
Europe, for example, embassies, trade and cultural organizations,
and news agencies. Individual entries in each volume list the following information: title of the library, its address, telephone and telex
numbers, hours, names of the librarian and appropriate specialists
on the staff, and a description of the collections focusing on their
history, size, character, and special features. If available, additional
material is included on access, interlibrary loan, copy facilities,
catalogs, and publications. Both volumes are indexed by library,
collection, and subject. Although the material in each volume is now
dated, both volumes can still be useful for researchers attempting to
locate special collections in these subject areas.

652. *A Directory of Rare Book and Special Collections in the United
Kingdom and the Republic of Ireland.* Edited by Moelwyn I. Williams
for the Rare Books Group of the Library Association. London:
Library Association, 1985. 664p. Index. ISBN 0-85365-646-0.

This work, the product of a project begun by the Rare Books Group
of the Library Association, attempts to serve as a guide for
researchers to the locations of rare book and special collection

material in the United Kingdom and Ireland. The emphasis is more on rare book collections, but the *Directory* does include information on special collections and manuscript holdings where they are deemed relevant. It includes material found in public and national libraries, university libraries, colleges and schools, cathedrals and churches, societies and institutes, and some private libraries. The *Directory* is arranged by region, beginning with England, followed by Northern Ireland, Republic of Ireland, Scotland, Wales, Channel Islands, and Isle of Man. Within each region or country the libraries and institutions are listed alphabetically under each city. Entries for each library include address, telephone number, hours, conditions of admission, research facilities, and a brief history. This is followed by a description of each collection, including material on its origin, history, size, and a chronological summary of its contents and subject fields. If available, information is provided on catalogs and published references. Williams' *Directory* is an excellent guide to rare book and special collection material in the United Kingdom and Ireland; it will be of definite value to researchers in the history of these countries.

653. *Libraries and Special Collections on Latin America and the Caribbean: A Directory of European Resources* (University of London, Institute of Latin American Studies monographs; 14). 2d ed. By Roger Macdonald and Carole Travis. London and Atlantic Highlands, NJ: Published for the Institute of Latin American Studies, University of London, by Athlone Press, 1988. 339p. Index. ISBN 0-485-17714-5.

This is a new edition of the *Directory of Libraries and Special Collections on Latin America and the West Indies*, compiled by Bernard Naylor, Laurence Hallewell, and Colin Steele (London: Athlone Press for the Institute of Latin American Studies, 1975). It covers Latin American and Caribbean holdings in Europe and includes three times the number of entries as the earlier edition, 195 from the United Kingdom and 272 from other European countries. Based mainly on information gathered from questionnaires, the work's greatest emphasis is on printed materials, although it contains information on discs, tapes, slides, maps, and postage stamps. The *Directory* is arranged by country, beginning with the United Kingdom, and then alphabetically by the other European countries. Individual entries are arranged by town and then by institution. Information includes the name and address of each institution, telephone, telex, and fax numbers, names of the librarian or Latin American specialist, history of the collection, size, and access, as well as material on finding aids, copying facilities, lending, and computer searching.

There is a title and subject index at the end of the volume. This work would be very useful for researchers attempting to find out information about Latin American holdings in European collections.

654. *Special Collections in College and University Libraries.* Compiled by Modoc Press. Introduction by Leona Rostenberg and Madeleine B. Stern. New York: Macmillan, 1989. 639p. Index. ISBN 0-02-921651-6.

This is the most recent guide to special collections, rare books, and manuscripts located in more than 1,800 colleges and universities in the United States. The compilers have adopted a broad definition of special collections, which includes not only the standard coverage of rare books and manuscripts but also specialized collections in libraries' main stacks and material in department libraries. Individual entries are arranged alphabetically by institution within each state. Information listed under each institution includes address, telephone number, institutional affiliation and enrollment, library administrators, and holdings. This is followed by descriptions of the special collections and rare book collections of each institution. There is an institution index at the end of the volume for easy access to individual college and university holdings. This guide will be essential for researchers searching for special collection material in United States libraries. It should be used along with Lee Ash and William Miller's work on *Subject Collections* [*see* 656].

655. *Special Collections in the Library of Congress: A Selective Guide.* Compiled by Annette Melville. Washington, DC: Library of Congress, 1980. 464p. Index. ISBN 0-8444-0297-4.

This work is a selective guide to special collections in the Library of Congress. It covers a total of 269 of the library's special collections, including collections of books and pamphlets, drawings, films, manuscripts, maps, music, musical instruments, prints, photographs, sound recordings, videotapes, and other nonbook material. The *Guide* does not include coverage of collections composed entirely of microforms and collections of personal papers and nonmusic manuscripts, which are covered by the *National Union Catalog of Manuscript Collections.* Based on information from Library of Congress publications and a wide variety of internal sources, the *Guide* is arranged alphabetically by the first word of the full collection title. The descriptions of each collection, which are really little essays, include the heading, as well as material on the collection's acquisition, size, scope and contents, subject strengths, items of particular interest, bibliographic control, and finding aids. At the end of each description there is a list of references that discuss the collection as a whole. Collections include the George and Ira Gershwin Collection, the Dime Novel Collection, and the Sigmund Freud Collection. An appendix at the end of the work lists collections arranged by the different divisions of the Library of Congress. Melville's work is a fascinating guide to the wide range of special collection material available for researchers at America's largest research institution.

656. *Subject Collections: A Guide to Special Book Collections and Subject Emphases As Reported by University, College, Public, and Special Libraries and Museums in the United States and Canada.* 6th ed., rev. and enl. Compiled by Lee Ash and William G. Miller. New York: R.R. Bowker, 1985. 2 vols. ISBN 0-8352-1917-8 (set).

Ash and Miller's work is the standard guide to special book collection material in the United States and Canada. The most recent edition is the sixth edition, which includes at least 6,500 new entries beyond those covered in the earlier volumes. Based on questionnaires sent to libraries, the volumes are arranged alphabetically by subject, with the subject headings adapted from the most recent *Library of Congress Subject Headings.* Within the subject headings entries are arranged by state, with information about the institution holding the collection and a description of the number and type of materials included; some of the descriptions are quite lengthy. This work is the largest and most definitive source for researchers seeking special collection information found in libraries located throughout the United States and Canada. It does not include local history material, but includes thousands of other entries on a wide variety of subjects.

14.

Guides to Microforms and Selected Microform Collections

Within the past 20 years, there has been a tremendous increase in the amount of material available for historical research in microform, including both microfilm and microfiche. This chapter is an attempt to make historians, graduate students, and under-graduate students in history aware of the potential use of these sources. There are three main purposes of this chapter: (1) to familiarize the reader with the main reference guides to microforms; (2) to list and describe the major history microform publishers and some of their key publications; and (3) to describe a selection of the major history research collections available in microform and their usefulness for historians.

Reference Guides to Microforms

657. *Bibliographic Guide to Microform Publications*, 1986–. Boston, MA: G. K. Hall, 1987–. Annual.

This annual guide, which began publication in 1987, contains information on all the microform materials cataloged during the past year by the New York Public Library and the Library of Congress, the two largest microform producers in the United States. The microforms covered in the *Bibliographic Guide* include both original microform publications—those materials filmed for archival or preservation purposes—and commercially available microforms purchased or received by these libraries. Material covered includes U. S. and foreign books and nonserial publications, government publications, pamphlets, and ephemeral material. The *Guide* also contains information on dissertations, technical reports, and manuscript collections from the New York Public Library.

The work is arranged by author, title, and subject in a single alphabetical sequence. Entries include information such as the bibliographic entry, number of reels, format, content statement, call number, and subject headings. This annual publication supersedes the *National Register of Microform Masters,* which was discontinued in 1983; it contains information on an extensive number of specialized microform publications available for historical research in these two libraries.

658. *Chinese Materials on Microfilm Available from the Library of Congress.* By James Chu-yul Soong. (Bibliographical Series: no. 11) Washington, DC: Center for Chinese Research Materials, Association of Research Libraries, 1971. 82p.

Although no longer current, this volume attempts to provide a single listing of Chinese books and serials on microfilm located in the Library of Congress. The guide is divided into two parts: (1) "Survey" and (2) "Checklists." Part 1, the "Survey," is divided into broad chapters by type of publication, for example, monographs, newspapers, periodicals, and translations. Each chapter in this part briefly describes the library's holdings. In Part 2, "Checklists," individual items are listed alphabetically by type of publication, such as monographs and newspapers. Individual entries in each chapter are arranged by title and include information on the number of reels and size of the collection. The first part of this work contains a good overview of Chinese material held at the Library of Congress. Soong's work is dated now, but its coverage of newspapers can be updated through *Newspapers in Microform,* and its listing of Chinese monographs and periodicals can be updated through the most recent *National Register of Microform Masters* (Washington, DC: Catalog Management and Publication Division, Library of Congress, 1965–1983).

659. *Guide to Microforms in Print. Author, Title.* Westport, CT: Meckler, 1978–. ISBN 0-88736-364-4. ISSN 0164-0747. Annual.

660. *Guide to Microforms in Print. Subject.* Westport, CT: Meckler, 1978–. ISBN 0-88736-363-6. ISSN 0163-8386. Annual.

This annual two-volume work, while perhaps more useful as a library acquisitions source, does provide a great deal of information to researchers about historical materials available in microform. The present series of volumes replaced three separate earlier publications: *Guide to Microforms in Print* (1961–1977), *Subject Guide to*

Microforms in Print (1962/1963–1977), and *International Microforms in Print* (1974/1975). There is an annual supplement updating the main volumes.

The *Guide* is international in its coverage of microform titles, including books, journals, newspapers, government publications, archival material, and collections. The *Author, Title* volume is arranged in a straight alphabetical listing, with both interfiled in one sequence; the *Subject* volume is arranged by broad Library of Congress subject headings, for example, history or political science. Entries are arranged alphabetically within these headings. Information given in each entry includes author, title, volume, date, price, publisher, and type of microform. This is definitely an international index, as the introductory sections are given in four languages—English, French, German, and Spanish. The *Guide* is useful to historians for determining whether a particular work or collection is available in microform. However, the subject index is very general, and researchers may first have to find the broader heading and then look alphabetically under their subject.

661. *Guide to Photocopied Historical Materials in the United States and Canada.* Edited by Richard W. Hale, Jr. Ithaca, NY: Published for the American Historical Association by Cornell University Press, 1961. 241p. Index.

This work serves as a guide to photocopies of historical material, both reproductions of publications and reproductions of manuscripts, available mainly on microfilm in repositories in the United States and Canada. The volume is arranged geographically by country, with the United States and Canada further divided by type of historical document, including government records, collections, church records, personal papers, business papers, census material, and other categories. The entries give full bibliographic information about the records, for example, author, compiler, collector or holder of the original material, type of material, dates, amount of material, and the location and type of photocopies. There is a name and subject index at the end of the work. Although a great deal of additional historical material has appeared on microfilm since this guide was published, it does serve as an initial guide to the location of these documents. However, it does not cover historical materials in locations outside the United States and Canada.

662. *Guide to Russian Reprints and Microforms.* New York: Pilvax Publishing, 1973. 364p.

The objective of this work is to provide a complete listing, as of 1 July 1973, of available Cyrillic Russian reprints and microforms. This includes items available from both foreign and U.S. publishers such as books, pamphlets, serials, and newspapers, but it does not include manuscripts. The main part of the *Guide* is basically an alphabetical author list, with the entries containing bibliographic information such as author, title, edition, and original place of publication. Following the bibliographic information, there is material on the source of the reprint or microform, type of reproduction used, publisher's serial or identification letter and number, and price. The second part of the volume is a title list that refers back to an entry number in the main part. Although broader in its coverage than just microforms, this guide includes information on more than 8,000 items and provides a good starting place for Slavic researchers trying to locate the availability of microform material in their research areas. Researchers, however, will want to contact the publishers for updated price information about particular material.

663. *An Index to Microform Collections.* Edited by Ann Niles. Meckler Publishing Series in Library Micrographics Management, 11; 13. Westport, CT: Meckler Publishing, 1984, 1988. Vol. 1, 891p. Vol. 2, 1,002p. ISBN 0-930466-75-6 (Vol. 1), 0-88736-061-0 (Vol. 2).

This two-volume work serves as an index to a total of 70 microform research collections, containing more than 20,000 items. The items indexed in the first volume were taken from the second edition of Dodson's *Microform Research Collections*, while those in the second volume were selected individually. Most of the collections included were those causing the most problems for users, especially those collections that contained a large number of individual monographs and had no adequate guide available. The collections indexed are wide-ranging and include material in history, literature, architecture, and religion. Each of the two volumes is divided into three parts: (1) an alphabetical list of each of the titles covered, along with a detailed contents list of the monographs in each collection; (2) an author index; and (3) a title index. Most of the information found in these volumes is taken from micropublishers' catalogs. This work, although selective, does provide detailed indexing for a wide range of microform research collections.

664. *Microfilm Resources for Research: A Comprehensive Catalog.* Washington, DC: National Archives and Records Administration, 1986. 126p. Index. ISBN 0-911333-34-7.

The National Archives is the major repository of America's historical records, and a large number of those records are available on microfilm. This catalog, which supersedes the earlier *Catalog of National Archives Microfilm Publications* (1974), serves as the most recent guide to these microfilm and microfiche publications. Covering more than 2,000 microform publications available from the National Archives, the guide is organized first by General Records of the United States government, followed by those of the individual branches—congressional, judiciary, and executive. These are followed by listings of the records of individual cabinet departments in the order of their creation, beginning with the Department of State. The last part of the guide contains the records of independent agencies, those relating to other governments, and miscellaneous records. Within these broad categories, the information is arranged by record group and lists a microfilm publication number as well as the number of rolls. At the end there is a general index, an alphabetical list of record groups, a numerical list of record groups, and a numerical list of microfilm publication numbers. For historians interested in more specialized areas of research, the National Archives has published other microfilm catalogs, including ones on American Indians, black studies, genealogical and biographical research, immigrant and passenger arrivals, military service records, and the population censuses.

665. *Microform Research Collections: A Guide.* 2d ed. Edited by Suzanne Cates Dodson. (Meckler Publishing Series in Library Micrographics Management, 9) Westport, CT: Meckler Publishing, 1984. ISBN 0-930466-66-7.

This is the definitive single-volume guide to large microform research collections, covering almost 400 items. Dodson has nearly doubled the number of entries contained in her first edition, *Microform Research Collections: A Guide* (Westport, CT: Microform Review, 1978). The *Guide* is obviously selective, but it provides the researcher with detailed information about a wide variety of major collections. Entries are arranged alphabetically and contain title; publisher; format; price; location of reviews (if available); arrangement and bibliographical control; listing of bibliographies, indexes, etc.; and scope and content. There is a detailed index that provides access by subject, title, author, editor, and compiler. For the researcher, there is a need for a new edition of this work to include the many recent collections now available in microform. Detailed reviews of these recent collections can be found in *Microform Review.*

666. *Microform Review.* Westport, CT: Meckler, 1972–. Quarterly. ISSN 0002-6530.

This is the outstanding journal covering microforms, and for the historian, it is particularly helpful for its definitive current reviews of research collections available in microform. Published quarterly since 1972, each issue of *Microform Review* contains a number of detailed reviews (the most recent issues had seven to eight) of collections available in microformat. The reviews, written by both teaching faculty and librarians, are lengthy—some run to several pages. They critically analyze the collection being reviewed, provide background, evaluate the microform format of the collection, and list any finding aids available.

There have been two cumulative listings of reviews published in *Microform Review, Cumulative Microform Reviews, 1972–1976* (Westport, CT: Microform Review, 1978), and *Cumulative Microform Reviews, 1977–1984* (Westport, CT: Meckler, 1985). These volumes make the researcher's task a great deal easier by arranging the reviews done from 1972 to 1984 into broad subject categories such as "Black Studies," "Government Documents," and "United States Cultural and Historical Materials." *Microform Review* is the best current source for reviews of new microform research collections.

667. *Newspapers in Microform. United States, 1948–1983.* 2 vols. *Newspapers in Microform. Foreign Countries, 1948–1983.* 1 vol. Compiled and edited by the Catalog Management and Publication Division, Library of Congress. Washington, DC: Library of Congress, 1984. Index.

This three-volume cumulation lists in separate volumes United States holdings of domestic newspapers and international holdings of foreign newspapers that are on microform through the end of 1983. These volumes replace earlier cumulative volumes for the United States and foreign countries, as well as additional annual supplementary volumes. The *United States* volumes are arranged by state, then city, and alphabetically by the title of the newspaper; the *Foreign Countries* volume is arranged by country, then city, and alphabetically by title. Within each volume the entries give information such as the date of publication, frequency, libraries that hold microform copies, and the dates of their holdings. Information is also given about the type of microform copy available, and there is a title index at the end of each set of volumes. For researchers, this three-volume set is extremely handy and useful for finding which libraries have microform copies of thousands of American and foreign newspapers and the extent of their holdings.

668. *Register of Microfilms and Other Photocopies in the Department of Manuscripts, British Library.* By Department of Manuscripts, British Library. (List & Index Society, Special Series, 9) London: Swift Printers, 1976. 239p. Index.

This work is useful for researchers because it reproduces in one volume a list of the microfilm and photographic copies of manuscripts acquired by the Department of Manuscripts of the British Library from 1948 to 1975. The *Register* is divided into two parts: (1) a list of microfilms acquired, arranged by order of acquisition, and (2) a list of photocopies of manuscripts received through the Board of Trade, also arranged in order of acquisition. There is an index to the photocopies at the end of the *Register*, but the first section of manuscripts is not indexed. The index to photocopies is not strictly alphabetical; the researcher has to search through an entire alphabetical listing to make certain that she/he has not missed a reference to the main listing. This volume does provide an initial starting point for locating individual documents and larger British historical collections in the British Library. However, it may now be largely superseded by some of the guides available through Chadwyck-Healey's *National Inventory of Documentary Sources in the United Kingdom and Ireland.*

669. *Union List of Canadian Newspapers.* Ottawa: National Library of Canada, 1988. Microfiche. ISSN 0840-5832.

This microfiche collection issued by the National Library of Canada provides the most complete listing to date of Canadian newspapers. The goals of this publication are to serve as the definitive tool for locating Canadian newspapers, to provide sufficient publication information for reference purposes, and to aid the interlibrary lending of newspaper resources. The union list consists of a sequentially numbered register and two indexes: a name/title index and a geographical index that lists the entries alphabetically by province and by city within the province. Newspaper holdings for more than 700 Canadian libraries are included.

Microform Publishers

Chadwyck-Healey, Ltd.
Cambridge Place
Cambridge, United Kingdom CB2 1NR

North American Office:
Chadwyck-Healey, Inc.
1101 King Street
Alexandria, VA 22314

Founded by Charles Chadwyck-Healey in 1972, Chadwyck-Healey is one of the leaders of the micropublishing industry and is international in its coverage, with offices in Great Britain, France, and the United States. Many of Chadwyck-Healey's historical collections are available on microfiche; the United States and Great Britain are the strongest areas of coverage. For researchers in American history, Chadwyck-Healey publishes the *National Inventory of Documentary Sources in the United States,* which includes detailed collection guides to federal records, the Manuscript Division of the Library of Congress, state archives, state libraries, state historical societies, academic libraries, and other repositories. They also publish a large number of collections in American history, including *American History and Culture,* which contains research studies done by the National Park Service from 1935 to 1984, and manuscript collections such as the *Papers of Robert M. LaFollette* and the *Papers of Charles Sumner.* In British History their publications include the *National Inventory of Documentary Sources in the United Kingdom and Ireland,* as well as an enormous microfiche collection of the *House of Commons Parliamentary Papers, 1801–1900.* Also useful for historians, Chadwyck-Healey publishes British government publications and nineteenth- and twentieth-century statistical sources.

Congressional Information Service, Inc.
4520 East-West Highway
Suite 800
Bethesda, MD 20814

Congressional Information Service (CIS), which was founded in 1969, is the leading micropublisher of government documents, including federal, state, national, and international publications. In addition to its strong indexing of government documents, such as the *Serial Set Index,* CIS publishes extensive collections of United States legislative publications on microfiche, such as *U. S. Congressional Committee Hearings, 1833–1969, U. S. Serial Set, 1789–1969,* and *U. S. Congressional Journals, 1789–1978.* CIS also publishes a number of executive branch publications on microfiche, including *Presidential Executive Orders & Proclamations, 1789–1983* and the *Federal Register* and the *Code of Federal Regulations.* For international coverage, CIS publishes the *International Statistics Library* on microfiche, which contains the statistical sources indexed in the *Index to International Statistics*. It also publishes a large set of individual statistical publications, with its *Current National Statistical Compendiums* series. CIS has also recently become active in the new CD-ROM technology with *Congressional Masterfile I*, which provides electronic access to four of its retrospective congressional indexes, and *Congressional Masterfile II*, which provides access to the most recent CIS congressional indexes.

Readex
58 Pine Street
New Canaan, CT 06840

Readex, one of the oldest of the microform publishers, was founded in 1948. It is best known as a publisher of United States and international documents and pioneered in the publishing of materials on microprint. Readex is the publisher of two major document collections originally on microprint, now microfiche, *United States Government Depository and Non-Depository Publications* and *United Nations Documents and Publications*, the latter including the Official Records of the U.N. since 1946. Recently, however, Readex has become involved in the publishing of research collections in American and British history. The American history collections include *Early American Imprints*, which reprints the text of all the titles in Charles Evans' *American Bibliography, 1639–1800*, Ralph Shaw and Richard Shoemaker's *American Bibliography, A Preliminary Checklist for 1801–1819*, and *Early American Newspapers*, which includes the full run of many eighteenth-century newspapers. Readex also has collections covering British history, including the *British Cabinet Records, 1837–1916*, and the *British Culture Series* for the eighteenth and nineteenth centuries.

Research Publications
12 Lunar Drive/Drawer AB
Woodbridge, CT 06525

Research Publications, which began publishing microform materials in 1966, mainly publishes research collections for academic institutions, as well as large numbers of newspapers, periodicals, and patents in microform. For the historian, this publisher is particularly strong in British, American, European, and international history. Its extensive British history collections on microfilm cover from the Medieval period to twentieth-century England. They include *Early English Newspapers, Politics, Religion, and Society in England,*

1650–1750, British Culture, and *British Cabinet Records.* United States history is well represented in Research Publications' collections, which cover from the colonial to the modern period. They include *Western Americana: Frontier History of the Trans-Mississippi West, 1550–1900,* the *Papers of William H. Seward,* the *Archives of the Works Projects Administration and Predecessors,* and the *Declassified Documents Reference System.* Also available from Research Publications is the *Eighteenth Century,* an extensive and wide-ranging collection based on the *Eighteenth Century Short Title Catalogue* (ESTC).

Scholarly Resources, Inc.
104 Greenhill Avenue
Wilmington, DE 19805

Founded in 1971, Scholarly Resources is a major microform publisher whose area of emphasis is in the humanities and social sciences. They have major microform collections in American history, British studies, Asian studies, black studies, and military history. In American history, their collections include *The Papers of Andrew Jackson, 1770–1845,* a collection of *Early American Newspapers,* and the *New American State Papers.* For twentieth-century American historians, their publications include the recent FBI files on Martin Luther King and the *Bureau of Social Hygiene Project and Research Files, 1913–1940.* In addition, Scholarly Resources is a distributor for all National Archives microform publications, including U. S. census material on microform. The company also publishes British historical documents, for example, the *House of Commons Sessional Papers of the Eighteenth Century* and *British Foreign Office Correspondence* concerning Japan, Russia, and the United States. They also have major collections in diplomatic history, specifically Latin America; these include the *U. S. Department of State Decimal Files* for Latin America, which contains twentieth-century U. S. diplomatic correspondence with individual Latin American countries.

University Microfilms International
300 North Zeeb Road
Ann Arbor, MI 48106

University Microfilms International (UMI), a subsidiary of Bell & Howell, is the oldest of the major history microform publishers, beginning micropublishing in 1938. Already heavily involved with doctoral dissertations and newspapers, UMI now publishes an extensive number of American and world history research collections on microfilm and microfiche. For researchers in American history, UMI publishes large sets such as the *American Culture Series,* an overview of American books and pamphlets from 1493 to 1875, and the *American Periodicals Series,* which covers significant American magazines from 1741 to 1900. UMI also publishes the papers of historical figures such as Aaron Burr, Daniel Webster, and Jane Addams. In British history, UMI's publications include the *Early English Books* series, covering from 1475 to 1700, based on the works of Pollard, Redgrave, and Wing. It also publishes a large *Pre-1900 Canadiana* collection and a large set on *Russian History & Culture.*

University Publications of America, Inc.
44 North Market Street
Frederick, MD 21701

University Publications of America (UPA) is the newest of the major microform publishers, first publishing in microform in 1975. UPA's strongest emphasis is on American history microform research collections and on twentieth-century American history materials. University Publications' research collections include collections on politics (*John F. Kennedy Presidential Oral History Collection*), radicalism (*Department of Justice Investigative Files on the Industrial Workers of the World*), women's studies (*Papers of Eleanor Roosevelt*), black studies (*Martin Luther King, Jr., FBI File*), and presidential documents (*Minutes and Documents of the Cabinet Meetings of President Lyndon Johnson*). UPA also publishes a number of international collections, including *Confidential U. S. State Department Central Files* on countries such as China, Mexico, the Soviet Union, Great Britain, and Israel, and *U. S. Military Intelligence Reports* on other countries, for example, Germany, France, and Japan. Unlike Research Publications and Scholarly Resources, UPA's greatest weakness is that it has little pre-twentieth century material and very little in terms of British, Canadian, and Russian primary-source materials.

Major Historical Microform Collections

670. *American Culture Series, 1493–1875.* Ann Arbor, MI: University Microfilms International. 643 reels of microfilm.

This interdisciplinary series is a massive collection on microfilm of Early American books and pamphlets from 1493 to 1875. Covering

5,850 titles, the collection is divided into two parts—*ACSI*, which covers from 1493 to 1806, and the much larger *ACSII*, which covers from 1806 to 1875. The titles included in this series were selected from David R. Weimer's *Bibliography of American Culture* (Ann Arbor, MI: University Microfilms, 1957) and cover many different subject areas, including history, literature and languages, science, economics, philosophy, politics and law, military and naval history and science, art and architecture, anthropology and sociology, education, journalism, and music. History is the largest part of the collection, with more than 1,500 titles, and the selection includes primary material on colonization, exploration, frontier life, the American Revolution, and the Civil War. There is an excellent finding aid to the collection, *American Culture Series, 1493–1875: A Cumulative Guide to the Microfilm Collection American Culture Series I&II*, edited by Ophelia Y. Lo (Ann Arbor, MI: University Microfilms International, 1979). The guide provides author, title, subject, and reel number access to this collection. For the historian and specialist in American studies, this collection provides access to a wide range of primary-source materials.

671. *American Periodicals Series, 1741–1900*. Ann Arbor, MI: University Microfilms International. 2,770 reels of microfilm.

This series provides access to the complete text of more than 1,100 American periodicals published from 1741 to 1900. The series is divided into three parts: Series I, which is the smallest of the three, running from 1741 to 1800; Series II, covering from 1800 to 1850; and Series III, which includes material from 1850 to 1900. Beginning with the origins of American journalism, this collection includes Benjamin Franklin's *General Magazine*, Thomas Paine's *Pennsylvania Magazine*, William Lloyd Garrison's *Liberator*, as well as standard publications such as the *North American Review* and *Godey's Lady's Book*. Many of the magazines contained in this collection are indexed in *Poole's Index to Nineteenth Century Literature* and the *Nineteenth Century Readers' Guide to Periodical Literature, 1890–1899*. There is also a separate guide to the collection, *American Periodicals, 1741–1900: An Index to the Microfilm Collections* (Ann Arbor, MI: University Microfilms, 1979), which provides title, subject, editor, and reel number access to the material in this series. This collection has a wealth of information for historians of the colonial, revolutionary, Civil War, and Reconstruction periods in American history.

672. *Columbia University Oral History Microfiche Collection*. Westport, CT: Meckler Publishing, 1973–.

The *Columbia University Oral History Collection*, begun by Allan Nevins, is the largest ongoing oral-history archive, containing interviews with major figures in twentieth-century American history. A number of memoirs from this collection are now available on microfiche from Meckler Publishing. This is an ongoing project and currently six parts of the collection are available—a total of 1,149 individual memoirs—including memoirs from twentieth-century leaders in areas such as politics, media, science, economics, business, journalism, and the arts. There are printed guides available for the first five parts, but the most recent general guide is still Elizabeth B. Mason and Louis M. Starr's *The Oral History Collection of Columbia University* (New York: Oral History Research Office, 1979), which provides name and subject access to the collection. This has recently been supplemented by a brief publication, *Columbia University Oral History Microfiche Collection: A Cumulative Index to Memoirs in Parts I–V* (Westport, CT: Meckler Publishing, 1985), which is strictly an alphabetical listing of names and locations. The Columbia collection is a must for social, economic, and political researchers of twentieth-century America.

673. *Documents on Contemporary China, 1949–1975.* White Plains, NY: Kraus International Publications. 525 microfiches.

This specialized research collection on modern China was originally published by Johnson Associates in 1977, in cooperation with the Social Science Center of the Columbia University Libraries. The collection is divided into five parts: (1) "Cultural Revolution: Red Guard Translations," (2) "Enactments of Party and Government," (3) "Research and Analysis Reports," (4) "Bibliography/Research and Leadership Information," and (5) "Provincial/Municipal Data." There is also a two-volume index to the five parts, which includes a bibliography of the items available on microfiche and detailed subject indexes to the documents. This set includes translations of primary documents and reports, as well as secondary studies on China. It is an excellent source for researchers interested in China during the Communist period, including the period of the Cultural Revolution, and is an example of the more specialized materials currently available on microfiche.

674. *Early American Imprints, 1639–1800.* New Canaan, CT: Readex Microprint Corporation, 1981–1982. 22,000 microfiches.

675. *Early American Imprints, 1801–1819.* 2d Series. New Canaan, CT: Readex (ongoing).

Charles Evans' *American Bibliography* (Chicago: the author, 1903–1934) is regarded as the major compilation of Early American books, pamphlets, and periodicals. This collection, published by Readex, contains the complete text of all the works listed in Evans, 39,162 titles, plus an additional 10,035 titles discovered since the publication of Evans' work. There is also a second series of microfiche, based on the work of Ralph Robert Shaw and Richard H. Shoemaker, *American Bibliography; A Preliminary Checklist for 1801–1819* (New York: Scarecrow Press, 1953–1963), which chronologically continues Evans' work through 1819. Readex has completed the filming of this second series through 1818. The company originally issued the first version of *Early American Imprints* on microcard during the 1950s and then in the early 1980s began making it available on microfiche. Historians of Early American history are fortunate to have access to this wealth of primary documentation, as well as excellent indexes to these collections. The two-volume work by Clifford K. Shipton and James E. Mooney, *National Index of American Imprints Through 1800, The Short-Title Evans* (Worcester, MA: American Antiquarian Society and Barre Publishers, 1969), corrected errors in Evans and added other titles. It serves as an index to the first Readex series. The multivolume work by Shaw and Shoemaker aids researchers working with the second series.

676. *Early English Books I, 1475–1640*. Ann Arbor, MI: University Microfilms International.

677. *Early English Books II, 1641–1700*. Ann Arbor, MI: University Microfilms International.

These two collections, based on A. W. Pollard and G. R. Redgrave's *A Short-Title Catalogue of Books Printed in England, Scotland, & Ireland, and of English Books Printed Abroad, 1475–1640* (London: Bibliographical Society, 1976–1986), and Donald G. Wing's *Short-Title Catalogue of Books Printed in England, Scotland, Ireland, Wales, and British America, and of English Books Printed in Other Countries, 1641–1700* (New York: Index Committee of the Modern Language Association of America, 1972–1988), attempt to reprint the complete text of every English book published in Great Britain or British North America from the invention of printing to 1700. The first collection is complete and includes almost all the 26,500 titles listed in Pollard and Redgrave. The second collection is still ongoing and, when completed, will include 50,000 titles. These collections provide an unparalleled primary-source collection for researchers in subject areas such as English literature, British and American history, philosophy, linguistics, and fine arts. There are reel guides, and a cross-index listing entry numbers from Pollard, Redgrave, and Wing is available for each collection.

678. *Early English Newspapers.* Woodbridge, CT: Research Publications (ongoing).

This is also an ongoing project to film a large collection of seventeenth- and eighteenth-century British newspapers and to make them available to researchers in one location. The newspapers in this collection are drawn from two large archival collections at the British Museum and the Bodleian Library at Oxford. Although the collection mainly covers the seventeenth and eighteenth centuries, recently titles printed in London and its suburbs through 1900 have been added. The collection includes newspapers such as the *Gentleman's Magazine,* the *Gazett'eer,* and the *New Daily Advertiser.* There is a brief guide to the collection, *Early English Newspapers: A Bibliography and Guide to the Microfilm Collection,* compiled by Susan M. Cox and Janice L. Budeit (Woodbridge, CT: Research Publications, 1983). However, this work is arranged alphabetically by title and does not provide any kind of subject access. It does give information about publication dates, title changes, and reel locations. This collection brings together a wide range of primary-source material for historians of Stuart and Hanoverian England.

679. *The Eighteenth Century.* Woodbridge, CT: Research Publications, 1983–.

The *Eighteenth Century* is an ongoing microfilm project based on the *Eighteenth Century Short Title Catalogue* (ESTC), a machine-readable data base of works printed in any language in Great Britain or its territories, or in English anywhere in the world, between 1701 and 1800. Ultimately, the ESTC will contain 500,000 items and 200,000 will be available in this collection, making it one of the largest microfilm projects ever. The collection has been organized into eight broad subject areas: religion and philosophy; history and geography; social sciences; law; literature and language; fine arts; science, technology, and medicine; and general reference and miscellaneous. It includes a wide variety of materials such as books, broadsides, tract books, and sermons by individuals such as David Hume, Edmund Burke, and Thomas Paine. Currently containing nearly 3,400 reels of microfilm, this collection is accessible through temporary unit listings and is arranged by main entry. There are also separate volumes, *The Eighteenth Century: Guide to the Microfilm Collection* (Woodbridge, CT: Research Publications, 1984–), which supersede the unit listings and provide better access by main entry, title, and broad subject area. This collection is indispensable for historians of the Enlightenment and eighteenth-century England.

680. *Latin American and Caribbean Official Statistical Serials, 1821–1982.* Alexandria, VA: Chadwyck-Healey.

This collection, which contains more than 4,000 microfiche, represents an attempt by Chadwyck-Healey to publish historically the statistical volumes issued by the governments of the Latin American and Caribbean countries from the earliest efforts to the early 1980s. To accomplish this, Chadwyck-Healey reproduced statistical volumes from the holdings of libraries in Great Britain and the United States. The aim of the collection is a good one, but the title is a bit misleading, in that most of the material covers the twentieth century, with much less country coverage available for the nineteenth. Also, the coverage for each county varies, depending on when statistical compendia first began appearing on a regular basis. Despite these problems, this set does open up a great deal of historical statistical material on Latin America and the Caribbean. Chadwyck-Healey has also published several other large statistical sets for other areas of the world, including *African Official Statistical Serials, 1867–1982* and *European Official Statistical Serials, 1841–1984.*

681. *National Inventory of Documentary Sources in the United Kingdom and Ireland.* Alexandria, VA: Chadwyck-Healey.

With the publication of this microfiche set and its American equivalent, the *National Inventory of Documentary Sources in the United States,* Chadwyck-Healey has performed a real service for historians. It has published many of the local finding aids, previously only available at the repositories themselves, for locating in detail what material is available in individual collections at particular locations. Chadwyck-Healey is publishing these inventories or finding aids for national and county record offices; national, university, and public libraries; and private, special, and other repositories in Great Britain and Ireland. This is a long-term project that is being produced on microfiche at the rate of 3,000 fiches per year. The microfiche is published in units, with a new cumulative index for each unit. Each cumulative index contains a list of finding aids and a name and subject index. This collection is quite expensive, but it will eventually provide researchers with access to the finding aids of many of the archives and libraries throughout the United Kingdom. Researchers will not have to make unnecessary trips or spend months trying to find out whether a particular collection would be appropriate for their research.

682. *National Inventory of Documentary Sources in the United States.* Alexandria, VA: Chadwyck-Healey. Part 1, *Federal Records* (1,911 microfiches); Part 2, *Manuscript Division, Library of Congress* (889 microfiches); and Part 3, *State Archives, State Libraries, State Historical Societies, Academic Libraries and Other Repositories* (ongoing).

This microfiche collection does the same thing for American history as the *National Inventory of Documentary Sources in the United Kingdom and Ireland* does for those countries. It provides access to many of the finding aids (registers, calendars, inventories, guides, etc.) to archival repositories in the United States. The *National Inventory* is divided into three parts: (1) "Federal Records," which includes records in the National Archives, Smithsonian Institution Archives, and the Hoover, Roosevelt, Truman, Eisenhower, Kennedy, Johnson, and Ford presidential libraries; (2) "Manuscript Division, Library of Congress"; and (3) "State Archives, State Libraries, State Historical Societies, Academic Libraries, and Other Repositories." Each of the first two parts is complete and has a printed index; the third part is still ongoing at the rate of ten units a year, which are accompanied by a cumulative index on microfiche. This is a wonderful tool for historians seeking to find out whether a particular collection meets their research interests, but it is important to keep in mind that the inventory is dependent upon the cooperation of all the libraries involved in making their finding lists available for filming. This is also an expensive project, which may dissuade some libraries from acquiring it. For the historian, the *National Inventory* has certainly made it more convenient to learn more about a collection, without having to travel to or contact the archive.

683. *Pre-1900 Canadiana.* Ann Arbor, MI: University Microfilms International.

This ongoing microfiche project claims to be the "most comprehensive collection of Canadian research materials in existence," and it will eventually include almost 57,000 monographs and pamphlets printed prior to 1900. The collection covers a wide range of subject areas, including history, geography, native American studies, sociology, psychology, anthropology, economics, religion, philosophy, law, political science, education, and science. Title lists are available for the collection as a whole, as well as each unit, and libraries can purchase individual segments of the collection, such as history and geography. The records in the collection are also being added to the

OCLC data base, which will improve access to these records for many libraries. This collection will provide access to an enormous amount of pre-1900 Canadian primary-source material in a single location, making things much easier for the researcher in Canadian history. After 1990, this collection will be distributed by the Canadian Institute for Historical Microreproductions.

684. *Russian History and Culture.* Ann Arbor, MI: University Microfilms International, 1978–.

With this still ongoing collection, University Microfilms International is providing researchers in Slavic studies and Russian history, politics, literature, and culture with access to the Slavic collection of the Helsinki University Library, recognized as the best Slavic collection outside the Soviet Union for the period 1820–1917. The goal is ultimately to make available 5,000 scarce titles from the Helsinki collection, of which more than 2,000 have so far been published on more than 8,000 microfiche. These titles are being selected by the staff of the Slavic and East European Department of the University of Illinois Library, and one of their major goals is to avoid duplicating Russian material already in American and Canadian libraries. The collection includes books in eight main subject areas: politics and government, industry and trade, military history, literature, biography, education, state and law, and social questions. There is an author, subject, and title index to that part of the collection already published. This is a valuable collection of diverse sources for researchers in nineteenth and early twentieth century Russian history.

685. *U. S. Congressional Committee Hearings on Microfiche, 1833–1969.* Bethesda, MD: Congressional Information Service.

Congressional Information Service (CIS) is the major indexer and micropublisher of United States government documents. One of its major document collections is the *U. S. Congressional Committee Hearings on Microfiche*. This massive collection, which covers the period from 1833 to 1969 (23d-91st Congress), contains nearly 31,000 publications on more than 82,000 microfiche. The collection contains a full-text copy of virtually all U. S. House and Senate hearings published during this period. It is divided into four groups of hearings, depending on when different collections of hearings were located and reproduced on microfiche. The four groups are (1) Group 1—Hearings contained in the U. S. Senate Library's bound collection of hearings, 1869–1934, and the Senate Library's bound *U. S. Serial Set* collection, 1833–1934; (2) Group 2—Hearings not contained in the U.S. Senate Library, 1839–1934, found in the Library of Congress and other locations; (3) Group 3—Hearings contained in the U.S. Senate Library bound collection, 1935–1969; and (4) Group 4—Hearings not contained in the three previous groups identified by CIS researchers examining other major collections and sources. Historians should use the *CIS U.S. Congressional Committee Hearings Index* to access material in this collection.

Index

References are to page numbers.